The First Definitive Study

Enochian chess' fascinating history begins in the late 1800s, when occultists Wynn Westcott and MacGregor Mathers updated the Enochian system of magic for the Hermetic Order of the Golden Dawn, and incorporated a four-handed chess game originally dubbed Rosicrucian chess—later dubbed Enochian chess, due to its derivation from the Enochian Tablets of Dr. John Dee.

Since the publication of the secret rituals of the Golden Dawn in the 1930s by the late Israel Regardie, there has been much speculation about Enochian chess' system of play, since the published manuscripts lacked the information necessary to actually play the game. But now, Chris Zalewski has made Enochian chess accessible as a "working game," with all the examples, rules and directions you will need to enjoy playing it.

Whether you want to explore Enochian chess as a divinatory tool rich with magical associations and kabbalistic analogies or are just intrigued by a four-handed variant of a "normal" chess game, you will find this book thorough, to-the-point and the most complete and authoritative text on the subject ever published.

About the Author

Chris Zalewski was born in 1956 in Hastings, New Zealand. She is a keen amateur artist and bodybuilder, has a diploma in herbal medicine, runs an herbal clinic and is president of the Wellington Astrological Society. In early 1980, she was initiated into the Golden Dawn, with her husband Pat, by ex-members of the New Zealand temple, Whare Ra. Her study of the Enochian chess game for the last 14 years was acknowledged by the late Israel Regardie as taking the game to an area that was quite beyond him. Her other interests include alchemy and other forms of esoteric healing. She resides with her husband in Wellington, where she has a long-standing tradition with the Golden Dawn through their Thoth-Hermes Temple.

To Write to the Author

If you wish to contact the author or would like more information about this book, please write to the author in care of Llewellyn Worldwide and we will forward your request. Both the author and publisher appreciate hearing from you and learning of your enjoyment of this book and how it has helped you. Llewellyn Worldwide cannot guarantee that every letter written to the author can be answered, but all will be forwarded. For more information about the Golden Dawn or to ask a question write to:

Ra-Horakhty Temple, Hermetic Society of the Golden Dawn
31849 Pacific Highway South, Suite 107
Federal Way, Washington 98003

To write to the author, address:

Chris Zalewski
c/o Llewellyn Worldwide
P.O. Box 64383-895, St. Paul, MN 55164-0383, U.S.A.
Please enclose international postal reply coupon.

Free Catalog from Llewellyn

For more than 90 years Llewellyn has brought its readers knowledge in the fields of metaphysics and human potential. Learn about the newest books in spiritual guidance, natural healing, astrology, occult philosophy and more. Enjoy book reviews, new age articles, a calendar of events, plus current advertised products and services. To get your free copy of the *Llewellyn's New Worlds of Mind and Spirit,* send your name and address to:

Llewellyn's New Worlds of Mind and Spirit
P.O. Box 64383-895, St. Paul, MN 55164-0383, U.S.A.

Llewellyn's Golden Dawn Series

Enochian Chess of the Golden Dawn

A Four-Handed Chess Game

Chris Zalewski

1994
Llewellyn Publications
St. Paul, Minnesota 55164–0383, U.S.A.

FIRST EDITION
First Printing, 1994

Cover painting by Richard Dudschus
Illustrations by David Stoelk and Richard Dudschus

Library of Congress Cataloging in Publication Data
Zalewski, Chris
    Enochian chess of the Golden Dawn : a four-handed chess game /
Chris Zalewski
        p. cm.—(Llewellyn's Golden Dawn series)
        Includes bibliographical references.
        ISBN 0–87542–895–9 : $12.95 ($17.50 Can.)
        1. Hermetic Order of the Golden Dawn—Rituals.   2. Enochian magic.
    3. Chess—Miscellanea.   I. Title.   II. Series.
    BF1623.R7Z33   1994
    135'.4—dc20   93–47223
                                                                         CIP

Llewellyn Publications
A Division of Llewellyn Worldwide, Ltd.
P.O. Box 64383, St. Paul, MN 55164-0383

About Llewellyn's Golden Dawn Series

Just as, 100 years ago, the original Order of the Golden Dawn initiated a powerful rebirth of interest in the Western Esoteric Tradition that has lasted through this day, so do we expect this series of books to add new impetus to the Great Work itself among an ever broadening base of sincere students.

> *I further promise and swear that with the Divine Permission, I will from this day forward, apply myself to the Great Work— which is: to purify and exalt my Spiritual Nature so that with the Divine Aid I may at length attain to be more than human, and thus gradually raise and unite myself to my Higher and Divine Genius, and that in this event I will not abuse the great power entrusted to me.*

With this oath, the Adeptus Minor of the Inner Order committed him/herself to undertake, consciously and deliberately, that which was ordained as the birthright of all Humanity: TO BECOME MORE THAN HUMAN!

It is this that is the ultimate message of Esotericism: that evolution continues, and that the purpose of each life is to grow into the Image set for us by our Creator, to attain and reveal our own Divinity.

These books will themselves make more easily accessible the Spiritual Technology that is inherent in the Golden Dawn System. It is a system that allows for individual as well as group endeavor; a system that works within or without an organized lodge; a system that is based on universal principles that will be shown to be global in their impact today.

And it is practical. The works in this series will be practical in their application. You need neither travel to the mountaintop nor obtain any tool other than your own consciousness. No garment need you other than that of your own imagination. No authority need you other than that of your own True Will.

Set forth then into the New Dawn—a New Start on the greatest adventure there is: to become One with the Divine Genius.

Other Books by Chris Zalewski:

Herbs in Magic & Alchemy
   (Prism Press, 1990)

With Pat Zalewski:

Z-5: Secret Teachings of the Golden Dawn
   Book II: The Zelator Ritual 1=10
   (Llewellyn Publications, 1992)

Equinox and Solstice Rituals of the Golden Dawn
   (Llewellyn Publications, 1992)

Other Books in Llewellyn's Golden Dawn Series:

By Pat Zalewski:

Golden Dawn Enochian Magic

Z-5: Secret Teachings of the Golden Dawn
   Book I: The Neophyte Ritual 0=0

Kabbalah of the Golden Dawn

By Israel Regardie:

The Golden Dawn

By Chic Cicero and Sandra Tabatha Cicero:

Secrets of a Golden Dawn Temple

Acknowledgments

A thank you to Karl for the many games played while I was researching the game; to Kevin for his games and objective opinions; to Pat for his help and encouragement in writing this book; and to those who wish to remain nameless.

Dedicated to Percy Wilkinson

Table of Contents

Figures

Tables

Foreword

Many years ago when I first encountered the Golden Dawn through Israel Regardie's four volumes, I remember becoming especially drawn to the Enochian chess described there. Like many others studying this material, I tried to construct a chess set and set of boards, but there did not seem to be enough information in Regardie's gathering of material for me to be able to follow this through. However, the system still interested me and I kept hoping that someone would eventually publish a more complete description of the game.

In 1987 while visiting R.A. Gilbert to discuss a few publishing ideas, he was kind enough to show me a box belonging to W. Wynn Westcott, one of the co-founders of the Hermetic Order of the Golden Dawn. In this box was a complete set of Enochian chessmen consisting of beautifully colored thick cards cut into the shapes of the chessmen. It was truly exciting to be able to handle these, and I became keenly aware that what I held in my hands that afternoon was the originally designed set of chessmen as worked out by Westcott, the archetype from which the later sets had been copied. In that moment as we gazed at these chessmen, Gilbert and I decided that we must find some way of publishing this set of cards.

At that time I had been able to structure my work through the Hermetic Research Trust and had some funds to undertake publications. However, these could not cover the expense of full-color printing, and we decided to produce a very small edition using color photocopying. In fact only 50 copies were produced. Together with these facsimiles I published a small book into which I gathered all the material I could find on this Enochian or Rosicrucian chess. Despite a great deal of searching for sources, I felt unhappy at not having found a coherent set of rules for play. What rules could be found in the Order papers were fragmentary and obscure and could not possibly provide a practical basis for a playing strategy. So I felt my little book rather incomplete. I felt much as I had done when first discovering Enochian chess in Regardie's book, having in my hands part of a beautiful esoteric system but lacking the key with which to activate it and bring it to life.

While I was compiling material for my book, Pat Zalewski had been kind enough to send me color photographs of the Enochian chess set used in the Whare Ra Lodge (which was derived from the Golden Dawn impulse that Dr. R.W. Felkin, one of the important later figures in G.D. history, had brought to New Zealand when he moved there in 1917–18). These Enochian chessmen were almost an exact copy of the Westcott originals.

Pat Zalewski also informed me that Chris Zalewski was writing a book on the Enochian chess game and had worked out a coherent set of rules for play. It was not possible to include any of Chris's material in my publication, but I eagerly awaited the publication of her book. I was surprised and pleased to be asked to write this short foreword to her book, and a copy of the manuscript arrived shortly after. In this I was delighted to find a complete working set of rules which Chris has constructed by many years of actual experimental playing with different variations of the game.

The rules she presents here provide a basis for playing a coherent game of Enochian chess, and one can see definite strategies and goals for the play of the game. However, I was also pleased to find that Chris had worked extensively upon the parallel divinatory aspect of Enochian chess and provided a system for using the game as a divinatory tool. This book also incorporates practical advice on constructing a chess set and documents much of the theoretical material on the occult system underlying the game. This book is perhaps most valuable in that it provides the reader for the first time with a working set of rules for Enochian chess, and I feel sure many occultists will be delighted to use her insights and ideas in their own work with this elaborate esoteric system.

ADAM MCLEAN

Preface

The first introduction both Chris and I had to Enochian chess was through the published Golden Dawn papers of Israel Regardie. At the time, we thought that this material was hardly more than adequate; there were quite a number of gaps. Chris worked for a number of years on the Enochian chess game trying to reconstruct the rules. Being extremely keen on standard chess play, she found herself continually over the years coming back to try to do more research into the Enochian game. After we were initiated into the Golden Dawn (under its New Zealand name "Emerald of the Seas"), we both found ourselves in contact with members of the now defunct Whare Ra Temple, which was the last of the temples to survive after the great Golden Dawn schism in 1900.

As it turned out, very few people in the Whare Ra Temple knew how to play Enochian chess or had even made their chess sets. We were eventually helped in this area by an elderly frater by the name of Percy Wilkinson, who was one of the few to have made his Enochian chess set and learned to play. Wynn Westcott's notebook on Enochian chess happened to be at Whare Ra, and we had the opportunity to study a copy of it. We found out that, like Regardie's published papers on the subject, it was very incomplete. As far as I can make out, Enochian chess was not introduced into the Golden Dawn for study until the Practicus Adeptus Minor level, or third level of the 5=6 grade, where the first part of the Y papers was given out. If the reader will refer to my *Secret Inner Order Rituals of the Golden Dawn* (Falcon Press, 1988, p. 174), where the grade requirements for the Practicus Adeptus Minor grade are given, it says:

> 14. The thorough elementary knowledge of the Formulas of the Awakening of the Abodes, by means of the Play or Raying of the Checkers of the Lesser Angles of the Enochian Tablets.

Although we are told by occult historian Ellic Howe that this grade was never implemented, a number of its papers, including the above chess papers, obviously were given out in some temples of the Stella Matutina at 6=5 level. In our copy of Wynn Westcott's chess notebook, Ritual Y, Second Part, was "Issued to such Z.A.M's as are in the fourth Stage (the Philosophus Adeptus Minor Grade) by Order of the Chief Adept G.H. Frater D.D.C.F." If this was the case, then very few in the Golden Dawn, with the exception of MacGregor Mathers or his wife (who were 6=5) and Westcott, would have known about Enochian chess unless they dabbled in it unofficially.

In his *Complete Golden Dawn System of Magic,* however, Regardie published certain papers belonging to Leigh F. Gardner. The natural assumption by the reader is that the papers he published were *all* Gardner's. If that is the case, the Enochian chess material must have been given out at the second level of the 5=6 grade (Theoricus Adeptus Minor), which Gardner held. He would not have been given the papers for a higher level.

Yeats made the comment that he played Enochian chess with Mathers, his wife and a spirit, in Paris, though he was only at the first level of the 5=6 grade. There appear to be some exceptions to Westcott's rule, therefore. Exactly how widespread it was is anyone's guess. One would have to have a list of manuscripts circulated to the various temples to find out. There is also a possibility that the papers were circulated at the first stage of the 5=6 level but individuals were not examined in it until much later. It appears that when Mathers was expelled from the Golden Dawn, a number of papers held for the Practicus Adeptus Minor Grade fell into the hands of those who had never been fully instructed in it. This of course applies to a number of papers, such as "The Ring and the Disc" etc., but it appears that, while some of Mathers' papers were seized, others were not.

Enochian chess does not appear to have been a secret, but its component parts were, I think. In the *Golden Dawn Companion,* R.A. Gilbert lists the Enochian chess material as part of the Second Order papers but does not state which grade the Y papers were for. In the same book, the Y papers are listed under the Stella Matutina as part of the Theoricus Adeptus Minor Grade, but the comment is made that this is part of the 6=5 work. As far as I am aware, the second level of the 5=6 grade only existed briefly, if at all, in the Stella Matutina, and certainly not in the New Zealand Whare Ra Temple. Regardie's publication places the chess papers at the *first* level of the 5=6 grade, through insinuation, and others have assumed the same ever since. Clearly Westcott intended to add more to the Enochian chess papers for higher grades of the Golden Dawn, but unfortunately did not have the opportunity to do so before he demitted from the Order in the mid-1890s.

We were often told by former Whare Ra members who did make their chess sets that game play was almost impossible because of the lack of rules. Since there was no doubt that Westcott based the Enochian chess game on the Indian game, Chaturanga, Chris went back to the original sources, as contained in the *Tithitattava* and in the works of Duncan Forbes, Edward Falkener and H.J.R. Murray, plus some original sources quoted by the latter. Translations and sources were provided by various members of the Indian Society here in Wellington.

By 1980 the first set of coherent rules was worked out after many hours of game play, with Enochian chess games being played a number of times each week until the early hours of the morning by Chris and her chess associates. Frankly, by that stage, I felt I was seeing Enochian chess in my sleep. It appeared at one time that whatever room of the house I was in, I was always tripping over an Enochian chess game. Chris eventually won out, and I adopted the philosophy "if you can't lick 'em, then join 'em." When the rules had been reworked a number of times, they were passed around to selected friends to play by mail. We feel sure that at least one set was sent across the Pacific to members of one occult organization that prefers to remain nameless.

In 1981 both Chris and I put some of our findings in a small volume titled *Enochian Chess*. But even with the later efforts of Regardie, we found no takers. In hindsight, that work was very inferior to the book you now hold. Gradually, over a period of time, Chris rewrote the original manuscript. She retained very little; in essence, it became a completely new book. Since my input was almost nonexistent, we both felt that this work would be better published under her name alone rather than the two of us as in the original manuscript.

In 1983 when Israel Regardie first came to New Zealand, he was astounded at the development to which Chris had taken the game of Enochian chess, as he mentioned in his introduction to our unpublished book on the Golden Dawn Tarot. Chris was originally uncertain as to whether to publish the Enochian chess book in two volumes, the first on game strategy and the second on divination. However, she decided that it would not be a publishable book in that form and opted for a basic introduction to the two areas.

When Chris first put this book together, it was outlined in such a manner that those interested in a four-handed chess game, but with no occult leanings, would find the book as interesting as would an occultist. The book is organized so that the chess enthusiast can skip the chapters on occultism and simply reap the benefits of Chris's vast experience of the game in all its variations.

In 1988 Adam McLean from the prestigious *Hermetic Journal* asked me to write a small section on the Enochian chess game for his forthcoming publication on the subject. McLean had, through the efforts of Bob Gilbert, found Westcott's chess pieces and was also selling chess sets. I immediately sent over photos of the Whare Ra chess pieces. For the most part, according to McLean, they were identical with Westcott's except for being more detailed. McLean astutely made the comment in his book that he felt the lack of chess rules did not mean that the Adept had to do for himself, but that the rules were simply unfinished. Since a number of authors to date have tried to look for some special esoteric significance for this fact, I can concur with McLean that he was quite correct in his assumption. If there were rules for this game, they would have been in Westcott's chess notebook. They were not, nor did anyone out here know of them. Also, according to a member of Whare Ra who was friendly with a high Alpha et Omega member in England, they did not exist in the A.O. temples under Mathers, either.

It has often been said that the oriental game of mah-jong is a game for mystics. For Enochian chess, I say doubly so. Having been both a player and a watcher of this game over the years, I do not doubt that what is in this volume is all there is on the subject.

I am continually struck by the inner transformation that the game brings about after exposure to a particular Enochian chessboard. When we made our first Enochian chess set, the pieces were sculpted from clay and we opted for an entire pantheon per board. The remarkable thing about the process of making the pieces was that they were done through a process of automatic sculpting. This is much akin to the automatic writing method where the person becomes a vehicle for some force or another. The pieces were literally made this way; my hands hardly made any conscious effort.

I have tried many times over the last decade to duplicate this process but have failed. It only occurred when the original pieces were being made. Chris also underwent a similar experience when painting the pieces and boards. The actual painting of the chessboards and the making of the pieces in fact becomes a very mystical experience during which a number of inner transformations occur. I do say this lightly, and for this reason I would urge you to try to make your own set rather than buying one.

Chris is continually working and updating the game based on her experiences. No doubt over the years future publications will also follow suit. Like ordinary chess, this game needs exposure and many different viewpoints for it to be explored and most of all for it to be accepted by the general public. Westcott actually told R.W. Felkin that the game could be played by those outside the Order provided they did not give away the esoteric associations. Since Regardie's publication, however, this hardly matters. Almost anyone can play if they wish, though I would be extremely hesitant about playing with people on an Enochian chessboard if they had never been exposed to the Tablets before, as the colors can have quite an effect. Enochian chess only becomes Enochian chess when one uses a fully colored Enochian chessboard. That makes the distinction between it and other games of four- or two-handed chess.

There are three basic levels in Enochian chess. The first is game strategy, the second is divination and the third relates to a personal transformation due to working with the other two. It is my personal conviction that when one plays a game of Enochian chess as a straight chess game, then one should forget about all the conscious paraphernalia and simply let the subliminal messages being sent to the psyche take over. Too much emphasis, I feel, is placed on being aware of hidden meanings in the game, such as attacking along certain lines that have astrological significance. While this may relate to divination, it certainly does not have relevance in straight game play. Quite a number of students, when they first play Enochian chess, look immediately for some mystic meaning in the game. As a result, they completely miss the whole point of the exercise. They get so bogged down in trivia that they are lost in the part and forget the whole. In my opinion, this was a very real problem in Golden Dawn work and the downfall of a number of temples.

P.J. ZALEWSKI

Wellington, N.Z.
1990

To the Reader:

How to Use
This Book

This book has been divided into four parts. Parts I and II are for those of you who are only interested in Enochian chess as a "game" rather than in the esoteric and divinatory use of the chess set.

Part I is the Book of Earth and introduces Enochian chess to the reader. It shows the reader how to go about constructing the chessboards and sets of chess pieces. It also provides a way of constructing a four-handed chess set without all the colors and symbology for the non-occultist.

Part II is the Book of Air and gives the rules and strategical use of Enochian chess. It explains the method of play and how to record your game play. Opening, middle- and endgame play is discussed, and game examples are provided. You are advised to have your chess set constructed before studying Part II, because much of what has been written, such as game-play examples, can only be fully understood when you personally move the pieces on the board while reading the text.

Parts III and IV have been written for those interested in divination and the esoteric sciences connected with Enochian chess. If you are interested in these areas, it is assumed that you have some grounding in the symbology of the occult or that you are interested enough to obtain the necessary reference material so that you can understand these sections.

Those interested in Parts III and IV will no doubt wish to read Parts I and II to get a basic understanding of game play and to construct their boards and pieces.

Part III is called the Book of Water and covers the divination teaching in Enochian chess.

Part IV is called the Book of Fire, Training of the Adept. This section provides some of the magical teachings connected with Enochian chess.

I have written this book with the view that it is only a foundation for the serious student from which he or she can launch off into many areas of in-depth study. For those who do not wish to enter into studies on the subject but simply wish to enjoy the "game," I think you will find the information provided satisfactory. I would like to wish the reader enjoyable reading and many happy hours with Enochian chess, which I have had.

CHRIS ZALEWSKI

Part I
Book of Earth

Introduction

Constructing Your Enochian Chess Set

The Enochian System of Magic and Its Relationship to Enochian Chess

The Enochian system of magic[1] was first introduced to the world on any large scale through the works of various authors such as Heinrich Cornelius Agrippa,[2] Pietro d'Abano[3] and Johann Trithemius[4] in fragments of seals and a variety of angelic names given in connection with varying aspects of occultism. It was not until the late 16th century that Elizabethan scholar Dr. John Dee[5] considered that, since Bibli-

---

1. This was dubbed Enochian due to the fact that the dictating angel was Ave, who was mentioned in the Biblical book of Enoch.

2. See *De occulta philosophia,* n.p., 1533.

3. See *Heptameron oder de elemente der magic,* partly given in Agrippa's *Fourth Book of Occult Philosophy,* trans. Robert Turner, London: Askin Press, 1976.

4. See *Steganographia,* Frankfurt, 1606.

5. For information on Dee's life, see *John Dee: The World of an Elizabethan Magus* by Peter J. French (Routledge & Kegan Paul, 1984).

cal man of the Old Testament could speak with the angels, why
not man in what was then modern times? Driven by an inner
desire to converse with God or his entities, he eventually found
an exceptional clairvoyant by the name of Edward Kelly. The
manner in which he was to make this contact was through a
"shewstone," or small crystal, in which visions would appear to
someone clairvoyantly inclined.

Over a number of years of working with Kelly, Dee recorded
all the information he received through these conversations. In
many instances, they explained rather fully the gaps in the
hierarchies of the angelic entities given many years earlier by
Agrippa and the like.[6] In the next half century some of Dee's
diaries were published based on the manuscripts in the British
Museum library[7] and gained a certain notoriety in occult circles. This led many occultists to study the Dee manuscripts
even further.

In the late 19th century, Wynn Westcott and MacGregor
Mathers both worked diligently to update this system of magic
to integrate it into the Hermetic Order of the Golden Dawn,
which they had established.[8] As yet another subsystem to this
system of magic, they incorporated a four-handed chess game,
which they originally called Rosicrucian chess (later dubbed
Enochian chess), which was used for a simple game of chess and
for divination.[9] The main connection with the Enochian system

6. Manuscript references to Dee's diaries in the British Museum are Sloane
78, art 11–3188–3189–3191–3677–3678.

7. See *A True & Faithful Relation of What passed for many Yeers Between Dr.
John Dee and Some Spirits* by Meric. Casaubon, London, 1659.

8. See *The Magicians of the Golden Dawn* by Ellic Howe (Weiser, 1978), *Yeats's
Golden Dawn* by George M. Harper (Macmillan, 1974) and *My Rosicrucian
Adventure* by Israel Regardie (Llewellyn, 1977) for historical references. See
The Golden Dawn by Regardie (Llewellyn, 1971) and *Secret Inner Order Ritu-
als of the Golden Dawn* by Patrick J. Zalewski (Falcon Press, 1988) for infor-
mation on their rituals and teachings along with additional historical material.

9. See *The Complete Golden Dawn System of Magic* (Falcon Press, 1984) for
the Order's papers on the subject.

was that the boards that were used were derived from four major tablets that Dee constantly used in his original system of magic.[10, 11]

The four elemental boards are in fact broken down into the following categories: the large Central Cross which binds the four quarters together represents the refined power of the planets in the astrological signs. The cross bar of this Central Cross then gives the Holy Name[12] or controlling influence or force of the entire tablet. The four smaller crosses in each quarter mainly represent the energies of the planets, while the four squares above each smaller cross are the incorporeal elements. The squares below the small crosses are dubbed the Servient Squares and relate to the 12 signs of the Zodiac and the four elements proper. These are the squares used to construct the Enochian chessboards.[13] While the chess pieces themselves are Egyptian, the main framework from which they operate is the chessboards from the Enochian Tablets and their various associations to numerous forms of magic and occultism. They are considered Enochian by virtue of that fact.

10. For a breakdown of the functions of the Enochian hierarchies of each of these boards, see "How the Golden Dawn Works Enochian Magic" by C.R. Runyon, *Portal,* Winter 1989. This article is mainly an edited transcript of a lecture given by Pat Zalewski in Los Angeles in January 1988.

11. In the National Library of Ireland, manuscript 13568(2), quoted in part in *The Sword of Wisdom* by Ithell Colquhoun (Putnam's, 1975), a Celtic variation of Enochian chess is given by William Butler Yeats. The only real similarity between this game and Enochian chess is the fact that there are four elemental boards, but these bear no relationship to the Enochian Tablets. There are no references to Enochiana in the original Yeats manuscript; without it, the game simply becomes a Celtic chess game. See "W. B. Yeats' Celtic Version of Enochian Chess" by Pat Zalewski, *Magus,* Autumn 1981.

12. Reading from left to right.

13. The shaded areas are the ones shown in figure 1.

THE FOUR ANGELIC WATCHTOWERS

Key:

The lightly shaded squares are the Servient Squares from which the chessboards are made up.

The more darkly shaded squares are the Kerubic Squares.

The small crosses in the corners of each Tablet are the Calvary Crosses.

The large cross in the center is called the Central Cross.

d	o	n	p	a	T	d	a	n	V	a	a
o	l	o	a	G	e	o	o	b	a	u	a
O	P	a	m	n	o	O	G	m	d	n	m
a	b	l	s	T	e	d	e	c	a	o	p
s	c	m	i	o	a	n	A	m	l	o	x
V	a	r	s	G	d	L	b	r	i	a	p
o	i	p	t	e	a	a	p	D	o	c	e
P	s	u	a	c	n	r	Z	i	r	z	a
S	i	o	d	a	o	i	n	r	z	f	m
d	a	l	t	T	d	n	a	d	i	r	e
d	i	x	o	m	o	n	s	i	o	s	p
O	o	D	p	z	i	A	p	a	n	l	i
r	g	o	a	n	n	P	A	C	r	a	r

FIGURE 1—FIRE TABLET

There are a number of variations in the Enochian Tablets used within the Golden Dawn and its later offshoots. The version given here is taken from the New Zealand Whare Ra Temple after the Tablets were "corrected" by Euan Campbell, a former member of that temple who reached the rank of 9=2. Campbell persuaded Mrs. Felkin, who was then in charge of Whare Ra, to change the letters from the Golden Dawn version to those presented here in the 1930s, after his return from England, where he had taken a year's sabbatical to study the Dee manuscripts in the British Museum library.

T	a	O	A	d	v	p	t	D	n	i	m
o	a	l	c	o	o	r	o	m	e	b	b
T	a	g	c	o	n	z	i	n	l	G	m
n	h	o	d	D	i	a	l	a	a	o	c
f	a	t	A	x	i	u	V	s	P	s	N
S	a	a	i	z	a	a	r	V	r	o	i
m	p	h	a	r	s	l	g	a	i	o	l
M	a	m	g	l	o	i	n	L	i	r	x
o	l	a	a	D	a	g	a	T	a	p	a
p	a	L	c	o	n	d	x	P	a	c	n
n	d	a	z	N	z	i	V	a	a	s	a
i	i	d	P	o	i	s	d	A	s	p	i
x	r	i	n	h	t	a	r	n	d	i	l

FIGURE 2—WATER TABLET

r	Z	i	l	a	f	A	y	t	l	p	a
a	r	d	Z	a	i	d	p	a	L	a	m
C	z	o	n	s	a	r	o	Y	a	u	b
T	o	i	T	t	x	o	P	a	c	o	C
S	i	g	a	s	o	n	r	b	z	n	h
f	m	o	n	d	a	t	d	i	a	r	i
o	r	o	i	b	A	h	a	o	z	p	i
c	N	a	b	a	V	i	x	g	a	z	d
O	i	i	i	t	T	p	a	l	O	a	i
A	b	a	m	o	o	o	a	C	u	c	a
N	a	o	c	O	T	t	n	p	r	a	T
o	c	a	n	m	a	g	o	t	r	o	i
S	h	i	a	l	r	a	p	m	z	o	x

FIGURE 3—AIR TABLET

b	O	a	Z	a	R	o	p	h	a	R	a
u	N	n	a	x	o	P	S	o	n	d	n
a	i	g	r	a	n	o	a	m	a	g	g
o	r	p	m	n	i	n	g	b	e	a	l
r	s	O	n	i	z	i	r	l	e	m	u
i	z	i	n	r	C	z	i	a	m	h	l
M	O	r	d	i	a	l	h	C	t	G	a
o	o	c	a	m	c	h	i	a	s	o	m
A	r	b	i	z	m	i	i	l	p	i	z
O	p	a	n	a	B	a	m	S	m	a	L
d	O	l	o	F	i	n	i	a	n	b	a
r	x	p	a	o	c	s	i	z	i	x	p
a	x	t	i	r	V	a	s	t	r	i	m

FIGURE 4—EARTH TABLET

It is very difficult to explain simply the Golden Dawn's use of the four Enochian Tablets. A detailed analysis of the Order's Enochian system is provided by Israel Regardie in his *Complete Golden Dawn System of Magic* and by Pat Zalewski in *Golden Dawn Enochian Magic* (Llewellyn, 1990). Briefly, however, the Golden Dawn considered that any force invoked or evoked for ritual had to be limited and controlled by a very powerful neutral force. The structure of the Enochian Tablets gave the magicians of the Golden Dawn that control.

It is the hidden or subliminal aspects of the chessboards that turn the mundane into the magical, a term I do not use lightly. I seriously suggest that, if you wish to study the Enochian chess game, you should first make a thorough study of the Order's Enochian system. This well-spent effort will definitely afford you a better concept of how the game is played.

Chaturanga

ithout doubt the origins of the Enochian chess game were fused in the ashes of the Indian game of four-handed chess called Chaturanga.[1,2] It was recorded as being played four or five thousand years ago,[3] though its actual origins are obscure. Some noted chess historians have attrib-

---

1. For a full study on Chaturanga, see H.J.R. Murray's *History of Chess* (Oxford, 1913), which covers the subject exhaustively and corrects many of the errors that occur in the previous work of Duncan Forbes and Edward Falkener. The brief rendition of the subject given here is merely an introduction to it as the foundation of Enochian chess.

2. *Chatur* = "four," *ranga* = "member."

3. See Sir William Jones, *Asiatic Researches* 2, 1788, wherein he places the game's origin at around 4,000 years previous to the current date. In his *History of Chess* (1860), Duncan Forbes places it around 4–5,000 years ago. My own researches place it around the 5th or 6th century AD. Anything earlier is pure speculation.

uted the invention of the game to Sita, a concubine of Ravana, king of Celyon (or Sri Lanka as it is now known). As tradition has it, she used to watch the warlords of the king plan their strategy to defend the city of Lanka against the onslaught of Rama, her former husband. Each day miniature troops were moved into their attacking positions and the king would order counterattacks. Ravana noted a pattern forming that could be detected. Using the prospects of chance to find the outcome of the battles, a die was used. She began by modifying certain aspects of army strategy that she had learned. She found, with great accuracy, that she could predict the outcome of the ensuing battles around her. The pattern was then set, using dice and miniature pieces to predetermine the outcome of battles in much the same manner as war games are played today.

The pieces utilized were a rajah (king), elephant (castle), horse (knight), ship (bishop) and four pawns for each corner section of the board. These corner sections were red, green, yellow and black. The king, castle and knight move the same as they do in modern chess, while the bishop always moves two squares diagonally. The king cannot be checkmated, but is simply taken like any other piece. However, all his forces are then captured by the enemy—or even by his ally if they are in the way. If both the king and an enemy king are captured, they can by mutual consent be restored to the game.

In this very early game, dice were used to decide what piece to move. It seems most unlikely that a chessboard of 64 squares was used with the war game from the outset, but the board does resemble that used in a very early Indian game of racing called Ashtapada.[4] It is thought that this board was eventually adapted for Chaturanga around the 6th or 7th century. Some authors such as Stewart Culin *(Chess and Playing Cards,* 1898) consider the board to be a breakdown of the four seasons.

To get a clear description of the game as it was originally played is almost impossible except for one shining example in

---

4. See Thomas Hyde, *De ludis orientalibus* (1694).

the *Tithitattava.*[5] The text takes up where Vyasa (the narrator of the poem) tells Prince Yudishthira (grandson of Brahma) how to play Chaturanga after he lost all his possessions playing dice and went to learn the science of gambling from learned Vyasa.[6]

> Explain, O supereminent in virtue, the game on the eight times eight board:
> Tell me, O my master, how the Chatarunga may be played. Vyasa replied:
> On the board of eight squares place the Red forces in the East, the Green forces in the South, on the West station the Yellow forces and the Black combatants in the North.
> To the left of the Rajah, O Prince, place the Elephant, then the Horse, the Ship; and then four Foot-soldiers in front.
> Opposite, place the Ship in the angle, O Son of Kunti; the Horse in the second square, the Elephant in the third and the Rajah in the fourth.
> In front of each place a Foot-soldier. On throwing five, play a Foot-soldier or a Rajah; if four, the Elephant:
> If three, the Horse; if two, then, O Prince, the Ship must move. The Rajah moves one square in any direction.
> The Foot-soldier moves one square forward, and takes diagonally; the Elephant can move at will—North, South, East, or West.
> The Horses move awry, crossing three squares at a time; the Ship moves diagonally, two squares at a time, O Yudishthira.
> The following, O Prince, are various positions and actions in the game:

---

5. Edward Falkener states that the version he quotes in his *Games Ancient and Oriental, and How to Play Them* (Dover, 1961) comes from the *Mahabharata,* which is incorrect. I have in my possession a full copy of this ancient text, and the dice game is only mentioned in the "Sabha Parva" section, twice, and briefly at that. For the text presented here, I have used the Albrecht Weber translation and that of Falkener. I am indebted to Mr. Rajas of the Wellington Indian Society, who brought two other versions in Sanskrit to my attention. Both of these differ slightly. Based on this, some modest adjustments have been made to this version of the text, which for the most part is identical with Falkener's. Murray gives a version as well in his monumental *History of Chess.*

6. The game play here is counterclockwise.

Sinhasana, Chaturaji, Nrtipakrishta, Shatpada, Kakakashtha, Vrihannauka, Naukakrishtapracaraka.

The Foot-soldier and the Ship may take; or run the risk, O
Yudhishthira; the Rajah, Elephant and Horse may take,
but must avoid being taken.

A player should guard his forces with all possible care. The
Rajah, O Prince, is the most powerful of all.

The most powerful may be lost, if the weaker, O son of Kunti,
are not protected. As the Rajah's chief piece is the Elephant, all others must be sacrificed to save it.

To enable the Rajah to obtain Sinhasana or Chaturaji, all
other pieces, even the Elephant, may be sacrificed.

If a Rajah enters the square of another Rajah, O Yudhishthira, he is said to have gained Sinhasana.

If he gains the Sinhasana, he takes the Rajah. He gains a double stake: otherwise a single one.

If a Rajah, O Prince, mounts the throne of his ally, he gains a
Sinhasana, and commands both forces.

If a Rajah, in seeking Sinhasana, moves six squares away, he
exposes himself to danger, however secure he thinks
himself.

If you still preserve your Rajah, and the other Rajahs, you
obtain Chaturanji.

In gaining Chaturanji, and taking the other Rajahs, you gain
a double stake: otherwise, a single one.

If a Rajah takes the other Rajahs on their own thrones then
his stakes are fourfold.

If both a Sinhasana and Chaturaji are obtained, only the latter can be reckoned.

If you have taken a Rajah, and your ally has lost one of his,
you may propose of prisoners.

But if you have neither of the other Rajahs, and your ally has
lost one, you must try to take one of the other Rajahs.

If a Rajah has been restored, and is taken again, O Yudhishthira, he cannot be destroyed.

When a Foot-soldier reaches an opposite square, other than of
a Rajah or Ship, he assumes the rank of the piece corresponding to each square.

If Chaturaji and Shatpada, O Prince, are both obtainable,
Chaturanji will have preference.

If the Shatpada is reached on the square of the Rajah or Ship,
it does not have the privilege of Shatpada.

When a Foot-soldier, after many moves, gains the seventh

square, the defenceless forces on the opposite side can easily be taken.

O Son of Kunti, if the player, however, has three Foot-soldiers remaining, he cannot take his Shatpada—so decrees Gotma.

But if he has only one Foot-soldier and a Ship, the piece is called Gadha and he may take his Shatpada in any square he can.

If a Rajah has lost all his pieces before being taken, it is Kakakashtha, so decide all the Rakshasahs. It is a drawn game.

If the Gadha, on gaining the Shatpada and becoming a fifth Rajah, is taken, it is misfortune for the pieces which remain who will have to fight the enemy.

If this happens a second time, the conqueror then sweeps off all the pieces.

But if, O Prince, Kakakashtha and Sinhasana occur together, it is counted as Sinhasana, and is not called Kakakashtha.

When three Ships come together and the fourth Ship completes the square, the fourth Ship takes the other three ships.

This fourth Ship is called Vrihannauka.

Never place an Elephant where it can be taken by another Elephant.

But if impossible to make any other move, then, O Prince, Gotama says it may be done.

If you can take both the hostile Elephants, take that to the left.

Chaturanga found its way into Persia around 550 AD during the reign of Naushirawan and it is here that it underwent a drastic change into a game that was eventually called Shatranji. The actual history of how the chess game came to Persia is recorded in the *Karnamak-i-Artakh Shatr-i-Papakan,* the origin of which is estimated at 600 AD. Later works of poetry such as *Shahnama* also describe chess history as well. During this time there is evidence that the use of dice was done away with and the four corners were changed to two straight lines facing each other, though in India it remained basically the same. In the book *Enochian or Rosicrucian Chess of Wynn Westcott,* edited by Adam McLean, McLean makes the observation that

Westcott must have made himself very familiar with Chaturanga from *The History of Chess* by Duncan Forbes. The alliance of the game with the elements is very plain to see, and the differences between the two games consists merely of a thin veil and a different power base.

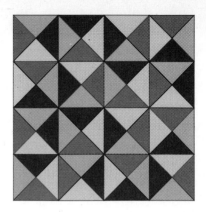

Constructing
Your
Chessboards

This chapter discusses the construction of the Enochian chessboards and the coloring and attributions given thereon. The meanings of the attributions described below are discussed further in Part III.

Four chessboards are constructed for Enochian chess. They are derived from the Servient Squares of the Angelic Watchtowers, which are the four elemental Enochian Tablets. For those who wish to investigate this Enochian system further, I suggest you read *The Golden Dawn* by Israel Regardie and *Golden Dawn Enochian Magic* by Pat Zalewski, both published by Llewellyn Publications. Each chessboard is identical in size, with 64 squares in each, set out 8-by-8, just as a normal chessboard. However, the difference between each of the four boards is seen in their pattern of coloring and the attributions painted thereon.

There are many different materials that can be used for your chessboards: heavy cardboard, hardboard, wood, canvas, fabric material etc., but the most effective, if used for anything other than a simple chess game, is a surface that can be made to shine with strong, bright (flashing) colors. Suitable coloring materials must also be obtained. The most common are high-gloss enamel paints of the three primary colors (red, blue and yellow), black, white and the three colors that are complementary to the primaries: purple, orange and green. If you do not have a high gloss, spray or paint on a high-gloss lacquer after the boards have been painted and dried.

To paint straight lines freehand is extremely difficult and you may prefer not to paint your boards. A method that avoids painting is to cut your pyramid shapes out of shiny colored paper or card and paste them onto your boards, then cover the boards with a strong, clear plastic for a smooth, shiny finish. Whatever materials you use, your purpose should be to aim for an end product that is flashing in color, hence the term "flashing tablets," which produce a talismatic effect.

The four Enochian chessboards are considered elemental boards and are individually identified as follows:

Chessboard 1 is associated with the element of Earth and therefore is referred to as the "Earth Board."

Chessboard 2 is associated with the element of Air and therefore is referred to as the "Air Board."

Chessboard 3 is associated with the element of Water and therefore is referred to as the "Water Board."

Chessboard 4 is associated with the element of Fire and therefore is referred to as the "Fire Board."

Before we continue it is necessary to point out that all four boards are not used at once in the same game. Only one board at a time is used during any particular game. Therefore, if you are constructing this set purely for strategical game play and not for use in divination or as part of your occult studies, I suggest you only construct one chessboard, preferably the Earth Board. In fact, I would further advise that, instead of constructing your board with the color system and occult attributions as described below, you should use the method given on page 30 under the heading "Alternative Method of Constructing Your Enochian Chess Set."

If you draw a horizontal line directly through the middle of each elemental board, and another vertical line through the middle from top to bottom, your boards will then be divided into four equal sections of 16 squares each. These sections are representative again of the four elements, showing four principle actions of each element, and are referred to as the "Lesser Angles." The top left-hand angle in each board is the Air Angle. The top right-hand angle in each board is the Water Angle. The bottom right-hand angle is the Fire Angle, and the bottom left-hand angle the Earth Angle. These divisions then, within each board, signify an element within an element. For example:

Fire Board:
>   Fire Angle of Fire Board (lower right) = Fiery part of Fire
>   Water Angle of Fire Board (upper right) = Watery part of Fire
>   Air Angle of Fire Board (upper left) = Airy part of Fire
>   Earth Angle of Fire Board (lower left) = Earthy part of Fire

Water Board:
>   Fire Angle of Water Board (lower right) = Fiery part of Water
>   Water Angle of Water Board (upper right) = Watery part of Water
>   Air Angle of Water Board (upper left) = Airy part of Water
>   Earth Angle of Water Board (lower left) = Earthy part of Water

Air Board:
>   Fire Angle of Air Board (lower right) = Fiery part of Air
>   Water Angle of Air Board (upper right) = Watery part of Air

Air Angle of Air Board (upper left) = Airy part of Air
Earth Angle of Air Board (lower left) = Earthy part of Air

Earth Board:
Fire Angle of Earth Board (lower right) = Fiery part of Earth
Water Angle of Earth Board (upper right) = Watery part of Earth
Air Angle of Earth Board (upper left) = Airy part of Earth
Earth Angle of Earth Board (lower left) = Earthy part of Earth

It would suffice at this point to say that the four boards representing the four elements are simply reflections of the four aspects of nature. A good example of this is to apply the qualities of heat and dryness to Fire, cold and moisture to Water, heat and moisture to Air, and cool and dryness to Earth. These are of course the cornerstones on which the esoteric sciences are built and have been recognized as such since the beginning of recorded history.

Each square of the boards is divided into four flat faces, and if you look down onto a square, it has the appearance of a pyramid shape, which in fact is what it is. Each face of a chess square is then the face of a vast pyramid of power. There are four schools of thought as to the make-up of these pyramid squares. The original Golden Dawn Enochian chess set pyramid squares had truncated tops. The squares were colored according to their attributions, but the actual attributions were not drawn thereon until the Adept began using the game for divination, when the attributions became necessary. The truncated tops were left blank without the Enochian letters from the Tablets inscribed on them. One of the reasons the Golden Dawn did not use the Enochian letters on the chessboards was simply because, if all the Servient Squares were placed together and the angelic hierarchy that binds them (i.e., the great Central Cross, Calvary Cross, and Kerubic Squares) were omitted, there would be a slightly chaotic situation in which the power emitted by the chessboards would only be from the lower angelic forces fragmented in each particular corner. If you decide to place all the attributions on the boards, I suggest that you place the symbol of Spirit (✹) in the truncated pyramid top. These forces are then bound together to an acceptable level through the unseen forces of Spirit.

Another way is to omit the use of the white truncated pyramid top completely, as shown by Regardie. If this is done, a white border must be placed around the outside of each board to contain the forces therein. In this case there are some who still paint on the attributions and others who prefer to leave the attributions off. In my own experience I have found that, for those who are fully familiar with the symbology of the Enochian chessboards, and what square represents what, it is not necessary to draw the attributions. They act merely as a visual reminder as to what each square represents. If you prefer to have your flashing boards without their attributions painted on them, perhaps you could draw up a reference chart that you can keep near your boards when playing.

Ultimately it must be up to the individual person who makes a chess set to decide on the design. Examples of each element board, the colors and attributions drawn on the squares, are given in the following diagrams. Although all given symbols are drawn onto your boards in the order given in the following diagrams, some of the symbols therein also double as codes as to what color is given to each triangle within each square. These are:

△ symbolizes Fire and its triangle is colored red with all symbols drawn thereon in green.

▽ symbolizes Water and its triangle is colored blue with all symbols drawn thereon in orange.

△ symbolizes Air and its triangle is colored yellow with all symbols drawn thereon in mauve.

▽ symbolizes Earth and its triangle is colored black with all symbols drawn thereon in white.

The truncated top of each pyramid is colored white and any symbol thereon is black, although the old Golden Dawn manuscripts show no symbol drawn thereon.

The actual size of the chessboards is entirely up to you, but they should be in proportion to the size of the chess pieces that you construct.

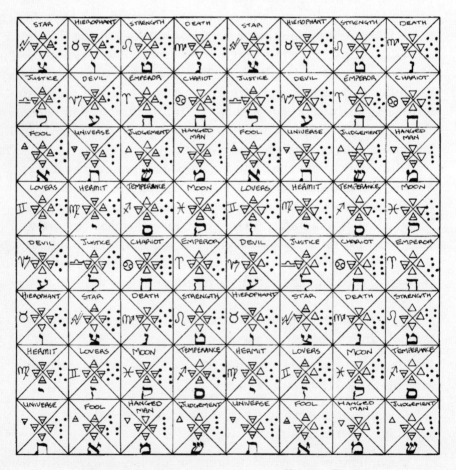

FIGURE 5—SYMBOLOGY OF THE EARTH BOARD

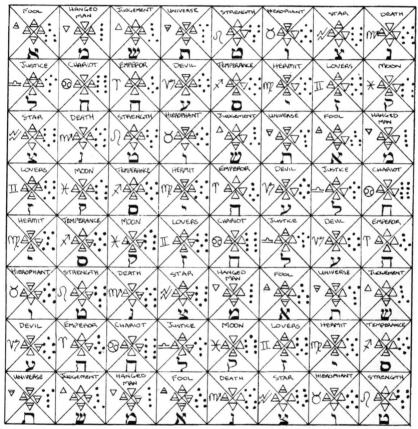

FIGURE 6—SYMBOLOGY OF THE AIR BOARD

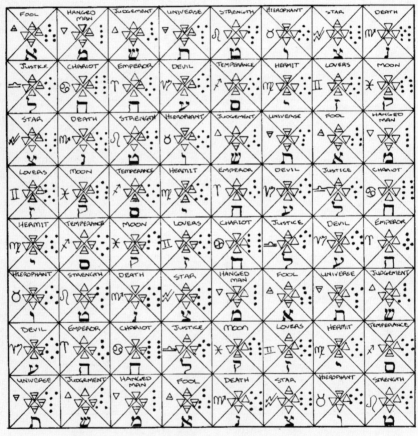

FIGURE 7—SYMBOLOGY OF THE WATER BOARD

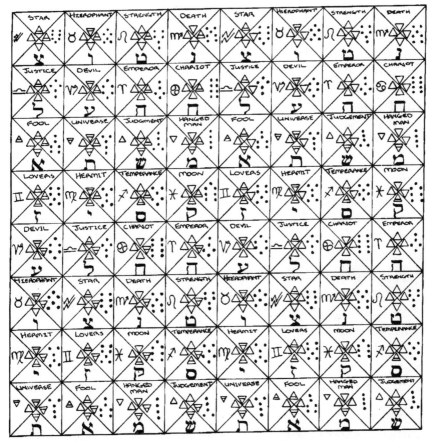

FIGURE 8—SYMBOLOGY OF THE FIRE BOARD

The formula that gave the layout of the attributions, as given in figures 5 to 8, is through four specific permutations of Tetragrammaton.[1] Tetragrammaton refers to the divine name as given in Hebrew Kabbalistic teachings and is identified in the English language by the letters YHVH (Hebrew יהוה), which simply means "to be" or "in existence."[2]

Y is the word "Yod" and representative of the elemental force of Fire. There are three signs of the Zodiac associated with the Fire element, and they are Aries (♈), Leo (♌) and Sagittarius (♐). Fire is considered a positive/masculine energy.

H is the word "Heh" and representative of the elemental force of Water. There are three signs of the Zodiac associated with the Water element, which are Cancer (♋), Scorpio (♏) and Pisces (♓). Water is considered a negative/feminine energy.

V is the word "Vau" and representative of the elemental force of Air. There are three signs of the Zodiac associated with the Air element, which are Libra (♎), Aquarius (♒) and Gemini (♊). Air is considered a positive/masculine energy.

H (final), which will be subsequently abbreviated as "Hf," is the word "Heh." This is different from the first "Heh" and is representative of the elemental force of Earth. The three signs of the Zodiac associated are Capricorn (♑), Taurus (♉) and Virgo (♍). Earth is considered a negative/feminine energy.

The astrological system of quadruplicities is also associated with the Tetragrammaton; these are the Cardinal, Fixed and Mutable signs. Cardinal is an initiating, active energy and likened to the Fire element and therefore the Yod force. Fixed is a set, concentrative but penetrating energy and is likened to the Water element and therefore the "Heh" force. Mutable is

---

1. These four permutations of the Name are associated with four tribes of Israel which are in turn associated with the four Cardinal signs: Aries, Cancer, Libra and Capricorn.

2. See *The Holy Kabbalah* by A.E. Waite (1929), *The Kabbalah Unveiled* by S.L. MacGregor Mathers (Routledge and Kegan Paul, 1926) and *Kabbalah* by Charles Poncé (Straight Arrow, 1973) for further information on Tetragrammaton.

changeable, flexible but harmonious, and likened to the Air element and therefore the "Vau" force. The Earth element (Hf) is made up of the other three elements and therefore represents the four elements in their more manifested form. Each of the four elements has one Cardinal Zodiac sign, one Fixed sign and one Mutable sign, therefore showing the different phases and manifestations of each element.

The attributions on the squares of the chessboards are worked out through a rank and column formula using the letters of Tetragrammaton. The order of Tetragrammaton on each board is worked out using the letter of the element of each angle as the starting point. However, there is a set direction in which each board is read, shown by the arrows in the diagrams below. For example, the Air and Water Boards are read from right to left horizontally in the upper quarters and left to right horizontally in the lower quarters (mirror image). The Fire and Earth Boards are read left to right horizontally in the upper quarters and left to right horizontally in the lower quarters. To get the vertical order of Tetragrammaton, the corner letter of the active angles (Fire and Air Angles) goes to the fourth square down and the rest of the letters from the angle are read in duplicate to the horizontal towards the corner. The corner letter of the passive angles (Earth and Water Angles) goes to the corner square and the rest of the letters are read duplicate to the horizontal out from the corner.[3]

---

3. "The Book of Concealed Mystery," found in the Mathers translation entitled *The Kabbalah Unveiled,* throws much more light on the various aspects of Tetragrammaton and shows the placing of the chess pieces, discussed later in this book, which, when seen through the eyes of an Enochian chess player, opens up new levels of game tactics.

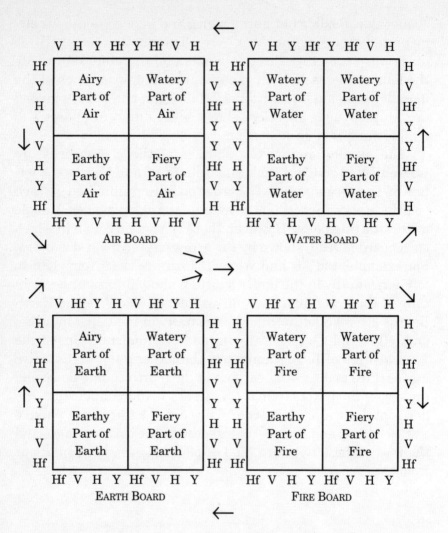

FIGURE 9—ORDER OF TETRAGRAMMATON APPLIED TO THE
ENOCHIAN CHESSBOARDS

The formula for working the attributions to the chess squares is the order of Tetragrammaton through a column and rank system. The top of the boards are always the Air and Water Angles. The columns are the vertical rows of squares, and the ranks are the horizontal rows of squares.

TABLE I—ASTROLOGICAL ATTRIBUTION TO TETRAGRAMMATON

Rank	Column			
	Y **Cardinal**	**H** **Fixed**	**V** **Mutable**	**H** **Element**
Y	♈	♌	♐	△
H	♑	♏	♓	▽
V	♎	♒	♊	△̶
Hf	♑	♉	♍	▽̶

For reference, the pyramid faces of each chess square may be numbered thus:

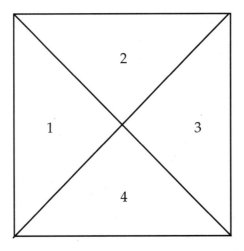

FIGURE 10—PYRAMID FACES OF A CHESS SQUARE

Triangle 1 shows the element color of the element board (e.g., red for Fire Board, blue for Water Board, yellow for Air, black for Earth), symbol of the element and astrological attribution (Zodiac sign—see Table I) in complementary color.

Triangle 2 shows the color of the elemental association of the letter of Tetragrammaton ruling the column and the ele-

ment symbol itself. Also shown is the Tarot trump that relates
to the astrological attribution of triangle 1 (refer to figures 1 to
4 for the complete associations and their relationships).

Triangle 3 shows the elemental color of the Lesser Angle of
the board together with its symbol and geomantic figure, which
is associated with the Zodiacal sign of triangle 1.

Triangle 4 shows the elemental color of the letter of Tetragrammaton ruling the rank and its elemental symbol, and the
Hebrew letter associated with the Tarot trump of triangle 2.

Therefore, referring back to Table I, where two Yods meet,
you will know that the square they meet in will be associated
with Aries (Cardinal Fire force), and all other attributions on
that square will be similarly associated; e.g., Tarot trump, The
Emperor; geomantic figure, Puer; Hebrew letter "Heh." Where a
Heh and a Vau meet, the square will be attributed to Aquarius
and all the other attributions follow.

Alternative Method of Constructing Your Chess Set

For the chess enthusiast and those who do not want to pursue
the esoteric side of Enochian chess, or go to the trouble of making elaborately colored boards, you can purchase two very cheap
modern chess sets. Take one board and color the edges or outside borders of the four quarters each in a different elemental
color. In this way each angle will represent an element, similar
to the Enochian chessboards. For example, the top left-hand
quarter of the board will have its border colored yellow, the top
right-hand colored blue, the bottom right-hand colored red and
the bottom left-hand colored black. The chessboard itself
remains with black and white squares.

The coloring of the borders enables angle identification for
your four sets of chess pieces. From the two sets of modern
chess pieces bought with the boards, divide them up into four
sets of five pieces and four pawns each; i.e., one king, queen,
knight, bishop and rook and four pawns per set. Each elemental

set can be identified by coloring it the color of the elemental angle that it represents. A pocket four-handed chess set can be created this way.

It is important for you to realize that, once the flashing colors of the boards and pieces are omitted, the game ceases to be an Enochian chess game and becomes simply a four-handed chess game. I personally have one such set that I use quite regularly when working out game strategy or playing simply for pleasure. One would use the fully constructed flashing set for divination play. I do not wish to give the impression that I use the small set all the time; I do not. Each has its place, and experiencing the full impact of the Enochian set even for game strategy on a regular basis is a must, but a small set is handy when one is traveling or playing by correspondence, because it is not good from an esoteric viewpoint to leave a fully colored Enochian set exposed unattended for any length of time.

Constructing the Chess Pieces

Enochian chess pieces and pawns are constructed in the images of Egyptian god pantheons. Like the chessboards, these pieces represent certain energies and archetypes (which are discussed in length in Part III, Divination). There are four sets of pieces and pawns, each set representing a different pantheon and each a particular element, thereby ruling an elemental chessboard.

There are two schools of thought as to the sets of chess pieces. One uses an Egyptian pantheon of five pieces and four pawns per set, each representing an angle of the chess board, thereby playing the four pantheons on one board: the Fire pantheon set on the Fire Angle, the Water pantheon set on the Water Angle and so on. The other method plays one pantheon per board, and the element of the angle upon which each set plays is identified by the color of the base of each piece.

Within the Golden Dawn, the most common approach was to have the four different pantheons playing on one board, one pantheon in each corner. This, however, was done to save time and effort: constructing a complete pantheon for each different board required a great deal of work, and only a few within the Golden Dawn attempted this. However, it has become common practice to simply use one pantheon on all boards (the main pantheon attributed to the Earth Board) and ignore the others. One of the reasons for this is that the Earth pieces are in fact the main god-forms and the others are merely variants of them. This is all very well when playing the game as a form of strategy, but when you get into divination, this method shows limitations. The quick and easy method of four pantheons played together on one board, for each of the four boards, is probably far better suited for the chess game overall.

The size of your chess pieces and the material used to construct them is entirely up to you. In the old Golden Dawn, two-dimensional figures were made up on hard cardboard and stuck onto or slid into a small piece of grooved wood that acted as a stand to hold the cards upright. Many people, however, used the card cutouts flat on the chess boards. I prefer to use three-dimensional figures. These can be made out of modeling clay, fiber glass, ceramics, wood, marble etc. The choice is yours, just as long as you use a material that can be easily painted with flashing colors.

The coloring of the chess pieces may also be done two different ways. The first and easiest way is to color the front and base of the piece with the color of the element of the angle it represents; e.g., red for the Fire Angle, blue for the Water Angle, yellow for the Air Angle and black for the Earth Angle. The back of the piece is colored according to the element represented by the piece itself; e.g., King, white for Spirit; Knight, red for Fire, the Yod force; Queen, blue for Water, the Heh force; Bishop, yellow for Air, the Vau force; Rook, black for Earth, the Heh(f) force.

The second method of coloring is more imaginative and is taken from the "Colouring of the Gods of Egypt who rule above the Pyramids of the sixteen servient Angels and squares."[1]

---

1. From the "Concourse of Forces" manuscript, which is partly given in Regardie's *Golden Dawn*.

TABLE II—GOD-FORM NAMES AND THEIR PIECE ATTRIBUTIONS[2]

Piece	Fire Set	Water Set
King	Chnupis Kneph	Ptah ha Pan-Lses
Knight	Ra	Sebek
Queen	Sati-Ashtoreth	Thouriest
Bishop	Toum	Hapimon
Rook	Anouke	Shooen (Shooeu-tha-ist)

Piece	Air Set	Earth Set
King	Socharis	Osiris
Knight	Seb	Horus
Queen	Knousou Pekht	Isis
Bishop	Shu Zoan	Aroueris
Rook	Tharpeshest-Jefine-pasht	Nephthys

Each set of five pieces for each pantheon represents the operation of Spirit and the four Elemental rulers, the five points of the pentagram, the five letters of YHShVH, the Tarot Ace and the Court cards. Each piece is either throned or standing, depending on what sex it represents, using the father, mother, son and daughter concept. The masculine or active principles are always on the move and hence are standing, while the feminine or passive principles are more stable. The power behind them both is of course the King, who as Spirit is more of a guiding force than a front-line figure. As such, he is throned.

The Pawns and Their Elemental Associations

The pawn's god-forms, images and names do not change, no matter what pantheon they are placed in front of. Therefore, you will have four identical sets of pawns per board. The angle

---

2. Some of these names differ from the Regardie publication. These current names are taken from copies of Wynn Westcott's chess notebook, which was at Whare Ra.

they belong to in play is defined by the color of their bases (black for the Earth Angle etc.). They are the vice-regents to the four elemental pieces, and thereby singularly associated. At the beginning of game play, a pawn is placed only in front of the piece it serves. These pawns are the four god-forms of the Children of Horus:

TABLE III—FOUR PAWNS AND THEIR ASSOCIATIONS

Image	Name	Regent	Elemental Representation	Prime Element
Hawk head	Kabexnuv	Knight	Fire, Air, Earth	Fire
Dog head	Tmoumthph	Queen	Water, Air, Earth	Water
Ape head	Ahephi	Bishop	Air, Fire, Water	Air
Human head	Ameshet	Rook	Earth, Fire, Water	Earth

The King has no single pawn; all the pieces and pawns of its angle are its vice-regents.

Coloring and Descriptions of the Chess Pieces

Not too long ago, Adam McLean published copies of the chess pieces of Wynn Westcott that had been uncovered by Bob Gilbert. The following diagrams are not copies of Westcott's chess pieces, but are taken from a Whare Ra chess set copied from that of a former chief of that temple. A photo of one of the Whare Ra sets was sent to McLean for purposes of comparison before he published the Westcott pieces.

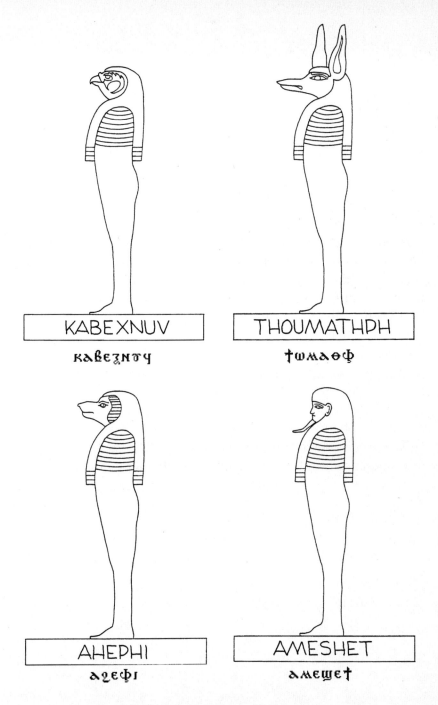

FIGURE 11—FOUR PAWNS

Earth Pantheon

Osiris—Spirit of Earth, Tarot Ace of Disks. Osiris (fig. 12) is classed as the Silent One, and represents Spirit. He is a bearded, mummified figure of a man who sits on a black and white throne. In his left hand he bears a yellow scourge and crook; in his right hand is a green phoenix wand. He wears a striped collar of red, blue, yellow and black to represent all the elements. On his white conical crown he has twin green feathers, with a red cross representing Spirit. His face and hands are green with black and white striped arm bands, and he has a black menat hanging from the back of his neck. His name in Coptic is pronounced Aeshoori. (Note: The name in English is written on one side of the base of the piece, while the Coptic letters are written on the other side of the base.) The central stripes on the King's arm bands relate to the element he represents, while the outer stripes are a complementary color. All arm bands, wristbands and ankle bands of the other god-forms represent the color of their sub-element, and the outer stripes represent the elemental angle.

OSIRIS

ⲏⲅⲱⲱⲣⲓⲥ

FIGURE 12—OSIRIS (EARTH KING)

Earth Pantheon *(continued)*

Horus—Fire of Earth, Tarot Knight of Disks. Horus (fig. 13) is the Fiery avenging force of Spirit. He stands ready to stride forward. He has a hawk's head and the crown of the North and South united, showing a red conical top with a white base and yellow plume. His nemyss is black with red knots. In his left hand he holds a green phoenix wand and in his right hand a green ankh. His skin is naturally colored, and he wears a black skirt with a red skirt wrap, shoulder straps and belt (which has a yellow pouch in front of it). The wristbands, ankle bands, arm bands and collar are black and red striped. The base on which he stands is black. His name in Coptic is Hoooor.

HORUS

ϩⲱⲱⲣ

FIGURE 13—HORUS (EARTH KNIGHT)

Earth Pantheon (*continued*)

Isis—Water of Earth, Tarot Queen of Disks. Isis (fig. 14) is the mother and beginning. She sits on a black and white throne holding a green ankh in her right hand and a green lotus wand with a red top in her left. Her headdress is a green symbol of the throne and nemyss, while her arm bands and wristbands are blue and black striped. She has a black gown and naturally colored skin. Her Coptic name is Eeisest.

ISIS

HICE

FIGURE 14—ISIS (EARTH QUEEN)

Earth Pantheon *(continued)*

Aroueris—Air of Earth, Tarot Prince/King of Disks. Aroueris (fig. 15) represents the Airy forces of Spirit. This god-form stands in human form holding a green phoenix wand in his left hand and a green ankh in his right. He has a black tunic with yellow belt, pouch and skirt wrap. The shoulder straps are also yellow, and the collar is a combination of yellow and black stripes, as are the wristbands, ankle bands and arm bands. The nemyss he wears is black with yellow knots, while the conical crown of the North and South united is white on a red base with a yellow plume and nose guard. His skin is naturally colored, and his Coptic name is Areeooueris.

AROUERIS

ⲀⲢⲎⲰⲦⲈⲢⲓⲥ

FIGURE 15—AROUERIS (EARTH BISHOP)

Earth Pantheon *(continued)*

Nephthys—Earth of Earth, Tarot Princess of Disks. Nephthys (fig. 16) the Bride and force of Earth. She sits on a black and white throne enclosed in a rectangular frame of the same color. Her robe is black and her wristbands and arm bands are black and white striped. In her left hand she holds a green lotus wand with a red top, and in her right she holds a green ankh. She wears a green nemyss with a green crescent symbol above a yellow, green and red rectangular headdress, which is the hieroglyph of her name. In Coptic her name is Neuphthusest.

NEPHTHYS

ⲚⲈ⳨Ⲫⲟ⳨ⲓⲉ⳨

FIGURE 16—NEPHTHYS (EARTH ROOK)

Air Pantheon

Socharis (Seker)—Spirit of Air, Tarot Ace of Swords. Socharis (fig. 17) is the Spirit of the force of Air, the Silent One. He is shown as a mummified form with the head of a falcon. He wears the white atef-crown with green and black striped feathers, a black nemyss and yellow menat. In his left hand he holds a yellow crook and scourge, in his right hand a green phoenix wand. The collar is yellow, blue and red striped. He has a red cross on his white robe, wears purple and yellow arm bands and sits on a yellow throne and base. His skin is colored green. In Coptic his name is Soukaourist.

FIGURE 17—SOCHARIS (AIR KING)

Air Pantheon *(continued)*

Seb—Fire of Air, Tarot Knight/King of Swords. Seb (fig. 18) is the avenging force of Air, He who held fast the wicked. This god-form has a human form, standing, with naturally colored skin. His nemyss is yellow with red knots, and a white goose, sacred to Amen-Ra, sits upon it. The tunic he wears is yellow with a red skirt wrap and belt with a yellow pouch. The shoulder straps are red and his collar, wristbands, ankle bands and arm bands are red and yellow striped. The base he stands on is yellow. In his left hand he holds a green phoenix wand and in his right hand a green ankh. His skin is naturally colored. In Coptic his name is Soubal.

SEB

ϥⲟⲩ ⲃⲁⲗ

FIGURE 18—SEB (AIR KNIGHT)

Air Pantheon *(continued)*

Knousou Pekht—Water of Air, Tarot Queen of Swords. Knousou Pekht (fig. 19) is a form of Nut, goddess of the sky. She sits on a yellow and purple throne and wears a yellow robe. Her collar is red, black, blue and yellow. Her arm bands and wristbands are blue and yellow striped. In her left hand she holds a green lotus wand with a red top and in her right a green ankh. Her urn headdress and nemyss are green, while the base is yellow. Her skin is naturally colored. Her name in Coptic is Knooou tha pekht.

KNOUSOU PEKHT

ⲐⲚⲰⲞⲨ ⲐⲀ ⲠⲈⲐⲎⲦ

FIGURE 19—KNOUSOU PEKHT (AIR QUEEN)

Air Pantheon *(continued)*

Shu Zoan—Air of Air, Tarot King/Prince of Swords. Shu Zoan (fig. 20) is a personification of the atmosphere. He stands as if striding forward and wears upon his head a blue and white feather and a yellow nemyss with mauve knots. His collar, arm bands, wristbands and ankle bands are yellow with mauve stripes. The shoulder straps are mauve and the tunic yellow, with a mauve skirt wrap and belt. In his left hand is a green phoenix wand and in his right a green ankh. The base is yellow. His name in Coptic is Zoo ooan.

FIGURE 20—SHU ZOAN (AIR BISHOP)

Air Pantheon *(continued)*

Tharpeshest Jefine Pasht—Earth of Air, Tarot Princess of Swords. Tharpeshest Jefine Pasht (fig. 21) is a form of Bast (Sekhmet) and represents the destructive powers of the Sun. This representation shows a lion-headed woman seated on a yellow and mauve throne surrounded by a yellow and mauve frame. She is wearing a red solar disk surmounted by a yellow uraeus serpent as a headdress with a red nemyss. Her skin is green. She holds a green lotus with red top in her right hand and in her left a green ankh. Her arm bands are black and yellow striped, and she has a black belt and yellow skirt. The base she sits on is yellow. Her Coptic name is Tharpheshst va Knooutha pe.

THARPESHEST JEFINE PASHT

ⲑⲁⲣⲫⲉϣⲅ ⳝⲁ ⲑⲛⲱⲟⲧⲑⲁ ⲡⲉ

FIGURE 21—THARPESHEST JEFINE PASHT (AIR ROOK)

Water Pantheon

Ptah ha (Ra) Pan-Lses—Spirit of Water, Tarot Ace of Cups. The Opener of the Day, Ptah ha (Ra) Pan-Lses (fig. 22) is a bearded, mummified man seated upon an orange and blue throne on a blue base. His robe is white with a red belt and cross. His nemyss is black with curved blue stripes on it. The menat is blue. On his nemyss there is a red band on which is a yellow lunar disk with curved horns. His skin is green, as is the phoenix wand in his right hand. A yellow crook and scourge are held in his left hand. His wristbands are blue and orange striped. In Coptic his name is Ptah Katheenkeest.

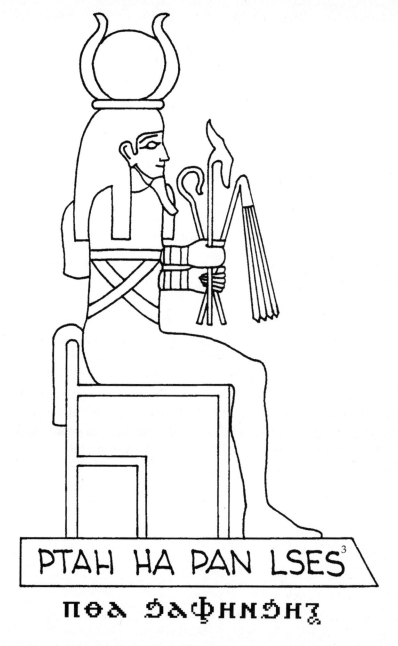

PTAH HA PAN LSES[3]

ⲡⲟⲗ ⲇⲗⲫⲏⲛⲑⲏⳤ

FIGURE 22—PTAH HA PAN-LSES (WATER KING)

_____

3. I have left the above name as was given in the Y manuscript, but the Coptic actually translates as Ptah Chaphen Chēx.

Water Pantheon *(continued)*

Sebek—Fire of Water, Tarot Knight/King of Cups. Sebek (fig. 23) is the Gatherer, a crocodile-headed man wearing a head-dress of two small red solar disks between the two blue and white striped plumes upon a green mount and ram's horns. Under this is a yellow band which sits atop a blue nemyss with red knots. His collar is blue with a red stripe running through it, as are his wristbands, arm bands and ankle bands. His tunic is blue with red shoulder straps, belt and skirt wrap, and he has a yellow pouch. In his left hand he holds a green phoenix wand and in his right hand a green ankh. His skin is green and the base he stands on is blue. In Coptic his name is Seba Knooou haourist tha mooou.

SEBEK

ϲⲉⲃⲁ ⲇⲛⲱⲟⲩ ⲅⲗⲟⲧⲣ
ⲓⲅ ⲑⲁ ⲙⲱⲟⲩ

FIGURE 23—SEBEK (WATER KNIGHT)

Water Pantheon *(continued)*

Thoueris (Taurt)—Water of Water, Tarot Queen of Cups. Thoueris (fig. 24) is Patroness of Childbirth and has a benevolent character. She has the head of a hippopotamus (which is partly combined with that of a crocodile) along with large human breasts, the body of a hippopotamus—which appears to be pregnant—the back of a crocodile and the feet of a lion. She is seated on an orange and blue throne which has a blue base. Her headdress has black cow horns with a red lunar disk between them, mounted on a yellow and black headpiece which in turn is mounted on a green nemyss. In her left hand she holds a green lotus wand with a red top and in her right she has a green ankh. Her collar is yellow with thin black stripes, and her arm bands and wristbands are orange with a blue stripe above and below. The robe she wears is blue. Her Coptic name is Theeooour ist Thamooou.

THOUERIS

ⲑⲏⲱⲟⲧⲣ ⲓⲥ ⲑⲁⲙⲱⲟⲧ

FIGURE 24—THOUERIS (WATER QUEEN)

Water Pantheon *(continued)*

Hapimoun—Air of Water, Tarot King/Prince of Cups. Hapimoun (fig. 25) is god of the Nile. This representation shows a man standing, as if striding forward. He wears a green headdress of aquatic plants, which have red tops and yellow bands and buds over a blue nemyss with yellow knots. The collar he wears is yellow with blue stripes as are also his wristbands and ankle bands. His tunic is blue but has a yellow skirt wrap and belt. In each hand he holds two green water jugs. The name of the god-form in Coptic is Xopist tha mooou.

HAPIMOUN

ⳌⲞⲠⲒⲄ ⲐⲀ ⲘⲰⲞⲨ

FIGURE 25—HAPIMOUN (WATER BISHOP)

Water Pantheon *(continued)*

Shooen—Earth of Water, Tarot Princess of Cups. Shooen (fig. 26) is a form of Hathor, She that Nourishes. She is encased in a blue rectangle with an orange border. Her headdress is a pair of black bull horns with a red lunar disk between them, mounted on a green nemyss. She has naturally colored skin, a cow's head and a robust human body. Her skirt is blue, as is her shoulder strap. She has blue arm bands and wristbands with a black center stripe, and she holds a green lotus with a red top and yellow stripe in her right hand and a green ankh in her left. The throne she sits on is blue with orange lines. Her name in Coptic is Sheeooee tha ist.

SHOOEN

ⱳⱨⱳⰵⱅ ⰲⰺ ⰹⰵ

FIGURE 26—SHOOEN (WATER ROOK)

Fire Pantheon

Chnupis Kneph—Spirit of Fire, Tarot Ace of Wands. Chnupis Kneph (fig. 27) is the Molder of Men. This god-form is a throned, ram-headed, mummified man. The throne on which he sits is red with green lines and sits on a red base. His headdress shows twin green plumes mounted on a green conical hat with a red solar disk, surrounded by a band of yellow. At the base of the hat are two green ram's horns, which are only slightly arched upward. His nemyss is black, and his neck collar and menat are red with thin black stripes. The shoulder collar he wears is red, blue, yellow and red striped and has the same red-cross band of all the Kings. The wristbands he wears are red with yellow stripes at each end. His skin is green. In his right hand he holds a green phoenix wand and in his left a yellow crook and scourge. The name he has in Coptic is Knou phooeesh.[4]

---

4. Crowley, in *777*, has the Coptic names for the Fire King and the Fire Knight transposed.

FIGURE 27—CHNUPIS KNEPH (FIRE KING)

Fire Pantheon *(continued)*

Ra—Fire of Fire, Tarot Knight/King of Wands. Ra (fig. 28) is the Sun in fullness of strength. This representation shows a hawk-headed man striding forward. His skin is naturally colored. His beak is green, while his eyes are red. The headdress he wears is a red solar disk surrounded by a yellow serpent, which is mounted on a red nemyss with green knots. The collar is green with a red stripe on its borders, the same as his arm bands, wristbands and ankle bands. The tunic is red with a green skirt wrap, belt and purse. He holds a green phoenix wand in his left hand a green ankh in his right, and he stands on a red base. His name is Coptic is Phaouroo.

RA

Ⲫⲗⲟⲅⲣⲱ

FIGURE 28—RA (FIRE KNIGHT)

Fire Pantheon *(continued)*

Sati-Ashtoreth—Water of Fire, Tarot Queen of Wands. Sati-Ashtoreth (fig. 29) is the Purifier and Consecrator. Here, she is a woman seated on a red throne with green lines. She is wearing a white crown from which protrude a vulture's head and tail feathers of the same color. From this two black cow horns emerge. Her collar, wristbands, arm bands and shoulder strap are blue with red stripes at each end. The robe she wears is red, and her skin is naturally colored. In her right hand she holds a green ankh and in her left a green lotus wand with a red top. In Coptic her name is Isthaoureth.

SATI ASHTORETH

ιℇ૨ΔΟΤΡℇΘ

FIGURE 29—SATI-ASHTORETH (FIRE QUEEN)

Fire Pantheon *(continued)*

Toum—Air of Fire, Tarot King/Prince of Wands. This figure (fig. 30) shows a man striding forward wearing a headdress of both the North and South. The conical part is white while the base and back support are red, as is also a plume in the front portion. His nemyss is red with yellow knots, while his collar, arm bands, wristbands and ankle bands are yellow with red at each end. The tunic and shoulder straps are red, while his skirt wrap, belt and pouch are yellow. In his left hand is a green phoenix wand and in his right a green ankh. The base he stands on is red, and his skin is naturally colored. His Coptic title is Thoooum moooou.

TOUM

ⲐⲰⲞⲨⲘ ⲘⲰⲞⲨ

FIGURE 30—TOUM (FIRE BISHOP)

Fire Pantheon *(continued)*

Anouke—Earth of Fire, Tarot Princess of Wands. Anouke (fig. 31) is Mistress of the Gods, giver of power, health and joy. This representation shows a woman seated on a red throne with green stripes, the same as the rectangle she sits in. She wears upon her head a green crown of feathers, in which are red and gold feathers also. Her nemyss is gold and the band around it is red. Her skin is naturally colored and she has blue eyes. The collar, arm bands and wristbands are black with red stripes at each end. Her tunic is red. She holds a green ankh in her right hand and a green lotus wand with a red top in her left. The base on which the throne rests is red. Her Coptic title is Ooan oo Kist.

ANOUKE

ⲱⲁⲧⲱϭⲓⲣ

FIGURE 31—ANOUKE (FIRE ROOK)

Ptah

Spirit of Spirits, Ruler of Life and Death. This piece (fig. 32) is
only used in divination and has no strategical use except to
mark the divining square. All this will be discussed fully in Part
III of this book. The Ptah piece is colored white and is about half
the size of the other pieces. He is a standing form, bald and
bearded, holding in his hands a scepter and the emblems of life
and stability. His tight-fitting clothes have two holes where his
hands protrude, and a menat falls from the back of his neck.
The pedestal on which he stands is the sign of Maat.

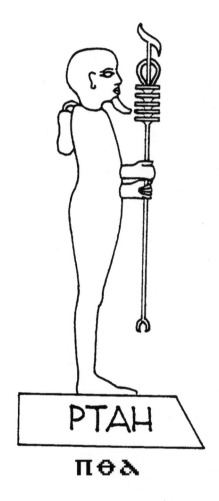

FIGURE 32—PTAH

Appendix to Part I
Table of Symbols and Associations

Zodiac Sign or Element	Planet Symbol	Geomantic Figure
Aries	Mars	Puer
Taurus	Venus	Amissio
Gemini	Mercury	Albus
Cancer	Moon	Populus
Leo	Sun	Fortuna Major
Virgo	Mercury	Conjunctio
Libra	Venus	Puella
Scorpio	Pluto (Mars)	Rubeus
Sagittarius	Jupiter	Acquisitio
Capricorn	Saturn	Carcer
Aquarius	Uranus (Saturn)	Tristitia
Pisces	Neptune (Jupiter)	Laetitia
Fire	(Saturn/Mars)	Cauda Draconis
Earth	(Venus/Jupiter)	Caput Draconis
Air	(Sun/Leo)	Fortuna Minor
Water	(Moon/Cancer)	Via

Part II

Book of Air

The Game, Its Rules
and Method of Play

Enochian Chess:
The Game

B y now you understand what Enochian chess is and where it
originated. Perhaps you have made your board and
pieces—or at least you understand what they look like—
from Part I of this book. Now it is time for you to get your
thinking cap on, place a chessboard in front of you with your
four sets of pieces and have some fun with the technical aspects
of Enochian chess.

Enochian chess is a strategically intriguing game. You can
spend many enjoyable hours on game settings, piece movements,
rules of the game, recording and game strategy. It is a four-
handed game, which means that four sets of pieces and pawns
are used in game play and four players are required. The four
players pair off into two pairs, with each pair being allies. One
pair operates the passive elements (Water and Earth) and the
other pair operates the active elements (Air and Fire). However,
two people can play if each player operates a pair of allies. For
example, if you are playing with the Water Angle set, your ally is
the Earth Angle set. Your opponents will be the Air and Fire sets.

The object of the game is to paralyze your opponents' play by capturing their Kings. You and your ally thereby become victors. Enochian chess is played very much like ordinary chess with the exception of a few variations in the rules, which are tailored for four-handed play, and the starting positions of the pieces at the beginning of the game. Although there are formal rules given here, the question as to which player opens play is naturally a matter of choice between players, as is the direction of play. To explain, the order in which players make their moves can be either of two ways: deosil (clockwise) or widdershins (counterclockwise). These directions of movement have been matters of controversy for many years. There have been many variations in belief, and no doubt there will continue to be for many years to come. Suffice it to say at this point that playing deosil expands energy (raises consciousness) while playing widdershins contracts energy, drawing it down. Neither is classed as positive or negative; they are simply forms or a framework within which one operates.

Following are the official rules for Enochian chess, and how to record your games. The game strategy, opening play examples and commentaries, middle and endgame examples and commentaries which follow have been written in such a way that you will need an Enochian chess set in front of you if you are to derive full understanding. The intricacies involved in the commentaries on the game examples will be incomprehensible unless you actually see the pieces move across the board with the moves described.

You may find making fully colored boards and pieces a difficult task. If so, I suggest you make up a mock set, as described earlier, as a temporary measure.

Official
Rules for
Enochian Chess

1. The chessboards and their arrangements

1.1 There are four boards of play, each composed of 64 flat pyramid squares.

1.2 Each board is representative, through its pyramids of color (see "Constructing Your Chessboards," pp. 17–31), of one of the four elements (Earth, Air, Water and Fire) and is called an elemental board.

1.3 Each board is divided into four Angles of 16 squares each, with each Angle being representative of one of the four elements, identified by its respective color. Therefore each elemental board has one Angle of Air (upper left-hand Angle), Water (upper right-hand Angle), Fire (lower right-hand Angle), and Earth (lower left-hand Angle). An Angle is referred to herein as the elemental part of an elemental board. For example, the Airy part of Fire = the Air Angle of the Fire Board.

1.4   Placing the board so that you are looking towards the top, the squares viewed horizontally are called ranks and the squares viewed vertically are called columns.

1.5   Only one elemental chessboard is played on at a time for any given game.

2. The pieces and their arrangements

2.1   Each player starts with five pieces and four pawns associated with the element of the Angle being played; i.e., player 1 will be seated by the Earth Angle and operate the Earth set, player 2 will be seated by the Air Angle and operate the Air set, player 3 will be seated by the Water Angle and operate the Water set and player 4 will be seated by the Fire Angle and operate the Fire set.

2.2   Each set of chess pieces (pantheons) consists of a King, a Knight, a Queen, a Bishop, a Rook and four pawns.

2.3   On each corner square is placed a King, who shares his square with one other major piece. These corner squares are called Throne Squares.

2.4   On each of the sequential squares beside the King is placed one chess piece per square, the remaining three pieces in the order of Tetragrammaton according to the Tetragrammaton order of the element Angle of the board chosen to be played (see pp. 101–105).

2.5   On the column or rank directly in front of the four squares on which the pieces are placed, the pawns are sequentially positioned according to their vice-gerents.

2.6   On the Air Angle, the Air pieces and pawns are placed upon eight squares of the two upper ranks (i.e., two rows of four squares each). On the Water Angle, the Water pieces and pawns are placed upon the two right-hand columns. On the Fire Angle, the Fire pieces and pawns are placed on the two bottom ranks. On the Earth Angle, the Earth pieces and pawns are placed upon the two left-hand columns.

2.7   There are 16 opening positions for the chess pieces from which a game can be started: four positions per board, each derived from the order of Tetragrammaton in each Angle. (Because the Tetragrammaton on the Fire and Earth Boards is the same, as with the Air and Water Boards, in actual fact there are only eight opening positions.)

2.8   All four sets in each Angle must be placed according to only one position for all, in any given game; i.e., if the Earth of Earth setting is being used, all sets are placed in that setting.

3. How the major pieces and pawns move (the term "piece" will refer henceforth to "piece and/or pawn")

3.1   **King**—The King moves as in ordinary chess, one square at a time in any direction. To capture another piece, a King must land on the square occupied by the other piece and remove it from the board.

3.2   **Queen**—The Queen does not move as in ordinary chess. The Queen moves over three squares in any direction (taking into account the square she is on; therefore, she moves two squares in any direction), horizontally, vertically or diagonally, forward or backward, always leaping over any piece in her path. The Queen can only capture a piece on the last square on which she lands in any move, thereby removing the captured piece.

3.3   **Knight**—The Knight's move is the same as in ordinary chess: move one square in any direction, then forward one square diagonally; or one square diagonally and one forward; or two squares in a straight line and one across at a right angle. The Knight always leaps over any piece obstructing its progress but cannot capture it. The

Knight can only capture on the last square it lands on, removing the captured piece from the board.

3.4 **Bishop**—The Bishop moves as in ordinary chess, diagonally only, right or left, forward or backwards, any distance in a straight line. It cannot leap over any pieces; therefore, its move is stopped if it does not capture the piece obstructing its move. When the Bishop captures any piece, it lands on the square occupied by that piece, takes the captured piece off the board and remains on that square until moved again.

3.5 **Rook (Castle)**—The Rook moves as in ordinary chess, horizontally or vertically, forward or backward, in a straight line. The Rook can capture a piece on any square it moves to in a straight line, remaining on that square until its next turn. The Rook cannot leap over any obstructing piece in its way but has its move restricted unless it captures the obstructing piece. The Rook does not move diagonally.

3.6 **Pawns**—A pawn moves only one square at a time forward (not two squares on the first move as permitted in ordinary chess). The regular method of capturing another piece by moving one square diagonally, left or right, in the forward direction, is still used. Pawns do not move backward or at right angles to their direction of play as indicated from their opening positions.

4. The conduct of the game

4.1 Although the game is designed for four players, each operating one set of pieces, two players can play by utilizing each a pair of allies. The Actives (Air and Fire) are allies and the Passives (Water and Earth) are allies. If two people are playing, each player will operate one pair of allies.

(a) A player operating two sets of pieces cannot choose to move a piece from either set. When each Angle's turn comes around, a piece from the set for that specific Angle can be moved. An exception to this is rule 9.1.

4.2 The players must decide before the game is started as to what direction they will play, either widdershins or deosil. The original Golden Dawn version utilized the deosil direction of play, but experimentation with both directions shows that it can be played either way. However, the direction of play cannot be changed in the middle of a game.

4.3 The Angle for each player at the commencement of the game is decided by the throw of dice. The one who throws the highest number chooses the Angle he or she wishes to play. The players throwing the second and third highest numbers then choose their Angles, leaving the fourth player with the remaining Angle. If there are only two players, the throw of dice decides who plays the Passives and who plays the Actives: the highest number plays the Actives.

4.4 The player operating the pieces of the greater Angle commences the game. (The greater Angle is that of the element of the board being used; e.g., Fire Angle of Fire Board, Water Angle of Water Board, etc.)

4.5 At each player's turn to move, he or she must move one piece only, then wait for his or her next turn to again move one piece.

5. The definition of the move

5.1 A move is the transfer of a piece from one square to another which is either vacant or occupied by an enemy piece.

5.2 One cannot move to any square occupied by an allied piece or by one of his or her own pieces. (Rule 11.3 is an exception to this.)

5.3 No piece except the Knight and Queen may cross a square occupied by another piece.

5.4 A piece entering a square occupied by an enemy piece captures it as part of the same move, and the move ends at that point. The captured piece must be immediately removed from the chessboard by the player making the capture.

5.5 There is no castling.

5.6 There is no *en passant*.

5.7 A move is completed when a player's hand is removed from the piece being moved.

5.8 The touched piece:

(a) Provided a player warns the other players, he or she may adjust one or more pieces on their squares. However, the pieces must not be moved from any square to any other square until it is the player's turn.

(b) If a player, on his or her turn, touches one or more pieces, he or she must move or capture the first piece touched that can be moved or captured.

(c) If the move or capture is not possible after a piece has been touched, the player is free to make any legal move he or she chooses.

(d) If a player wishes to claim a violation of this rule, he or she must do so before touching any piece on the board.

5.9 When each player has moved once, it is considered a Set of Moves, or round of play.

5.10 Concourse of Bishoping: Enemy Bishops move on different courses; therefore, Bishops cannot capture enemy Bishops. Allied Bishops move on the same course. If three Bishops are on adjacent squares and the fourth Bishop moves into position to occupy the fourth square, this player completes the concourse of Bishoping, captures the two enemy Bishops and takes control of the moves of the ally Bishop. There are only five positions on the board where a concourse can occur:

4							3
	2	1			2	1	
	3	4			3	4	
			2	1			
			3	4			
	2	1			2	1	
	3	4			3	4	
1							2

5.11 Concourse of Queens: Rule 5.10 also applies when three Queens are on adjacent squares and the fourth Queen moves into position to occupy the fourth square.

6. Object of the game

6.1 To work as a team with your ally to capture the opponents' Kings, paralyzing their play. This is done through strategical play, encountering the opponents' forces, capturing them if you are able, but at the same time defending your own King and taking your ally's welfare into consideration.

7. Throne Square

7.1   Throne Squares are the corner squares where each of the four Kings resides at the beginning of play.

7.2   A King shares its Throne Square with a piece (Knight, Queen, Bishop or Rook) in the opening game setting. No other piece can mount that square while the King or sharing piece occupy it except in the event of capturing the King.

7.3   Once either the King or piece sharing the Throne Square moves from that square, during game play, neither can share that square or any other square for the duration of the game.

7.4   The King and the piece sharing the Throne Square do not move off the Throne Square together. Either piece can be moved, one at a time in separate moves, when it is that player's turn to move. For example, if a King is in check, only the piece *or* the King could be moved, not both.

7.5   No two pieces can share the same square except the two pieces on the Throne Square, and then only until one moves off.

7.6   A piece giving check to a King seated on its Throne Square also gives check to the piece seated with the King on the same square. When the King is captured, so is the piece sharing the square at the time (and vice versa).

7.7   If a player mounts his or her own King on the Throne of his or her ally, he or she assumes command of the allied forces together with his or her own and is free to move any piece that was under the ally's command during that Angle's sequential moves. This situation continues for the duration of play or until rule 8.9 operates.

8. The King: capturing and checking, endgame

8.1 A King is said to be in check when an opponent's next move is able to capture that King. The opponent must say "check" to warn the player threatened.

    (a) A King, when checked, if it cannot be freed from check, is captured on the following turn. The remaining pieces of that captured King are frozen (see 8.2).

    (b) A player is obliged to move his or her King when the King is attacked or checked. If the King is unable to move, then a piece must be strategically moved to aid the King.

8.2 When a King is captured (not "checkmated") by an opponent, he is taken off the board, but the King's pieces are left in the positions in which they are situated at the time of the King's capture. No one can move these pieces, and they are called Frozen Pieces. They must remain on those same squares for the duration of play (or until rule 8.5 is invoked), neither moving nor being attacked, and only blocking the squares they occupy; no other piece can move onto the squares occupied by the Frozen Pieces. Merely to check a King does not capture and freeze a player's pieces. The King must be captured and removed from the board. After a King has been checked, the King or the ally of the threatened King may be able to make a strategical move to prevent capture. For example, if the ally's next move is to threaten to capture an Angle by threatening a King or major piece, it would buy time for another round of play and give the initially threatened King time to move completely out of check, perhaps by using rule 8.6.

8.3 The remaining Ally continues to play and seeks to release the captured King by an exchange, as defined in rule 8.5.

8.4 The player whose King is captured by an opponent loses his turn to move, and no other player may take that turn.

8.5   Regaining the Throne: If an ally's King has been cap-
      tured by an opponent and a hostile King is then cap-
      tured, the player making the second capture may
      propose an exchange of prisoner Kings. The opposing
      player has the option of accepting or refusing.

      (a) The exchange cannot take place if the opponent was
          not the one that captured the ally's King.

      (b) A rescued King re-enters the board on his own
          Throne Square, or if that square is occupied, on the
          nearest square to the Throne Square that is not occu-
          pied and that is not threatened by any other piece.

      (c) The player who has been out of the game immedi-
          ately regains control of his or her previously frozen
          pieces when his or her King is restored.

      (d) This offer of exchange can be made when the hostile
          King is captured or thereafter when it is the move of
          the player making the capture. If refused, the offer
          can be made more than once.

      (e) Players with frozen pieces cannot negotiate King
          exchanges.

8.6   Checking: A King can move into check if already in
      check by another piece. The move might enable the ally
      or one of the King's own pieces to free the situation.

8.7   If an ally's pieces are frozen and a player manages to
      capture both opponents' Kings, or the ally has captured
      one of the opponents' Kings before being frozen and the
      player captures the other, that player is the victor. If a
      player and his or her ally capture both opponent Kings,
      then they are both the victors.

8.8   Allies do not continue to play against each other when a
      victory over both opponents has been established.

8.9   If an ally's pieces are under a player's control (according
      to Rule 7.7 or 11.3) and that player's King is captured,

the ally's pieces are then immediately released back to the control of their original player. The pieces of the captured King become frozen (Rule 8.2). If a player gained control of his or her ally's forces via Rule 11.3, then the ally's King regains his throne via Rule 8.5(b).

8.10 A drawn game is:

(a) When only Kings are left to play, all other pieces and pawns having been captured; i.e., four bare Kings (see Rule 8.14[b]). (A King is bare when all his pieces and pawns have been captured.)

(b) Two ally Kings are bare.

8.11 Stalemate: If a King cannot move to any square from an unchecked square without moving into check, the game is classed as a stalemate for that element and no move can be made by that element until his stalemate is freed by an ally. If the ally is out of the game (withdrawn or pieces under control of the partner) the game is drawn.

8.12 When a player has lost all of his or her pieces (including his or her King) and pawns, that player is out of the game. The turn of that player does not pass to the partner, who must continue to play with only one turn per round.

8.13 If the player is left to face two opponents with one set of pieces and the position seems hopeless, that player may resign, leaving the victory to the opponents.

8.14 The game terminates when:

(a) One side (both allies) captures both opposing Kings. This is a win (Rule 8.7).

(b) Drawn game (Rule 8.10).

(c) A drawn (Rule 8.11), resigned or stalemate game.

(d) In the case of an annulment according to Rules 12.2 and 12.3.

9. Withdrawing

9.1   If a player loses all pieces except the King, that player may withdraw from the game. In so doing that player may be leaving the ally to play alone, and in this case the remaining player takes the withdrawn player's turn as well as his or her own when moving his or her own pieces.

(a) The withdrawn player's King remains on the board and the remaining player takes control of it on the turn of that King's Angle.

(b) This rule does not apply if only two players are operating the four Angles (two ally sets each).

9.2   Any player can withdraw from a game at any time, other than described in rule 9.1, but in so doing that player forfeits control of his or her pieces and leaves them under the ally's control. The playing turn, however, is not shared with the remaining player's pieces as in Rule 9.1 but is continued as before, one turn per corner in each round of play.

(a) This rule does not apply if only two players are operating four Angles (two ally sets each).

9.3   In the case of two players operating two ally sets each, if a player loses all the pieces except the King of one of the sets he or she is operating, he or she may choose to play on with that King or withdraw that Angle from the game. In that case, the King of that Angle remains where it is as a frozen piece and the turns of the withdrawn Angle are relinquished; the player of the remaining Angle does not have use of the withdrawn Angle's moves. Therefore the remaining Angle must continue play with one turn per round of play as opposed to the opponents' two turns.

10. Pawns

10.1 If a pawn reaches an unoccupied or uncovered square on the opposite side of the board from that in which it faced at the commencement of the game, it is promoted to the piece to which it is vice-gerent.

(a) Promotion only occurs if the player has already lost one or more pawns.

(b) If a player still controls four pawns, promotion is delayed until a pawn is lost.

10.2 A pawn reaching a Throne Square is not promoted to a King; it can only be promoted to the piece originally sharing the Throne Square.

10.3 Privileged pawn: If a player has only a King, Bishop or Queen, and a pawn left (or a King and a pawn), then this pawn becomes a *privileged pawn* and, on reaching any square on the opposite side of the board, can be promoted to any piece (not including a King) at the choice of the player, even if that piece is already on the board. In this case a pawn is returned to the board and takes the role of the piece that is duplicated.

10.4 If a pawn at any time in the game comes to a different side other than the opposite side of the board from which it originally faced, that pawn must continue to move on its original forward course (as in ordinary chess).

10.5 A King does not have a pawn. The pawn in front of the King belongs to the piece sharing the Throne Square at the beginning of play. This pawn is already on a "side" of the board, as mentioned in Rule 10.4.

11. Allies

11.1 Only Fire and Air or Water and Earth are allies. The allies are diagonal to each other. Under no circumstances can Fire and Water, Fire and Earth etc. be allies. (One plays for him or herself but is always aware of the ally strategy. He or she should not hinder his or her ally's play but should strive to complement it. The allies can work together to achieve victory.)

11.2 A player does not capture his or her ally's pieces (Rule 5.2 prevents this) or check his or her ally's King (with the exception of Rule 11.3).

11.3 If a King is about to be taken, that player's ally may capture the King and gain control of both elemental sides. Each element must move in turn and not share moves. In this case the captured King is removed but his pieces and pawns are not frozen. This rule does not apply when only two players are playing instead of four.

11.4 Assuming command of ally forces. See Rule 7.7.

12. Illegal moves (any move contrary to the above rules)

12.1 If an illegal move is made, the positions of all pieces prior to the move are reinstated and the game is continued from that point on.

12.2 If several illegal moves are made, the game is annulled.

12.3 If during the game the opening positions of the pieces are found to be incorrect in any Angle, the game is annulled.

See Part III of this book for Rules 13 to 19, which are divination rules.

Setting Up Your Boards: Game Play Settings

Positioning of the Chess Pieces

The chessmen of the Enochian chess game are positioned around the edge of a board in the form of an ancient swastika (fylfot). This form of positioning is found in the game of Chaturanga and also coincides with a diagram of the swastika as found in the original Golden Dawn cipher manuscripts. This was originally simply a blank cross, but it was later filled in by Mathers for the 1=10 grade ritual of Zelator in the Order.

There are two swastika symbols found in ancient civilizations:[1] clockwise and counterclockwise in movement. The actual origin of the Hindu word "swastika" means "movement of life," with a positive emphasis. The Celtic swastika indicates

---

1. See *An Illustrated Encyclopædia of Traditional Symbols* by J. C. Cooper (Thames Hudson, 1979) for an in-depth look at this symbol.

good luck, while the the Roman one is a symbol of Jupiter.

The positive swastika, which is the way the chess pieces are placed on a board at the commencement of a game, shows a natural development coupled with celestial harmony authorized by divine power, all of which can be correlated with game play.

In ancient times different colored swastikas had different meanings in much the same way as colors are associated with various planets of our solar system. The multicolored chess pieces herein described show a combined harmony of color and perfect balance of the cycle of movement, a beautiful composite of the Yin/Yang aspect. A modern approach to placing the pieces shows an archetype in various stages of development, and the Enochian chess game should be played with this in mind.

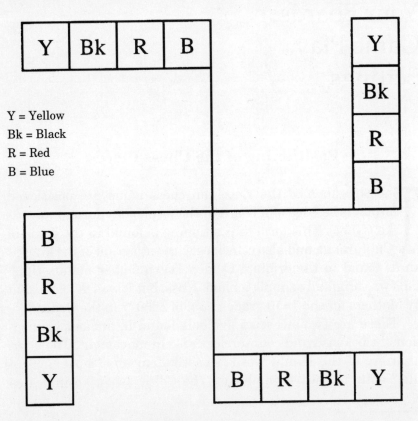

FIGURE 33—SWASTIKA PLACINGS OF THE AIR OF FIRE SETTING

Theoretically there are 16 different play positions in which the chess pieces could be placed at the commencement of a game. Each piece falls in line with a Tarot court card, geomantic figure, etc. A closer look, however, will show that, if the chess positions are based on the Kerubic Square associations of the Enochian Tablets, there are only eight different settings. The reason for this is that the Air and Water Tablets have the same order of Tetragrammaton applied to these squares, as likewise do the Earth and Fire Tablets.

In the diagram below, a chessboard is shown. Squares have been numbered showing the positions in which the chess pieces are to be placed. Following the diagram is a list of the different play positions for each chessboard. A number beside each chess piece, cross-referenced with the diagram, indicates the square where the piece will be placed.

Air   Water

1	2	3	4				1
							2
							3
							4
4							
3							
2							
1				4	3	2	1

Earth   Fire

FIGURE 34—PIECE POSITIONING FOR OPENING PLAY SETTINGS

In the following combinations of piece positioning, any combination, when chosen for game play, would be repeated in each Angle of the board being used. You do not place a different combination in each corner. The pawns for each elemental set of pieces are placed in front of the appropriate pieces to which they are vice-gerent (as given in Part I).

Fire and Earth Chessboards

Earth combination—otherwise known as the Earth of Earth setting if played on the Earth Board, or the Earth of Fire setting if played on the Fire Board.

	Square
King and Rook	1
Bishop	2
Queen	3
Knight	4

Air combination—Air of Earth or Air of Fire

King and Bishop	1
Rook	2
Knight	3
Queen	4

Water combination—Water of Earth or Water of Fire

King and Queen	1
Knight	2
Rook	3
Bishop	4

Fire combination—Fire of Earth or Fire of Fire

King and Knight	1
Queen	2
Bishop	3
Rook	4

Air and Water Chessboards

Earth combination—otherwise known as the Earth of Air setting if played on the Air Board, or the Earth of Water setting if played on the Water Board.

	Square
King and Rook	1
Knight	2
Queen	3
Bishop	4

Air combination—Air of Air or Air of Water

King and Bishop	1
Queen	2
Knight	3
Rook	4

Water combination—Water of Air or Water of Water

King and Queen	1
Bishop	2
Rook	3
Knight	4

Fire combination—Fire of Air or Fire of Water

King and Knight	1
Rook	2
Bishop	3
Queen	4

Which Board to Use?

The particular elemental board used will be relevant to the setting that is chosen for any given game with respect to game strategy only. However, for those who only have one board constructed (preferably the Earth Board), the question of which board to use will be irrelevant. Do not, however, look lightly on the value of having four elemental chessboards. Their importance, meanings and use are varied when using them for divination or magic. In these cases, it is the board that is first chosen for a game; only then is the choice made among the four settings applicable to the given board.

If you possess the four elemental chessboards, whether you play Enochian chess strategically, for divinatory purposes or otherwise, you should only play any given setting on its associated elemental board. For example, the Fire of Earth setting is played on the Earth Board, the Water of Air setting is played on the Air Board, the Air of Fire setting on the Fire Board, the Fire of Water setting on the Water Board and so on.

Further information on the meanings and use of the four elemental chessboards is given in Parts III and IV, since this information is relevant to the subjects therein.

Recording
Game Play

Within the original Golden Dawn system, one of the things that became a stumbling block for Enochian chess was that there was no method of recording game play. The method below is one that I worked out in 1980 when preparing the first draft of this book. Since then I have seen no need to improve upon it, and I personally find it more than satisfactory.

In recording your game, the letter of the piece, the Angle it moves to, the square number and letter and any other function must be written down. For example, K is the letter used for King, 1 = square one and a = square letter, so at the commencement of the game the King actually sits on 1a, and this may be written K1a. The abbreviations used are as follows.

F = Fire   W = Water   A = Air

E = Earth   P = Pawn   K = King

Q = Queen　　　　　B = Bishop　　　　　N = Knight

R = Rook (Castle)

x = Captured piece; e.g., NWldxP (Knight moved to Water
　　square 1d and captured a pawn)

+ = Check　　　　　++ = Captured King

* = Bad move

? = Questionable move

= Promoted pawn

When recording your moves, it is easiest to record only the square that a piece moves to rather than first writing in the square it came from; that square was made clear in moves previously recorded. It is also not necessary to establish what elemental piece has been moved (e.g., FN3d, Fire Knight to 3d), because each elemental Angle's move is recorded under its specific column (see diagram of play recording sheet). Therefore, move recording might look like this:

	A	**W**	**F**	**E**
6	...NW3d	R4a	Q1c	BF2dxN
7	NE4d	RF1d	P2dxB	P2c?
8	NA2d	RF2dxP	Q3c	K2b
9	QW3d...			

In move 6, the Air Knight moved to Water 3d and Water's Rook moved to 4a in the Water Angle. Since it is a Water piece, there was no need to record the Angle in which it was moving (i.e., its own). The Fire Queen moved to 1c, and Earth's Bishop captured a Knight on Fire Angle square 2d. In move 7, Air's Knight proceeded to move to Earth Angle square 4d. Looking back to move 6 you will see which square and Angle the Knight was moving from. Water's Rook moved from its own Angle to the Fire Angle, square 1d; Fire's pawn took a Bishop on square 2d of the Fire

Angle; an Earth pawn moved to 2c, which was considered a questionable move; and so on.

Below is a diagram of the recording codes set up on a chessboard. It is followed by two diagrams of a suggested format for a play-recording sheet.

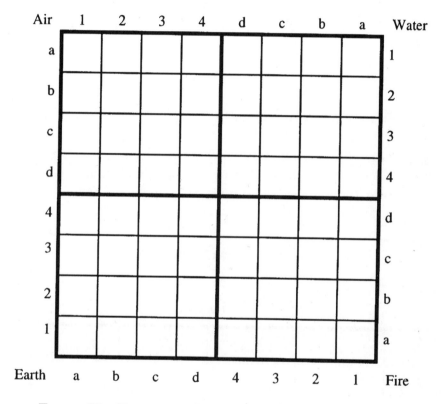

FIGURE 35—ENOCHIAN CHESS GAME RECORDING CODES APPLIED TO A CHESSBOARD

Enochian Chess Game Recording Sheet				
Date:		Board: Piece Setting:		
Move	Player 1	Player 2	Player 3	Player 4
1 2 3 4 5 6				

FIGURE 36A—FORMAT FOR A GAME RECORDING SHEET

Where "Player 1, 2, 3 and 4" have been written in, the element each player operates is written above. A space could be left under the date for the names of the players. For a divination game the following sheet could be drawn up.

Enochian Chess Game Recording Sheet				
Date: Question:		Board: Piece Setting: Ptah Square:		
Move	Player 1	Player 2	Player 3	Player 4
1 2 3 4 5 6				

FIGURE 36B—FORMAT FOR A DIVINATION GAME
RECORDING SHEET

These sheets have proven very helpful when recording games, since the moves for each set of pieces are kept clearly separate from the other sets. It is normally satisfactory to provide for 20 to 30 moves, but to be on the safe side I use sheets with space to record as many as 40 moves.

Game
Strategy

The challenge of eight different game settings, each providing a mass of variations in game play, can be quite exciting. I have provided in the following chapters some recorded games together with their analyses. I have attempted thereby to open up the world of Enochian chess to you, the reader, discussing opening moves of the eight settings[1] and middle/endgame play. These discussions address some of the weaknesses and strengths of play. When studying these eight settings, you may find that the most effective method by which you open your play can be analogous to the elemental character of the setting itself.

Enochian chess can be approached strategically from a two-handed chess (modern chess) point of view; e.g., the use of combinations, traps, double attacks, pins, forks etc. However, in a four-handed chess game, you must learn to work with an ally

---

1. See previous chapter on Game Play Settings (p. 101).

and be aware of the strengths of your pieces in each play setting. Develop your minor pieces and your defense to decrease your risk of losing valuable pieces. One common error is to exchange two pieces for a Rook, which leaves you with fewer pieces to maneuver. In all game settings, there is at least one piece that is the weakest—but it is not always the same piece. For example, the Queen's move is very limited and is suited to a more defensive, sacrificial role, but there are some play settings where the Queen's presence is quite strong.

Piece strength and value vary throughout the game and also continue to be dependent on the play setting you are working with at the time. For example, in one setting, a Knight may be very weak at opening play, but during middle-game play his value increases. Because of this, it is advisable not to make early sacrifices. Study your play settings, for they hold the keys.

Endgame play can be viewed a little differently, for here the Rooks hold the strength, and depending on what pieces your opponent has left in play, the Knight and Bishop hold equal footing, the Knight perhaps a little more.

Double attacks take place where one piece is covered by more than one attacking piece. This can cost you. Try to back up all your pieces and position them so that they cover each other. An undefended piece or pawn, even if not threatened, is ultimately vulnerable. There are also times where you must lose a piece to save your King, so try to get the Throne Square cleared of the piece sharing it or move the King if strategy dictates.

Organize your thinking; you are not looking ahead two to five moves as in ordinary chess. To look even one move ahead in Enochian chess, you have to take into consideration four different play positions and their possibilities. To look four moves ahead, you must consider 16 different play positions and their variations or probabilities.

Do not forget your pawns. A strategically placed pawn can severely hinder your opponents' play. Be careful of traps. Think twice if your opponent makes a seemingly non-offensive or foolish move; it could be bait. Try not to give check to an opponent if your checking piece cannot be backed up with a strong move by your own pieces or your ally's. So often I have seen players become extremely disadvantaged by premature checks.

As in ordinary chess, control over the center of the board is advantageous, but not easy. By keeping your pawns linked and eventually linking up with your ally's pawns, you can create a dividing line across the board. Double pawns or loose pawns are weak and become a liability; once they arise, they are difficult to alter.

Unlike ordinary chess, a player does not always have full control over his or her play, because chain reactions caused by forced moves often occur. This can lead a skilled player into difficulty, giving a less skilled player the upper hand. Therefore, you will find that even the best of players can be foiled if he or she is not extra careful. Enochian chess is not only a challenge to your intellect and concentration, but to many other hidden facets of your nature, which will be further discussed in Parts III and IV of this book.

Pins are frequent in Enochian chess. A pin involves three essential pieces: the pinning piece, the pinned piece and the target. A pinned piece cannot move without exposing an essential piece; e.g., a piece on the square in front of a King. Cross pins are even more vicious than pins; this is where the pinned piece is held from more than one direction or protects more than one piece. To defend yourself against a pin, you can either place a defender between the pinned piece and the target, lend additional protection to the pinned piece without unpinning, move the target or attack the pinning piece.

You will find that in all play settings the Bishops and Queens of the same element and of the ally element operate on different diagonals from each other. For example, in each element set of pieces, there is one Bishop and one Queen, and each operates on a different diagonal; therefore, they can never cross the same square. A Bishop moves along the same diagonal as its ally Bishop, but neither can capture an opponent Bishop because the opponent Bishops operate a different diagonal. Your Bishop can capture an opponent's Queen, since they operate on the same diagonal. Ally Queens move along the same diagonal,

but neither can capture an opponent Queen because they operate on the diagonal upon which their opponents' Bishops move,
but because of this your Queen can capture opponent Bishops.
The diagonals that Bishops or Queens operate on are dependent
on the type of play setting used at the commencement of the
game. The only time you have an opportunity to operate a Bishop on your Queen's diagonal is when your Bishop's pawn reaches the opposite side of the board, where an exchange occurs.

The movement of these pieces across an Enochian chessboard is discussed in a paper by Mathers called "Notes on Rosicrucian Chess" under the preceding subtitle "The Awakening of
the Abodes." This paper appears to have little strategical value
apart from an observation of piece movement. Enochian chess
divination and esoteric instruction have more use for this
paper; however, extracts have been quoted below.[2] While reading these extracts, the reader is advised to refer back to the earlier diagrams showing the attributions of the chessboards, or to
refer forward to the divinations section of this book, to the diagrams of the Zodiac on the boards.

> The diagonal lines of Bishop's move present peculiarities.
> Every Lesser Angle throughout the tablets has a diagonal line
> of four squares starting from its prime square; which are allot-
> ted respectively to Aries, Gemini, Scorpio and Earth (the non
> Osiris Squares). From these four squares the Bishops can
> move one square into a square of Libra, Sagittarius, Taurus or
> Water, these completing the series of squares in that Lesser
> Angle in which a Bishop can move. Let us call this the Aries
> system of diagonal squares. This diagonal is crossed by anoth-
> er which in the Airy and Watery Boards is composed of Can-

---

2. I personally disagree with some of the comments made in this paper and
have therefore only quoted a few extracts. Judging by the style, it appears that
Mathers worked a lot on theory. How much practice he had is anyone's guess.
In addition, the reference to black and white squares is not really applicable,
because the Enochian chessboards are not black and white. This shows that
the game was possibly originally considered using a plain black and white
board. Mathers states that the signs of the Zodiac are naturally allied. I do not
agree, because the signs he discusses are in fact in opposition to each other.

cer, Leo, Virgo and Air Squares, having as subsidiaries, squares of Aquarius, Pisces, Capricorn and Fire. In the Earthy and Fiery Board the second series of four form the diagonal and the first subsidiaries. Let us call this the Cancer series.

If we now examine the Boards we shall see that the Aries system of any Lesser angle is joined diagonally to the Aries systems of other Lesser Angles; and that the Cancer is also similarly joined to other Cancer systems. So that we have two systems of squares; the Aries and Cancer; of the whole, each containing four squares allotted to every sign it contains. This resembles the black and white systems of squares of the ordinary boards; and it is as if we allotted the White to Aries and the Black to Cancer. . . . The central squares of the Board contain 16 signs that are allotted to each lesser Angle. And it is only on these 16 squares that the pieces—except the Rook and the King—develop their full influence or defensive force.

The four Queens, the Watery portion of their respective Elements govern between them every Square of every board. But a Queen can never check another Queen for the following reasons. Each of these pieces govern 16 squares on the board, four in each Lesser Angle: and they are so placed as to divide the 64 squares equally between them. It follows, therefore, that there is only one of them that can check the Ptah[3] square. The 16 squares governed by any Queen are allotted to eight signs, two squares of each sign to every Queen. And the remaining two squares of the same eight signs are governed by the friendly Queen. And the other pair of Queens govern the 32 other squares similarly. The Queen of the Prime Player always governs the Water, Earth, Taurus and Scorpio squares of its own lesser angle, and also of the Lesser Angle of the same rank. In each of the two Lesser Angles, the Queen of the Prime Player governs the Sagittarius, Gemini, Libra and Aries squares.[4] The

---

3. The Ptah is the stationary piece used in the divination game. See Part III of this book for further information.

4. This would only be the case with certain piece settings such as Fire of Earth, Water of Water, Water of Earth, Fire of Air, Air of Air, Fire of Fire, Earth of Water and Earth of Earth. Otherwise, the Prime Player and Ally Queens would govern the Cancer System with the Opposing Queens governing the Aries System.

allied Queen governs the same squares in the opposite ranks of the Lesser Angles. Thus the Prime player's Queen and his ally together govern the Aries system of squares, and this is equally true of every board. The opposing Queens govern the squares of the Cancer system, against a passive prime player.

The opposing Queens govern the squares of the Cancer system in a similar manner. But there is a slight variation dependent on the position of the Prime Player. They together govern the Cancer system. If water or earth be the Prime Player, the opposing Queens govern the Air, Fire, Leo and Aquarius squares in their own Lesser Angles and in the others of the same rank; while in the other rank they govern Virgo, Pisces, Cancer and Capricorn squares. If Air or Fire be the Prime Player these two sets of squares are reversed. The Queen of the Prime Player, and, therefore of the attacked Lesser Angle, invariably governs therein the passive Kerubic and Elemental squares. The attacking Queens govern and have their bases, when active Elements attack—the active Kerubic and Elemental squares. When passive elements attack—the passive Cardinal and Common Sign Squares. The allied Queen, supporting the defence, has for her base the squares corresponding to those of the Prime Player, the passive Kerubic and Elemental squares. It also falls out that no passive Queen can, under any circumstances of Board or setting, check an active Kerubic, Cardinal, Common or Elemental square in her own rank of Lesser Angles, nor a similar passive square in the other rank.

It is to be seen that there are certain Signs whereon the Queens are strong and others whereon they are weak. In defence, the Queens, or Watery Forces of each element, are strong in the Water, Earth, Scorpio and Taurus squares of the irrespective domains. But in attacking, the vulnerable points of the hostile depends upon which elements are in operation. If Water be the Prime Player, and hence the point of attack, the Watery Queen can deliver a strong counter attack on Water, Earth, Scorpio and Taurus of Yellow-Air (being in the same rank), and on Aries, Gemini, Sagittarius and Libra of Red-Fire. While the friendly Water of Earth delivers attack on Aries, Gemini, Sagittarius and Libra of Yellow-Air, and water,

Earth, Scorpio and Taurus of Red-Fire. The Aries system then offers the strong points for the Airy portion of an Elemental Force in defence; and the Cancer system in offense.

The Watery forces of the elements never oppose one another, nor clash in their action. Each undulates onwards unaffected by and unaffecting undulations of the others. Each Queen will swamp an opposing force only when that force encroaches on the domain of the particular Queen. Every Queen has to fear the attack of the opposing Airy forces. But as the latter develop force as the matter proceeds towards ultimation, the Queen when protected is not likely to be destroyed by an opposing and threatening Bishop. The same is true as regards the hostile Knight's attack. This rule of play is generally sound except in the case of a Queen that can check the Ptah Square, which ability greatly enhances her value.

The Bishops of partners always govern the same set of squares; and the Bishop of the opposing sides govern opposite sets of squares. These sets are the same of those before mentioned as the Aries and Cancer systems. The Bishops of the Prime Player and his ally always govern the Cancer system; and those of the opponent always act on the Aries system. Hence if the Ptah square be of the Aries system, the airy parts of the opposing forces have great power; but if it be of the Cancer system the opposing aerial forces are impotent in direct attack and can only be operative secondarily. It follows, too, that the Bishops and the Queens are great opponents, since the Bishops operate over the same system as their opposing Queens. The Queens can only touch 16 squares while the Bishop can touch 32, giving the latter a greater superiority in this respect. But the Queen must be considered the equal of the Bishop from the power she possesses to hop over an intervening piece, which would arrest the approach of the Bishop. And further, the Watery piece is not hampered by the pawns in the opening, whereas the Bishop as a rule cannot act at all until one pawn has been moved.'

The Knights can all reach every square on the Boards, and therefore, operate over both the Aries and Cancer Systems. The Knight moves from one of these Systems into the other every time he is played. If he starts on a square of the Aries, the first, third, and fifth, etc., moves will bring him on to squares of the Cancer System. And in his first, third or fifth moves he can get to any Cancer System square on the board. His second, fourth and sixth moves will equally bring him to any Aries System square. There appears to be only one square on the board that requires six moves to reach. That is, if the Knight be in one of the corner squares he cannot cross the board diagonally into the opposite corner in less than six moves.

The Knight when placed in the corner square can only move to 2 others. The Knight when placed in the two adjacent squares can only move to 3 others. The Knight when placed in any other outside square can only move to 4 others. The Knight when placed in any other second row square can only move to 6 others. But in the central 16 its full power is developed and it can move to eight others. This gives the possible moves of a Knight as 336. There is a curious difference between the details of these 336 moves in the upper and lower Ranks of Tablets. The Air Board will be identical with the Watery. The Earthy Board will be identical with the Fiery.

Mathers goes on to say that the squares of certain signs are more often attacked by the Knight than others, for instance:

. . . the four Sagittarius squares in the Air and Watery Boards are attackable from no less than 24 squares, where the four Taurus squares are attackable from 18 squares. When playing the 16 central squares, each Knight governs 8 squares. These 8 squares, however, are not promiscuously arranged, but follow one rule in the Air and Watery boards, and another in the Earth and Fire.

In the former the 8 squares are allotted to 6 signs, two of which are moved to twice. Thus from the Earth square of the Water Tablet, the Knight moves to the following squares: Virgo, Leo, Capricorn 2, Cancer 2, Pisces, Aquarius, duplicating Capricorn and Cancer, and missing Fire and Air of the Cancer system. Or again from the Aries square, the Knight moves to Pisces, Aquarius, Air 2, Capricorn 2, Virgo and Leo, duplicating Air and Capricorn, and the missing Fire and Cancer. . . .

From the central 16 squares an attack is made on the Cardinal and Common Signs 10 times each; but on the Kerubic and Elemental Squares 6 times each. This is true of every board, and the reason is to be found in the position of the ranks; which in every case are disposed so that the uppermost and lowermost ranks are Kerubic and Elemental, while the two central ranks are Cardinal and Common. The same reason will explain the peculiarities of the curious differences between the columns—the number of times the Sign is duplicated, triplicated and missed.

This analysis of the moves from the 16 central squares seems to show a certain steadiness in the Earth and Fire Tablets, and is less seen in the Water and Air.

The same increase of steadiness is described here:

In Air and Water the extreme numbers are 24 and 18. In Earth and Fire the extreme numbers are 23 and 19. The moves of the Knight referred in a similar way to the remaining 48 squares show the same point, a great steadiness in the Earth and Fire boards than in the Water and Air. And this difference is seen in the outer row and not in the inner one. The 28 outside squares are attacked by 96 possible moves. The 20 next squares are attacked by 112 possible moves. The 16 central squares are attacked by 128 possible moves.

The Rook moves through columns as through ranks. She is able, therefore, to reach every square on the board, and is very powerful. But her movement is very ponderous, and it is a piece that is not moved many times in a game unless the forces of the other Elements have been absorbed in its working out. While the Aleph, Mem, and Shin forces are in full operation the Rook is easily attacked and with difficulty defended, unless she remain quiet, and act as a firm basis of support and defence to the side. If she however, make the mistake of entering early into action she is nearly sure to fall a prey to the more subtle forces whose proper sphere is attack.

If the more subtle forces do not bring about a solution of the question, and the matter has to be fought out to the bitter end, that is, if the Yetziratic and Briatic forces are absorbed and balanced in the matter, then do the ponderous forces of Assiah, the Knave, engage in powerful combat.

The Kings of Water and Earth stand in squares of the Aries System. The Kings of Air and Fire stand in squares of the Cancer System. If Water or Earth be the Prime Player the opposing Bishops attack the squares on which they stand. If Air or Fire be the Prime Player they do not.

The King is the Ace, and the King of the Prime Player being the piece on whose action that of all the forces depends, it is this King that, at every move he makes, causes a new whirl to be set up in the other forces.

The Pawns move on the Cancer and Aries systems, and they generate the whirl of the elemental forces in the direction of play.

Openings

In modern chess the "opening" is considered to be the moves made in the first phase of any game, commencing with the initial position and continuing until all sides have brought out their pieces and the middle-game is reached. In Enochian chess, due to the fact that middle-game play is sometimes reached within five rounds of play (i.e., five moves per player), without all the pieces having brought out into play, the opening play examples provided here are semi-openings, reproducing the first four to six or more rounds of play.

In the examples given below, "game recording" abbreviation codes are used, as described in the earlier chapter, "Recording Game Play." The commentaries on the game openings will not make much sense unless read in conjunction with the actual moves made on your chessboard. In this way you will be able to see the situation described in the text.

Earth and Fire Board Play Settings

Earth of Earth and Earth of Fire Setting (KR, B, Q, N)

One opening move would be to make an attacking move with either the Queen or Knight. However, this approach has been proven to result in a situation of vulnerability for the piece concerned, another piece of the same element or the ally. For example, Earth Queen's move to 3c or 1c forces the Fire Knight to move to either 3c, immediately threatening the Water pawn on W4b (Water Angle, square 4b). If the WP4b (Water pawn on 4b) moves to W4c, the Fire Knight on F3c (Fire Angle, square 3c) can eventually go to W4b, threatening the Water Bishop. The Earth Queen has nowhere of any consequence to move. Also, if she is on E3c, this will restrict her Bishop's and Knight's chances of movement from the back-row lineup. Hence the values of the Queen, Bishop and Knight diminish. The Fire Knight could have gone to E3d in response to the Earth Queen's first move, threatening the Earth Angle the same way as it would the Water Angle if it moved as described earlier. A move of this nature (in this case made by the Queen) is called a "chain-reactor."

If the Earth Knight makes the opening move to A3d or E3c, in both cases AP4b or FP4b is threatened. (It should be noted that this pawn's value would be the least, of all the pawns in this particular setting.) In the case of an opening move with a Knight, the following could take place. Earth Knight to 3c would result in blocking pawn movement necessary to release the Bishop. If Water did not follow up on Earth's move by attacking Air, therefore forcing Air to act in defense rather than attack, Air would then attack Earth with Knight to 3c, causing the Earth Knight move to burn out, for a pawn and Bishop would immediately be threatened. If the Earth Knight moves to A3d in its first move, a light but eventually unsuccessful attack would be made, if the move is declined by Air. If a Knight move is declined and the pawn is unmoved, the opponent may lose a pawn, but his or her position is left relatively unthreatened. It seems in some sequences of this opening, P4b must be sacrificed if an equilibrium is to be kept.

Pawn opening—Earth to move first: P3c opens the way up for the Bishop, but removes one opening for the Queen and Knight, leaving the Knight with one avenue of escape and the Queen two. An advantage is the Bishop on a direct line to its ally's P1b, discouraging the Air Knight from moving into the Water Angle due to the Earth Bishop's covering that diagonal.

If Earth opens with P1c, it would seem to be a totally defensive move, but if you look a little harder you will see that an attack by either of the opponents' Knights would be totally ineffective. For example:

	E	F	W	A
1	P1c	NE3d	P1c	P3c
2	P4c	NE4b	B1b	B4c
3	...			

It is a waste of time for the Fire Knight to continue its attack (which is also the case if Air makes the attack), as in the moves following the Earth Bishop would move out of threat to 1b and the Fire Knight would have no safe square to move to.

So far the main direction of attack seems to be the Bishops, at the supposed cost of the Knights, if they are successful. The question then arises as to the value of the pieces. Do the Bishops have more value than the Knights in this play setting, or is it just that the way is open for these moves to be made—the obvious? What is obvious, as you will see in the following examples, is that piece value becomes more evident after each opening move has been made. This will also depend on how each angle opens, which will result in the same or different piece values in each angle. It is important, though, to get as many pieces working as possible. The crunching point is, at what stage of the game? You will probably find in this setting that, after the initial flurry of attack, the Knight's move is very restricted as to what squares he can move to in safety. Such is also the case for the Queen. The only operational piece apart from these would be the Bishop, if freed from his position. A P2b must remain where it is, as the opposing Bishops are on a potentially direct line to the Kings. The Knight and Queen also have a stronger follow through if the Bishop is working with them. In addition, although the pawns seem rather passive in their approach, their moves create a defense, pending attack, plus providing openings for the back line and acting as probable backups. In conclusion, for the Earth of Earth and Earth of Fire settings, the strongest and most stable opening moves are by the pawns, followed by the Bishops. Although not directly attacking, they are creating a strong fortress from which to fire.

Example 1
Earth Board, playing widdershins

	E	F	W	A
1	P4c	P1c	P4c	P1c
2	P3c	B1b	P3c	B1b
3	P4d	N3c...see examples 1(a) and 1(b)		

This is a sensible opening for all parties: Earth and Water hold initial priority on the P4b, bringing it into use and thereby turning it into a pawn of importance, while Fire and Air concentrate on putting their Bishops on the 1b square, thus creating two firing lines right across the board—two important positions.

Example 1(a)

	E	F	W	A
3	—	—...	QF3d	Q3c
4	NA3d	K2a	B3b	P4c
5	NA4b...			

The Water Queen moves into the F3d square and exposes itself to the Fire Bishop. The initial intention is a quick break in the Fire lines by a QxP3b and QxB1b, leaving an opening for the Water Knight to pin the King. But Fire King to 2a foils Water's plan and results in a wasted move, as the Fire pawns could have pushed Water Queen back. Air, on the other hand, moves Queen to 3c and presses Earth, but Earth turns its forced move to its advantage. This situation brings into question the early move of the Queen as an aggressor rather than as a defense.

Example 1(b) shows an improved play on example 1(a) and gives some very interesting possibilities:

Example 1(b)

	E	**F**	**W**	**A**
3	—	—	...Q1c	N3c
4	B4c?	P4c	P4d	P2c
5	... see examples 1(b)(i) and 1(b)(ii)			

Water moves the Queen to 1c, forcing the Air Knight to the only safe square. Although this seems like an aggressive move, it is in the long run a defensive move which also protects the Water King from the obvious. Earth placed B4c in a position which threatens FP4b and the Fire Queen. The Fire Queen could have moved to E4d, but it would eventually have been pushed back or lost to Earth's pawns, or Bishop takes pawn, threatening the Knight and the Queen. Earth gets a piece and a pawn in exchange for a piece. So Fire offers its Queen in the hope of achieving an even exchange. Example 1(b)(i) shows this.

Example I(b)(i)
A straightforward exchange with Water next to move.

	E	**F**	**W**	**A**
5	BF3axQ	RxB ... and so on.		

Example I(b)(ii)

	E	**F**	**W**	**A**
5	PF4d?	N4a	B3c	P2d

Earth ignores the Queen offering and pushes a pawn forward. This was not such a good move, since the Fire Knight now finds a safe but threatening position. Water presents a threat similar to Earth, but Air ignores it and pushes P2c to 2d, gaining quite an advantage. Water and Earth will have quite a fight on their hands. At this point it appears that a B4c move by Earth is rather worthless unless it is going to capture a Queen.

Example 1(c)

	E	F	W	A
3	—	—	...Q1c	N3c
4	BA4d?	NW4b	B3b	NE4b...

The move EB4d is substituted for EB4c. This move threatens the opponents' Kings and threatens a possible break in their pawn lines. But it is not a serious situation, because Fire and Air still have their moves to make. This shows that Earth moved out too soon and put itself and its ally at an apparent disadvantage. So why doesn't Earth forget about moving the Bishop and keep it back behind the lines and utilize another piece? If you experiment further, you'll find the Earth and Water P4c opening to be weak; the P1c and B1b openings are much stronger.

Example 2
Using Air and Fire opening moves as in Example 1(b). Playing widdershins, Earth Board.

	E	F	W	A
1	P1c	P1c	P1c	P1c
2	B1b	B1b	B1b	B1b
3	N3c	P4c	N3c	P4c
4	QA1d	N3c*	P4c	P3c
5	NF4d	K2a	BE4c	P4d ...

This appears to be a good opening on all accounts, yielding many possibilities for an interesting game to follow; however, Fire may have made a fatal move with N3c. He or she should have moved P3c to prevent Earth moving Knight to F4d, which may start a chain reaction that could capture the Fire King.

Example 3
An opening that becomes a quick middle- and endgame. Playing deosil, Fire Board.

	F	E	A	W
1	P3c	N3c	N3c	P3c
2	B4c	P4c	P1c	QF3d
3	Q1c	NF4bxP	P1d?	B3b
4	P2c	P3c	PE4a	P2c
5	PxWQ	P4d	P2c	N2b
6	NE2c+?	BA4d	P2d	BE2cxN
7	B3b	BF3cxP+	PE4b	RF1cxQ
8	Resigns	QA3d	P4c?	BE4axP?
9	—	QW2d	Q1c?	BA3cxN+
10	—	RA1cxQ+	Resigns	

. . . a win in 10 moves. Although Earth was on the defensive by the second move, Water came immediately out as the aggressor. Air's attack is weak, which costs in the long run. Water sacrifices its Queen to make an opening for its Knight and threaten the Fire Queen. With NE2c, Fire panics and makes a blunder that costs the game. The Earth Queen makes room for the Earth Rook later, and the Water Bishop takes a pawn, a questionable move. But Air gives Earth time by moving Q1c, with Earth and Water finishing in glory. This is an example of Fire and Air not working in harmony when Water and Earth did.

Example 4
A variation on Example 3. Playing deosil, Fire Board.

	F	E	A	W
1	P3c	N3c	N3c	P3c
2	B4c	P4c	P1c	QF3d
3	Q1c	NF4dxP	B1b	B3b

	F	**E**	**A**	**W**
4	P2c	P1c	QW3d	QF1bxP
5	KxQ	B1b	R2a?	NF2cxP...

The opening is as in example 3, but in move 3 Air brought the Bishop to 1b instead of P1d. Water moves B3b to cover the Knight, and Fire threatens the Water Queen and Knight and makes an escape square for its own Knight. Earth opens up for its Bishop in an attempt to free up its back row, anticipating an ANE4b. Air puts additional pressure on Water, working in greater harmony with its ally, but it appears that Air has not advanced enough: the Fire King took the Queen to avoid a check with the Earth or Water Knight on F2c. The Earth Bishop moved to cover the Water Bishop. The Water Knight in move 5 continues the attack on Fire to gain a piece and pawn for its Queen. Fire is now at an extreme disadvantage. From this game play you can see that P3c and N3c have proved to be both an advantage and disadvantage. The key is to turn your questionable moves to advantage.

To open with the Queen's pawn opens the lines for one's Bishop, which appears to be the least vulnerable piece in opening play, therefore the most mobile and valuable. A P2c opening puts one's opponent in a position where he or she cannot move P4b without allowing an easy forward march. However, do not move P2c to 2d, as it will leave your opponent's Knight free to move to 3d, holding that position as a potential threat if your ally attempts to advance P3d. This is one reason why the Knight is not moved too soon in this opening, to wait and see which way your opponent is going to move.

Air of Earth and Air of Fire Setting (KB, R, N, Q)

This setting has proven rather deceptive in its opening play, showing the Bishop as a troublesome piece. It either becomes trapped in the early game or one has to play boldly, if not recklessly, to obtain an opening for it. This play setting does not leave too much room for a careful defensive opening that opens up a seemingly solid play. The opening is volatile, giving an apparently quick (Air) form of play. Early checks are tempting and easy—but not advisable, as shown below. It is far better to position your pieces and develop your game. The following examples are played on the Fire Board, moving widdershins, Air of Fire setting. You'll see that premature moves in this opening are tempting, as the pieces come into play quite quickly with early exchanges.

Example 1
A bad opening for Earth.

	F	W	A	E
1	P3c	P3c	P2c	QA1c+
2	NE2d	N2c	K2b	P2c
3	NE3bxP+	NA4axQ+	K1cxQ	K2b
4	NE2d	P4c	N4c	P4c
5	P2c	NW2c...		

Fire and Water open defensively, preventing an N2d attack. Air baits Earth but also opens up the lines for its Bishop, leaving Earth vulnerable to the Fire Knight. Earth cannot now move its Knight to open up protection for the Queen and has to move a pawn to provide an escape for its King. Water pushes forward with NA4a, taking the Queen and checking the King, but can do nothing to hinder Fire. However, Water skillfully keeps one step ahead of Air, as you will see with later pawn moves. Earth had to move P2c and K2b to push the Fire Knight and prevent a P1c attack from the Fire Queen and Rook, in the event of EP1c. This shows how a seemingly reckless opening can lure the opponent to a premature move that causes difficulties if each move is not carefully thought out.

Example 2
Fire Board playing widdershins.

	F	**W**	**A**	**E**
1	P3c	P3c	P3c	P3c
2	N4c	P2c	QW1c+	N2c
3	P2c	K2b	QW3axN	R3a
4	B2b	R3axQ	N4c	N4d
5	P2d	Q2a...		

A premature move for Water. The P3c opening prevents an N2d attack to 3b check. P2c is best moved after the Knight has moved from the back file. Here, Water moves P2c too early and loses its Knight. Earth and Fire are more cautious and position themselves for a stronger game.

Example 3
An opening where a Hoor defense, as in Example 3(a), or Counter-Hoor defense, as in Example 3(b), would have better been played.

	F	**W**	**A**	**E**
1	Q4c	NF2d	Q4c	NA2d
2	P2c	Q4c	P2c	Q4c
3	B3c	QxB	BF3cxQ	NA3bxP+
4	QW4bxP	NF3bxP+	K2b	NA2d
5	NE2d	P3c	BA4d	P1c
6	NE3b+...			

If Water had not moved NF2d, Fire would have been able to continue its advance on Earth with NE2d and RE1b+. Earth must also anticipate this and either ignore Air's attack, especially if Water does not ignore the bait, and move N4c to cover the opponents' Queens and attacking Knight square, or not move the Knight, so that 1b is covered by two pieces. But if Water ignored the Queen opening, Earth would also move NA2d. However, this could be a disadvantage (see above example). Fire and Air must move P2c to make an escape for their Kings if the opponent Queens go to 1c of their respective angles, or if the opponent's Queen moves elsewhere to open a line for the Rook. FB3c covers P4b, leaves an opening for its King and attacks the opponent's Knight. FR1b instead of B3c is a bad move, as the opponent's Q4bxP immediately causes difficulty.

Example 3(a)
Hoor defense.

	F	W	A	E
1	Q4c	NF2d	Q4c	N4c
2	P2c	P3c	N2c	Q2c
3	B3c	QxB+	N4d?	QF4bxP
4	K2b	QA4dxN	P2c	QxK++...

A King capture in four moves. Air erred by N2c; the move should have been P2c.

Example 3(b)
Counter to Hoor defense.

Air must move P2c in the second move, and not N2c as in the above example, to counter the Hoor defense and create some form of equilibrium.

	F	W	A	E
2	—	—	... P2c	QA1c+
3	B4d	R3a	K2b	QE4a
4	K2b	P4c	QE4bxP	P3c
5	BA4d...			

In move 2, the Earth Queen checked the Air King to force the Air King to block its Bishop. Fire takes the opportunity to get its Bishop out to 4d instead of 3c and forces a Water Rook move, therefore not giving Water a chance to put further pressure on Fire. In move 4, the Fire King becomes more active, preventing a Water Knight attack. A Water pawn pushes forward, chasing the Fire Bishop. Air takes an exposed pawn, and Earth moves defensively, preventing a Fire Knight to E2d. In move 5, the Fire Bishop makes WP1b vulnerable to Water, causing another forced move. At this point there are many possibilities for middle-game play.

Example 4

	F	W	A	E
1	P1c	N4c	P2c	Q2c
2	N2c	QF1cxP+	BF3c	NA2d
3	PxQ	RxP+	P3c	NA3b+
4	K2b	RF1d	K2b	NA1c
5	NW4cxN	PxN	R1a...	

The move P1c is a vulnerable opening, but thanks to Air foreseeing a King capture with EQF4b, Fire escapes. Fire's foolish opening leaves Air vulnerable, but Air manages to escape from this unscarred.

Water of Earth and Water of Fire Setting (KQ, N, R, B)

This opening play position provides a fluent defensive game in which you will find that, without good defense, an easy advantage can be obtained. But if the opposition plays well in defensive moves, the game can be long and difficult. Cooperation with one's ally is easy in this setting and is essential for a strong game. An early Earth Bishop to A2d would put pressure on FP4b and the Fire Rook, because the Water Bishop is on the same diagonal. The Fire Knight would have to respond, and eventually Earth and Water would get a Knight and pawn exchange for the loss of a Bishop. Fire can avoid this by moving P3c, which blocks the Water Bishop. Earth would then exchange a Bishop for a pawn. It may be a move you can attempt with an unsuspecting player, but not an experienced one. An early Knight move could be fatal for the Knight and sacrifice a pawn unnecessarily. For example, if EN1c, the Fire Bishop would capture EP4b, and in Earth's next move the Rook would have to move to safety. The move N3c is just as futile, because the Knight is a valuable piece for middle- and endgame play and the Fire Bishop would immediately capture it.

Example 1
Earth Board playing widdershins.

	E	F	W	A
1	P3c	P3c	P3c	P3c
2	P1c	P4c	B3b	Q1c
3	B3b	N4b	Q1c	B3b
4	P4c	B2c	P2c	P4c
5	N4b	P4d	P4c	N4b...

An interesting variation, which shows caution by all players. The P3c opening opens up the Bishop diagonals and blocks your opponents' Bishops. In move 2, EP1c seems to be a defensive and restrictive move; nevertheless, the strong FP4c begins to open up for a future FN4b and advancing Rook's pawn. Water also opens defensively, and Air attacks. After AQ1c, the Air Queen can go on next move to E4c, attacking the Earth Knight, so Earth's next move (move 3) must be B3b. Meanwhile, Fire and Water are working at moving their pieces out into play, Water moving forward more aggressively with Q1c and Air forced to move B3b. Move 4 shows all angles progressing in positioning their pieces. At move 5, Fire moves P4d to prevent a Water Bishop from moving to E3d, which would have eventually threatened the Fire Rook and Knight, and Air's Queen, or a Water Bishop to W4c threatening the Air Rook. Air moves its Knight into play at A4b, then goes to either 3d or W4d if Water moves P3c to 4d. On move 6, Earth opens up its Bishop line of fire with P4d.

Example 2
Earth Board playing widdershins.

An example of allies working together, but is the loss of a Rook and Bishop worth one piece and a doubled pawn?

	E	F	W	A
1	P3c	Q1c	P1c	Q1c
2	BA2d	P3c	Q3c	P3c
3	BA1cxQ	B3b	P2c	N1cxB
4	RA1cxN	P4c	QA4axB	P1cxR
5	P4c	P4d	QA4c	P1d
6	Q3a	B2c	QE4d	P3d
7	QA1dxP	BW4d+?...		

In order for Earth's attack to be successful, Water must be very careful to first block Fire and second to attack Air. Water ignores the Fire Queen's threat and restricts the Air Bishop's move instead by P1c. Air would have been better off to move P1c or 3c before its Queen moved. Fire gets the message and quickly moves with a P3c. It is characteristic of this play setting that Queens appear active in the opening. With only two pieces threatening A1c, Air decides there is no immediate threat, for it also has two covering pieces, Knight and pawn. Air therefore moves P3c, attempting to push the Earth Bishop away and open up its own lines. There seems to be little else it could do at this point. If the Air Bishop takes the Water Queen, it would only bring the Water Knight out into play and later make matters worse. Earth moves in with its attack, which initially looks weak and premature but eventually gains a piece. The Water Queen, however, is vulnerable to being chased around the board. The Fire Bishop move, however, was premature without backup and ineffectual unless planning to take the Queen.

Example 3
Fire Board playing widdershins. Queen opening ignored— Queen sacrifice.

Example 3(a)

	F	W	A	E
1	Q1c	Q1c	Q1c	Q1c
2	P3c	QA4axB	BxQ	BA2d...

This opening invokes a fluid effect. Each angle ignores the Queen threat, as in the opening play. The piece values of the Queen and Bishop are here considered equal; therefore, a simple Queen and Bishop exchange would be a wasted exercise with no significant gain. If the opening is ignored by all parties and Fire moves P3c in the second move, it will expose itself and its ally to exchanging their Bishops for Queens, but this sets off another chain reaction where all again lose Bishops and Queens. As mentioned earlier, a Queen and Bishop exchange is a wasted exercise.

A more stable opening is given in example 3(b), but here you must not completely duplicate your opponents' moves. The advantage lies with the angle that has the first move of each round.

Example 3(b)

	F	W	A	E
1	Q1c	Q1c	Q1c	Q1c
2	P3c	P3c	P3c	P3c
3	B3b	B3b	B3b	B3b
4	P4c	P4c	P4c	P4c
5	P3d	P3d	P3d	P3d
6	N3c	N3c	N3c	N3c
7	NE4d	NA4b	NE4b	NF4d
8	QW4cxP	QA4cxP	B4cxQ	NA4cxB
9	QA4bxN	PxQ	R4a	B4a
10	P1c	BF4d...		

Quite an organized arrangement, but the version given above from move 7 shows that, if Water had followed suit in move 7, Air would have also been able to do so, and Water and Earth would have suffered. Instead, Water and Earth force a situation that could turn out even all 'round. Bishops may not take Queens because the Knight is covering the 4c squares. However, Earth and Air respond by making a Queen-Bishop exchange. The Fire Queen takes the Water Knight, the result of an oversight by Water. But Water has not been beaten yet. Watch the potentials from this point on and play the rest out by yourself. Have fun!

Fire of Earth and Fire of Fire Setting (KN, Q, B, R)

This is a very exciting play setting which encourages early attacks and active openings; however, nothing ends up as it initially appears to be. Some very difficult games can be formed from this setting. You will see from the examples that an early Rook attack can open up your own Rook escape square. Bringing the Rook out too early can be dangerous. But this is one setting where the Rook will always play an important role in the opening. The Knights are restricted in opening moves and best left until later in this opening, and the Queens, although initially appearing weak, can be brought into useful play. They are still limited in their protectiveness, however, but as pieces of defense their role is functional. A better opening is given in example 3(b), where premature and failed Rook attacks shown in the first examples are not used.

Example 1
Fire Board playing widdershins.

	F	W	A	E
1	N2c	RF1d	N2c	RA1d
2	P4c	P4c	P4c	P4c
3	N4b?	B4b	RW1d	B4b
4	RE1d	N2c?	B4b	P2c
5	RE1c	P1c	R3a	K2b...

Fire and Air attack early, pushing the opponents' Rooks out. However, the Rook move is limited because of P4c and N2c covering the center. Earth and Water must move P4c to prevent

B3d, leaving two-to-one on the King-Knight's pawn, and also restricting their opponents' Knight moves. Air and Fire must also protect their Knights from B3d and also look at opening an escape route for their Rooks, as their opponents' P2b is not restricted from moving 2c. Fire's N4b is a questionable move and may cause restriction, but it does cover the Rook if it moves E1c. In move 4, WN2c prevents an R4d, but with the Earth Rook already on that line, a P2c may have been more effective.

Example 1(a)
Rook's Gambit declined.

	F	W	A	E
3	B4b	P2c	B4b	P2c
4	P3c	B2b	P3c?	P4d
5	P4d	P4d	P4d	BA3d
6	BA1c...			

If at move 3, Water and Earth move P2c before B4b and Fire and Air anticipate by B4b, the Rooks have a greater choice of escape squares. Then a pawn advance can take place to build up control of the central board. The Water Bishop moves 2b to help cover the center. However, what can Air do to escape the Earth Bishop attack? Move AN3a, or Fire Bishop to A1c? Water can prevent N3a by threatening the Air Rook. Air has to sacrifice its Knight. In move 4, Air should have moved B3c.

Example 2
Fire Board playing deosil.

	F	E	A	W
1	P4c	P4c	P4c	P4c
2	Q2c	B4b	B4b	Q2c
3	RE1d	RA1d	B3c	P3c
4	B4b	P2c	Q2c	RF1d
5	R2a	B3c	R2a	N3b
6	Q4a...			

An example where the Queen plays a more active role. P4c opens a Bishop to Rook attack, but a simple Q2c countermove prevents B4b, or later threatens the Bishop. If you are going to move to 4b, leave an escape square. The move P2c seems poor, because it blocks both Queen and Knight. A point needing mention is that an early Q2c defense would operate better in widdershins play.

Example 3
Fire Board playing widdershins.

	F	W	A	E
1	P2c	P3c	P2c	Q2c
2	B2b	N3b	B2b	P4c
3	Q4c?	P4c...See (a) and (b)		

In this opening, the players ignore the obvious but futile early Rook attack. Allies are working together, but Fire and Air have a greater control of the central board. Some variations of this are:

Example 3(a)

	F	W	A	E
3	—	—	...BF3c	BW2d
4	P1c	BF4cxQ	R3a	BE4b
5	R3a	R3a	P3c	P3c
6	PxB...			

The Air Bishop supports Fire by a threat to the Water Rook. This leaves the Water Rook trapped. Earth delays Air by a Bishop threat to the Air Rook. Fire can do very little to help as yet, and Water opens up an escape square for Rook. Air must move its Rook and so cannot follow through with a Bishop attack. The Earth Bishop then threatens the Fire Rook, forcing another move, and the Water Rook escapes capture. Fire gets a doubled pawn out of this exchange.

Example 3(b)

	F	**W**	**A**	**E**
3	—	—	…B3c	R4b
4	P1c	P3d	PW3dxP	P4d
5	QA3d	P3dxP	K2B	R4c
6	FQA1d…			

If Earth had moved A1c instead of E4b, the Air King would finally trap the Earth Rook, unless Earth or Water could buy some time to move out of difficulty. Water is keen to open up its Rook line and advance its pawns. Air responds. Fire is not moving characteristically and seems bound up as of move 5, showing Earth and Water coming in strong. What would you do in move 6? FQA1d? In both examples (a) and (b), FQ4c has proven to be a questionable move.

Air and Water Board Play Settings

Earth of Air and Earth of Water Setting (KR, N, Q, B)

The variations of effective openings available for this setting appear limited. Bishop to opponent's 2d offers little because of a P3c defense, and until your opponent's Bishop has moved from 4a, the Knights and Queens are restricted in movement. P2c cannot be moved before a 3c or 1c as the King would immediately be exposed. An early Q1c will force your opponent's Bishop to your 2d and can cause a loss of the Bishop if your ally works well with you, or an early no-gain exchange. P1c advance has been found more effective towards middle game. If a player opens P3c, player 2 (player 4 if playing deosil) must open 3c as well to provide an escape for its Bishop, as player 1 can follow with Q1c. Mistakes are easy in this setting, exactness being needed. B3b instead of 3c seems necessary as the player preceding you (following you if playing deosil) can immediately go Q1c then on to your 4c, threatening your Knight.

Example 1 gives a strong opening and seems to be the best alternative for a conservative player, but for other players Example 3 may be more enjoyable.

Example 1
Water Board playing widdershins. Pawn March.

	W	A	E	F
1	P3c	P3c	P3c	P3c
2	B3b	B3b	B3b	B3b
3	P2c	P2c	P2c	P2c
4	P1c	P1c	P1c	P1c
5	K2b	P1d	K2b	P1d
6	P2d	K2b	P2d	K2b...

This opening appears conservative and initially safe for all players. Each player is well protected and positioned, ready for a long fight ahead.

Example 1(a)

	W	A	E	F
3	P2c	P4c*	P2c	P2c
4	P1c	N4b	P1c...See examples	
			1(a)(i) and 1(a)(ii)	

Air moves P4c, a bad move which may cost Air some pieces later. If Water had moved QF3d in move 3, the Air Bishop would have had to capture the Queen to prevent further difficulty.

Example 1(a)(i)

	W	A	E	F
4	—	—	—	...N1c?
5	B4c?	N2c	P1d	P2d?
6	B3b	P4d	PF4bxP...	

Fire makes too many mistakes, which will weaken Fire and Air's positions for middle-game play. Water wastes two moves with B4c, but Earth comes on strong.

Example 1(a)(ii)

	W	A	E	F
4	—	—	—	...P1c
5	P4c	N2c	P3d	P4c
6	K2b	P1c	N3c	K2b
7	...			

If Fire had moved P1c and P4c, as in this example, Fire and Air would have had a stronger footing in further play. It would have also caused all the other players to reconsider their next moves. It is clear in this opening that bringing your Knight out too early can be inhibiting, but the following opening shows a different story.

Example 2
Air Board playing deosil.

	A	W	F	E
1	P3c	Q3c?	P1c?	P3c
2	B3b	P4c	P3c	B3b
3	P4c	N4b	B2c	P4c
4	N4b	N2c	P4c	N4b
5	P4d?	QA4a?	P4d	PA4dxP
6	PxP	PF4dxP	PxP...	

Water's pressure on the Air Bishop seems unnecessary, inasmuch as Air had already provided an escape. Earth did not follow up with the same move as Water so as to open up its lines for the Bishop. While Air and Fire bring in their 4d pawns to cover the center, Water sacrifices its Queen to hold Air up in its moves. Earth makes the exchange, but Air does not take the obvious course and moves the Queen to open up a second firing line, after first capturing an Earth pawn.

Example 3

Air Board playing widdershins.

	A	E	F	W
1	Q1c	BA2d	P3c	Q1c
2	BW2d	P3c	Q1c	P3c
3	BW1cxQ	Q1c	B3b	NxB
4	P3c	BxQ	QxB	RxQ
5	NxB	P4c...		

An Air Queen attack starts the game, but may be a mistake for the first move, because Water can now pressure Air. Then Fire must move P3c to protect P4b. With a Water Queen attack following, a chain reaction sets in. The Air Bishop must move W2d because N3c, which opens up protection for Air, exposes the Knight to capture by the Earth Bishop. Earth must, in move 2, go P3c because of Bishop crossfire to P4b. Air must capture the Water Queen because there is nowhere to run, and the same for the Earth Bishop. However, Earth must first force a Fire move, to prevent the Fire Queen from taking the Water Bishop. In move 4, Air could have moved P4c to avoid a pawn loss from an eventual NxP. Then NxN and BxN, with both Air and Water losing Knights. Air moves P3c instead, so the Earth Bishop must immediately capture the Air Queen because it has nowhere to go. By the time move 5 is over, the Passives would have two Queens, one Bishop and one pawn, the Actives two Bishops and one Queen.

Air of Air and Air of Water Setting (KB, Q, N, R)

This setting provides potential for many quick exchanges in the game opening. An early King attack can be allowed by P2c, which will prove to be a disadvantage if your ally does not back you up. For example, if in move 1, AP2c, Earth Knight to A2d, FP3c, WN2c, then in move 2 the Air King would move to 2b and save the day or move the Rook to W1d, in which case the Air Rook is lost (for example, 2 ARW1d NA3bxP+ FN2c WRF1d,

3 AK2b ENxAR. Or 2 AK2b EP3c FN2c WRF1d, 3 ARW1d). A
P1c move only adds to the block on the Bishop and is subject to
a Queen and Rook attack to check. A P4c seems of no particular
value in the first moves. Early Rook captures as shown in example 1 below can be avoided as shown in example 2.

Example 1
Air Board playing widdershins. Knights Charge:

	A	**E**	**F**	**W**
1	NW2d	N2c	RE1d	P1c?
2	NW3bxP+	Q4c	N2c	K1b
3	Q4c	K2a	NxR	K2c?
4	QW1cxP	QxFP	RA4c	N4c
5	NW1axB+	P4c?	RW3d	K1b
6	QA4c+	QF2d	RW4d	KxN1a
7	RxK++...			

Fire and Air start off aggressively. Earth tries to delay Fire's
forward moves by threatening the Fire Rook and pawn. Fire
ignores the pawn threat and attacks the Water Rook, knowing
that Water's next move must be K1b. However, the Water King is
not out of the heat yet, as you will see in moves 3 and 4. In move
4, if WP2b had taken the Air Queen on square W1c and immediately checked, then a King capture would have followed. Earth
seems helpless because of an early N2c, but, in move 5, could have
moved N4d instead of P4c and prevented the Fire Rook move.
Air's discovered check was well done, with the help of the Fire
Rook, forcing the Water King to 1b. If in move 5 the Earth Rook
had sacrificed itself by RA1bxP+ this would have given Water
King time to capture Fire Rook and move out to a free square.

If in move 3 Water Queen takes Knight instead of K2c, in
move 5 Fire Rook would have had to go W3b, for example:

	A	**E**	**F**	**W**
5	—	—	...RW3b	K2a
6	QA4c	N4d	RW4bxP	K3a

	A	E	F	W
7	QF3d+	NA2d	Q2c	K2a
8	K2a	RxP	RxQ+	K3b
9	NxK+...			

In move 5, the Water King cannot capture the Air Knight or Queen because they are covering each other; e.g., the Rook covers the Queen and the Queen covers the Knight. The move WP2b cannot capture the Queen because it will expose the King, and there is nothing Earth can do at this stage to restrict Fire. The Water Queen has nowhere to go: only the King can be moved, because the Knight covers a crucial 3a square. On move 6, the Air Queen must move away from the pawn's threat. Moves 7 and 8 show a probable direction of play. Water hoped an Earth to Air attack would hinder an immediate capture, but Air ignored the bait.

The following two examples show you a defense against the Knight's charge.

Example 2
Air Board playing deosil. Knight's Charge Defense, playing deosil.

	A	W	F	E
1	NW2d	Q4c	N2c	NA2d
2	Q4c	RF1d	P3c	NA3bxP+
3	K2a	K2a	N4d	NA2d
4	P2c	N2c	P2c	NA4cxQ?
5	RW1bxP	R3a	NxN	P2c
6	R4a	NxN	Q4c...	

The Queen comes out to 4c so the King can move to 2a and cover any attack on 3b. Earth must put pressure on Air instead of Fire to save the Water Rook, because Air must be slowed down in its attack. Otherwise NW3bxP in move 2 or 3 would create a crossfire to the Water King and Rook. Fire continues threatening Water, but it does not hold back the threat to Air. The Earth Knight captures the Air Queen, which was not covered, and Air has to move its Rook rather than chase the Knight with its King. As you will see, the struggle continues from moves 4 to 6.

Example 3
Air Board playing widdershins. Knight's Charge defense, widdershins:

	A	**E**	**F**	**W**
1	NW2d	NA2d	N2c	RF1d
2	Q4c	RA1bxP+	Q4c	Q4c
3	K2a	R3a	QW4bxP	K2a...

The Knight's charge opening is deflected comfortably by defense. However, Earth takes a pawn but fails a King capture. Fire and Air fail their King capture but obtain a pawn.

Example 4
Water Board playing deosil.

	W	**F**	**E**	**A**
1	N4c	P2c	N4c	P2c
2	R3a	B4d	R3a	B4d
3	NE4d	P4c	NW4d	P4c
4	NA2d...			

Although N4c covers your opponents' 2c, preventing a Knight to Rook threat, it allows your opponents' Bishops to come into play early in the game with a Knight chase. In move 2, Earth and Water must move R3a to avoid a pawn fork on the opponent's 2d. The Fire and Air Bishop's 4d moves prove annoying, although not difficult, since P3b is covered with Rooks to 3a. Fire and Air chase the Knights too hard, however, and return the threat to themselves with a Knight's forced move to their 2d, even as they do the same. See 4(a) below.

Example 4(a)

	W	**F**	**E**	**A**
4	—	...NE2d	NF2d	NW2d
5	RxP+	K2b	RxP+	KxR
6	NxAK++	K3c...		

Water and Earth are one step ahead and capture the Air King, freezing Air's pieces. What Fire and Air should have done was:

Example 4(b)

	W	F	E	A
4	—	...P3c	NF2d	P3c...

Earth Knight to opponent's 3b+ is a wasted move, since K2b leaves the Knight out on a limb. It will eventually end up at 3c, with Earth's pieces undeveloped and Fire and Air controlling the middle board.

Example 5
Water Board playing widdershins.

	W	A	E	F
1	P3c	N2c	RA1d	P3c
2	N2c	R3a	P3c	P2c
3	Q4c	P3c	P2c	P2d
4	QF1c+	P4c	P4c	K2b
5	R3a	P4d	P2d	RE1d...

This opening was played with caution as the main factor. By move 6, all are into middle-game play with no casualties.

Water of Air and Water of Water Setting (KQ, B, R, N)

Although a very difficult game for a clean opening, if played carefully this is an opening that is slow but which provides some solid play. If looking from an Air Board widdershins play perspective, P3c must not be your first move because of a vulnerable 2c square where your opponent's Earth Knight could go to your 2c and check, followed by his ally's Q1c or N1c. Your P1b cannot capture the Earth Knight because it will expose your King to immediate capture. As in most openings, P4c is vulnerable. Deosil play, however, shows a P3c move to be quite acceptable, because by the time the opponent you are facing gets his or her turn, your ally's Bishop is covering square 2c.

If you commence with a Queen opening, it pressures your opponent's Knight, but unless you play this carefully your pieces could wind up under pressure. For example, AQ1c would attract the Earth Knight to A3d. At your next turn, your Queen must go 3c to avoid NxQ, which would eventually leave you with a doubled pawn if your ally cannot move to help. Therefore, Q3c seems better as a first move.

Pawn advances provide a strong play in this setting, and a more defensive role for the Knight is advantageous.

Example 1
Water Board playing widdershins.

	W	A	E	F
1	Q3c	NW3d	Q3c	N3c
2	P4c	NW4b	P1c	P1c
3	P1c	P1c	B1b	B1b
4	B1b	P4c	P2c	P4c
5	P2c	B1b	R2a	P2c
6	P2d	Q3c	N2b	P2d
7	N2b	BE4d	P2d	R2a
8	QxB	R2a	B3d	PxQ...

Queen openings must be played very carefully to avoid being a liability. A WQ3c opening forces Air to move its Knight. The Air Knight counterattacks, but Water is not worried because its P1b is covered by two pieces, and a P4c will avoid a pawn capture and force the Air Knight to move again. Earth follows suit to its ally, but Fire retaliates by adding to Air's threat to Water. This results in a Knight hook (Air NW4b and Fire N3c), which restricts the amount of safe squares for Water. The first advance for all sides, although unsuccessful, establishes positions, so the Fire and Water Angles take Earth's lead and establish their Bishop diagonals. Air must delay B1b to avoid an Earth Knight move to A3d; Fire also advances P4c. So far the central board is covered from all angles, although Fire and Air have a slight advantage. In move 5, Water makes an escape square for its Knight and the other angles continue to position themselves. As you will see in moves 6 and 7, each player continues to bring his or her pieces out, positioning them with a small exchange in move eight. This opening leads to a long and interesting game.

Example 2
Air Board playing widdershins.

	A	**E**	**F**	**W**
1	P1c	P1c	P1c	P1c
2	B1b	B1b	B1b	B1b
3	P3c	P4c	P2c	N3c
4	P4c	Q3c?	N2b	P2c
5	BE4d	BF4d?	P3c	K2a
6	P2c	BE1b	P2d	P2d
7	N2b	P2c...		

This Pawn opening allows each player to open up Bishop diagonals and advance their pieces. Once AP3c, the Earth Knight would have moved 2c+, but now that the Air Bishop is in 2b, this would be futile. EQ3c inhibits Earth's forward march and is therefore a questionable move. In move five, the Air Bishop makes a play for the Water Knight, so Earth reciprocates, but against Fire—a foolish gesture, because P3c is not blocked. Water cannot move its Knight because of a discovered check, so moves the King instead. The strong advance of Air and Fire pawns could lead to a strong game on their part. In move 7, although the Fire Bishop could move W4d so that both Bishops threaten both Water and Earth, a Water Knight move brings danger to Air King by a Water or Earth NA2c, King and Rook fork. Then in move 8, the Water King cannot capture the Fire Bishop because of Air Bishop cover. Water can bide its time, and P3c solves that problem, trapping the Fire Bishop.

Therefore, a follow-through with the Fire Bishop is not advisable; FP4c to 4d is a better move. In Air's turn, it would have to be 4d, opening up the Fire Bishop line to A3b to add additional cover to the pin in the fork, although a K1b would have done just as well.

Example 3
Air Board playing widdershins.

	A	E	F	W
1	P1c	P1c	P1c	P1c
2	B1b	B1b	B1b	B1b
3	P4c	P4c	P4c	P4c
4	K2a	N3c	P2c?	N3c
5	P3c	BF4d+	Q3c	B3d
6	NxB	NF4b	K2b	PxN...

This is another version of a Bishop diagonal opening. In move 3, P4c seems best because a Bishop to the opponent's 4d would only have to retreat, and a P4c prevents a Knight to 3d. In move 4, the Earth and Water Knights must move instead of pawns because of a possible Knight pin. Move 5 sees the Earth Bishop lineup and Fire attack, so the Air Knight must capture the Earth Bishop. The move FP2c turned out at this point not to be so good, because Water and Earth were still positioned to move and threaten Fire.

Example 4
Water Board playing deosil. Rose of Air.

	W	F	E	A
1	P3c	P3c	P3c	P3c
2	B3b	B3b	B3b	B3b
3	P2c	P2c	P2c	P2c
4	N2b	N2b	N2b	N2b
5	P2d	P2d	P2d	P2d...

The P3c opening is no danger in deosil play because, by the time the player to the right of you gets his turn, your ally's Bishop covers your 2c square. If in move 2, Water had moved B4c, Air still would have had to move B3b to get a free square for the Rook, but 4c is a bad move because Water would eventually suffer a check. B3b prevents N2c+. P2c opens up a route for the Knight, and P2d keeps the opponents' Knight or Bishop away from their 4c. The pattern on the board formed by the pieces and pawns resembles a flower. The opening provides for an interesting but tricky game.

Fire of Air and Fire of Water Setting (KN, R, B, Q)

This setting is another difficult one for successful opening variations. P2c and P4c in succession would invoke a check from the opponent's Queen on your 3c, then a possible Knight loss, because only one piece at a time can be moved from the Throne Square. If your opponent threatens your Queen with N2c, it would be wise to go 2c instead of 4c; otherwise you would get something like example 1(b). The play from this setting is restrictive, showing the type of restriction one would assume for Fire in a Water element, but not so in an Air element. However, notice the play examples on the Air Board, which operate a little quicker but still have to be carefully thought out to prevent disorder among the pieces.

Example 1
Water Board playing widdershins.

Example 1(a)

	W	A	E	F
1	P2c	N2c?	Q2c	P2c
2	B2b	P4c	P4c	P3c
3	P3c	B4b	B4b	Q4c
4	P4c	B3c	P3c	N3b
5	N3b	N3a	P4d	QW4b
6	P2d	Q2c	BA1d	P2d
7	Q2c	P1c	N3b	PW4cxP

	W	**A**	**E**	**F**
8	QxP	BW1d	N2d	QW2bxB
9	RxQ	BW3bxN...		

Water opens to free its Bishop. Air threatens Earth with its Knight, but this could be premature because it limits its own Queen's escape. In move 2, Air has to go P3c because P4c would cause the Water Queen to move to F3c+. The Fire Bishop to 2b would leave P4b unprotected. Move 3 brings the pieces out, and the Fire Queen to 4c threatens WP4B while moving the Fire Queen away from the Earth Bishop's attack. Moves 4–5 show an effort by all the players to position their pieces, advancing to take an advantage on moves 6 and 7. Air takes more pressure from Water and Earth, and Fire comes to the rescue and turns the advantage to Fire and Air.

Example 2
Water Board playing widdershins.

	W	**A**	**E**	**F**
1	N2c	Q2c	N2c	Q2c
2	P4c	P1c	P4c	P1c
3	P3c	P4c	P3c	P4c
4	P1c	P3c	P1c	P3c

Example 2(a)

	W	**A**	**E**	**F**
5	P4d	PxP	P4d	PxP
6	PxP	BW3d	PxP	BE3d...

Example 2(b)

	W	**A**	**E**	**F**
5	K1b	P4d	PxP	N3b
6	R1a	PxP	BA3d	BE3d
7	P3d	K1b	N3a	N2d...

This opening shows how the Queens gain in strength if the Knight opens. An early Knight and Queen opening limits pawn movement, which may leave you at a loss for moves. Move 3 for Water or Earth, although tempting, should not be Bishop to the opponent's 3d, because the Bishop will eventually be lost; e.g., 3 BF3d* P4c P4d P4c, 4 R3a B4b Q4c PxB. So here Water and Earth move P3c in move 3. In example 2(a), P3d in move 5 would be alternately a restrictive move, so Water and Earth move P4d. That too was not good, however, because the Knights get into strife by move 7; the Queen's defense is too strong and pins the Knights. In example 4(b), all players escape from early strife and the game can continue with no early handicaps. Water missed a chance in move 7 to effect an exchange that may have given Earth and Water points up with a BF4cxP, because the Earth Bishop would have followed through after the Fire Queen captured the Water Bishop.

Example 3
Air Board playing deosil.

In move 1, if players one and three open P4c, player four is advised also to open P4c; otherwise you may get something like this:

Example 3(a)

	A	W	F	E
1	P4c	P2c*	P4c	P2c*
2	BF2d	B2b?	B4b	Q4c
3	BxQ	P3c	B3c...	

P2c allowed the Air Bishop to move to F2d, threatening the Water Queen. Water assumed that, when moving its Bishop from the back line, the remaining Rook cover would be satisfactory. Not so. FB4b doubles the attack. The Earth Queen moves out to a pawn cover, threatening the Fire Bishop. ABxWQ is safe because the Water Rook will be lost if Water reciprocates. The Fire Bishop moves away from the Earth Queen threat.

Example 3(b)
Defense against P4c opening.

	A	**W**	**F**	**E**
1	P4c	P4c	P4c	P4c
2	B4b	Q2c	B4b	Q2c
3	B3c	P3c	B3c	P3c...

Example 4
Air Board playing deosil.

	A	**W**	**F**	**E**
1	P4c	P4c	P4c	P4c
2	B4b	B4b	B4b	B4b
3	P3c	Q2c	B3c	Q2c
4	B3a	P3c	P2c	P3c
5	P2c	N3b	P1c	N3b
6	N3b...			

By move 3, the defense (Water and Earth) must not move P3c; otherwise Air will move P3d, then EB3a, FP3d, WB3a, and then Air Bishop takes Queen, EP2c and Fire Bishop takes Queen. So Earth and Water must move Q2c. Thereafter, all players position their pieces for a strong game.

Experiment with openings and see what you can come up with.

Middle-Game
and
Endgame

Enochian Chess middle- and endgame play can be as complex as opening play, if not more so. Middle-game play directly follows the opening. It is where strategical patterns of moves are made to obtain an advantage over your opponents. Piece value can change depending on players and the opening game, but players must always try to preserve pieces and pawns that may be of value in the endgame. Within the opening, middle-game and endgame play combinations are also used. Combinations are considered variations or groups of variations of moves that force opponents' moves with the objective of obtaining an advantage. Combinations usually require a piece or pawn sacrifice.

In the middle-game, players must build up their attack power while at the same time creating a well-defended King. Enochian chess players will find it difficult, as is not so much the case in conventional chess, to make successful attacks and capture a King if the opponents are working well together, even if the player's own ally is working well with him or her, which is essential in most cases. You always have to watch your back. Unlike ordinary chess, there are enemy forces coming up from behind you as well as in front of you, and the odds can turn against you very quickly. Try not to sacrifice too many pieces, as you only have four pieces and four pawns to work with. Your ally cannot always be there to help. Always keep your pieces and pawns in touch with each other as well as with your ally's pieces and pawns to ensure that cover or support is always near.

Try not to move automatically without reflection. Even if you have previously worked out your next move, check the board again for hidden threats; look ahead to sequences of moves. Do not abandon control of the center to your adversary or give up open lines. Seize them and hold them. Moves that require a hasty retreat are a waste of time, so work toward realizable plans in your game; don't just make what seems to be the best move at the time. Keep enemy pawns blockaded to prevent an advancing line. Create weaknesses in your opponents' play without weakening your own position; then follow through with an attack. Make pawn sacrifices only if it creates a disadvantage for your opponent, because pawns are valuable in the endgame. They are a force to be reckoned with if they are used well in middle-game play.

Endgame (or ending) play is the phase which follows the middle-game. Endgames are when the play results in a forced win, draw, withdrawal or stalemate. The character of endgames is such that there are few rather than many pieces/pawns present, and they can be quite unique in their combinations, depending on the expertise (or luck) of the players. To play a good endgame shows great composing skill on the part of the player. Endgames are strategically different from middle-games: patience is required for very careful analysis of the strategic value of each move. A pawn may have just as much value as a piece. Because of a limited number of pieces and pawns available, or because some of your remaining pieces are blocked, you may have to move from a good position to a bad

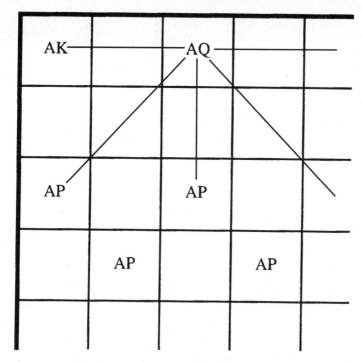

FIGURE 37—QUEEN'S DEFENSE
AIR ANGLE, FIRE OF FIRE SETTING
THE AIR QUEEN COVERS SQUARES 1C AND 3C

one. The defense may also try for a stalemate or a draw, defeating the purpose of a win.

Some interesting patterns form in endgames; however, they are relative to the pieces left playing. The Queen is usually of little value in the endgame accept as a defense, as for example in figure 37 above.

If two allied Queens remain, they can, if carefully played, work together and become stronger than a single opponent's Knight. In figure 38, on the following page, a Queens' fork prevents any movement from the Knight without its being captured. Therefore, in this instance, allowing your Knight to work from the outer squares of a board rather than from the center handicaps you if two opponent Queens are still operating.

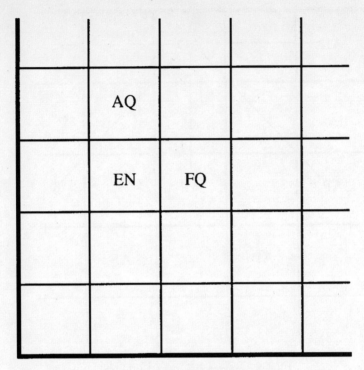

FIGURE 38—QUEENS' FORK
THE KNIGHT CANNOT MOVE TO ANY SQUARE THAT IS NOT
COVERED BY EITHER THE AIR QUEEN OR FIRE QUEEN

Try to use your King more as an active piece in endgame play: the King can be used defensively and aggressively, as you can see in some of the following examples.

Example 1
Earth Board, Water of Earth setting, playing widdershins.

	E	F	W	A
1	P3c	P3c	P3c	P3c
2	P1c	P4c	B3b	Q1c
3	B3b	N4b	Q1c	B3b
4	P4c	B2c	P2c	P4c
5	N4b	P4d	P4c	N4b

	E	**F**	**W**	**A**
6	P3d	NE4d	PF4dxP	P4d?
7	PA4dxP	P3d	K2b	P3d
8	N2c	Q3c	P2d	B2c
9	NxN	P1c	QA4a	PxN
10	B4a	PW4c	B2c	N3d
11	BA2d	B3d	RF1d	BxWQ
12	PF4c	R2a	PxAB	RxWP
13	PF3dxFB	K1b	N4b	Q3c
14	BF4b	R1a	K3a	QW1d
15	BF3cxQ	K2a	BxAQ	RxWB
16	BW4a	K3b	K2a	RA3a

Example 1(a)

	E	**F**	**W**	**A**
17	RF2c	R2a	K1a	NE4a
18	PW4d	K3a	P3d	RE2c
19	K2a	PW3c	PA4c	RE2bxP+?
20	K3a	K3b	N3d	PE3d
21	KxN	R4a	NA3b+	K2a
22	RE3dxP	K2a	P1c	RE2a+
23	RE3a	R4dxP+	NA2d	RE2c
24	K3b	RW4dxP	NA1bxP	RF3b
25	BW2c	K1b	PA3c	P2c
26	PF2d	RF4c+	NA2d	RF3c
27	K2b	K2c?	RW2a	K3a
28	PF1c[†]	K3b	NE4d	R2c
29	RxFR	KxR	NW4c+	RW4b
30	RW4a	Resigns	R2b	Resigns

[†]Pawn promoted to a Rook.

Refer to the Water of Earth opening, example 1, page 135, for commentary on moves 1 to 5. In move 6, Earth threatens the Fire Knight, which must move. The Fire Knight goes to E4d, knowing that any Water pawn advance would be counter checked by Air,

Air   Water

AK		AR	WQ			WP	
AP	AP		AN	WP		WK	WN
AQ	AB				WP	WB	WR
			EP				
			AP	WP	FP		
ER	EB		EP		FQ	FB	FP
	EP					FP	
EQ EK		EP			FR		FK

Earth   Fire

FIGURE 39—PIECE POSITIONS AT MOVE 9 IN EXAMPLE 1

leaving F3d free for advancing forces. Water opens up the back ranks by taking a Fire pawn. Air also opens its ranks, but leaves its pawn vulnerable, as shown in move 7, EPxAP, covered by a Bishop and a Knight. Fire ignores the Water pawn and moves its Rook's pawn forward. Water must not move P3d because of a subsequent Air Bishop check to the Water King. Water also cannot move B4c, pinning the Air Rook and threatening the Air Knight, because the Fire Knight covers W4c. The Water King therefore comes forward to add cover to the Queen. The Air pawn ignores possible capture by the Earth pawn and goes forward as bigger bait. As you can see, in only two rounds of the game since opening play, all players keep the pressure on each other to prevent a sound attack from being established.

The pawn triangle in the center holds quite strongly—two Earth pawns with one Water pawn at the point of the triangle.

But if the Earth Knight were to take the Fire Knight, the Air pawn would have to take the Earth Knight, filling the center of the triangle and pinning both the Earth and Water pawns, although it would be a floating pawn itself if the Air Bishop's cover were removed.

By move 9, the Fire pawn sitting on 3d has been a handicap to Water, preventing Knight and Bishop movement. Water tries to give Air a choice of pieces to capture in order to save the Earth Knight, but Air ignores the bait and makes the pin in the triangle. This could cost Water, so Earth adds a threat with its Bishop, although this puts the Bishop under threat also. Watch how this struggle is played out.

By move 14, Fire is in trouble. If Fire moves P2c, a checkmate follows in two moves. The only other piece that can be moved is the Rook, making way for the King. Water and Earth are safe, and Air is poorly positioned. Up to this point, Fire and Air have not played well. Water, however, has nowhere to move while waiting for Earth to remove the Fire Queen, which is playing a key role, so Water must make a miscellaneous move with the King; any other move would put Water in jeopardy.

At this point, Water and Earth are up by one piece and one pawn.

All players made mistakes in this game, the greatest of which was failing to watch their backs. In any game where allies concentrate too much on one opponent, there is a danger that the other opponent will sneak up from behind. In move 15, if Fire had counterattacked by capturing the Earth Bishop with its pawn, a quick Fire King capture would have followed: both the Earth and Water Rooks would have been lined up together with the Water Knight on the Fire pawn on 1c. Move 16 sees the Fire King play as an aggressor, preventing Water and Earth from moving in.

By move 18 in example 1(a), Earth and Water are finding a Fire King capture difficult. Pawns are cleverly used by all players to hold an advantage. In move 19, Air overlooked a King fork and could lose a Knight. The Water Knight moved out to put some pressure on Air, since Air was hindering effective

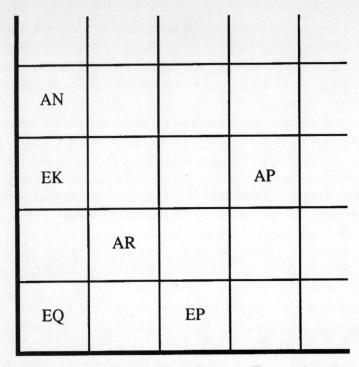

FIGURE 40—EARTH KING FORK IN EARTH ANGLE

Earth moves. Fire and Air turn the attack in their favor on moves 22 and 23. However, this turns again against Air, who miscalculated his or her attack on the Earth King and left itself with a King fork, as shown in figure 40.

However, the Fire Rook comes to the rescue, again changing the advantage. This is an example of how a turn of events can occur in this game, with the input from two additional players. But the struggle does not end at move 23, for endgame play makes more free squares available for maneuvering and leaves all players working for an advantage. Having more free squares to choose from can make players careless, whereas in fact which square you position each piece on can be crucial to the success of your game.

Another point to note here is the Earth Queen, which has not moved once in the whole game, yet even unmoved plays a key defensive role for Earth in the endgame. The Rooks play a strong role in the endgame providing you can keep them free from being pinned in, as the Water Rook was for most of this game.

Earth's move in move 27 might have been Q3c to protect the Earth King and also threaten the Air Rook, but Earth moved its King instead. In move 28, Earth exchanges a pawn for another Rook, giving Earth and Water a further advantage. Move 29 brings a Knight fork to the Fire Knight and Air Rook. Air chooses to save its Rook, but move 30 brings the newly exchanged Earth Rook into play, combining with the Water Rook to threaten the Air Rook, which has nowhere to go. Air and Fire resign.

In example 1(b), given below, in move 17, Earth moves BF3c instead of RF2c, and Fire retaliates with PxB, but Earth and Water still win because Fire and Air erred early in the game and lost too many pieces. However, in the next few moves, Air certainly tries hard to change the odds.

Example 1(b)

	E	**F**	**W**	**A**
17	BF3c	PxB	RF1cxP	R3b+
18	RF3cxP+	K2b	K1a	NA4b
19	RF2c+	K3b	RF1axR	NW1c
20	Q3a	K4b	RW3a	P1c
21	K1b	K3b	NF1c+	RE4c
22	P2c	K4a	P3d	RE4b+
23	K2a	PW3dxP	K2b	NA4b
24	P2d+	KE2d	R2dxP	N2c
25	RE3b	Withdraws	R1d+	K1b
26	R4bxR	Air Retires		

On move 23, Fire attempts to create a bare King by sacrificing its last pawn. In so doing, Fire can withdraw and leave its moves to Air, who has more pieces in play, thereby giving Air an advantage. Earth anticipates this and pulls its Rook away from the Fire angle in move 25 to reinforce its own forces. With ally cooperation, Water and Earth double-team Air. This does not give Air a chance to get going with its extra moves received from

Fire, and the Air Rook is captured. Air retires, conceding defeat. Once the Rook is captured, the odds are heavily against it; for example, one Knight against two Rooks, a Knight and a Queen.

Example 2
Fire Board, Fire of Fire setting, playing widdershins.

	F	**W**	**A**	**E**
1	P2c	P3c	P2c	Q2c
2	B2b	N3b	B2b	P4c
3	Q4c?	P4c	BF3c	BW2d
4	P1c	BF4cxQ	R3a	BE4b
5	R3a	R3a	P3c	P3c
6	PxB	N2d	R4a	N3b
7	P2d	P4d	P3d	B3a
8	N2c	Q2c	N3b	Q2a
9	PW4b?	R3b	BA3c	P2c
10	P1d	NxB	P4c	B1c
11	BA3cxN	PA4d	P1c	R3a
12	BA2b	P3d*	P1d	BF4cxP
13	RW2cxQ	K2a	RW1d	Q4a
14	RW4c?	P2c	RA4a	QA3c+
15	BxQ	PxB	N1c	N2d
16	K2b	K2b	NE4b	P3d
17	NW4a+	K2a	NA3cxP	PF4bxP
18	NW3c+	K1a	NW2d...	

Example 2(a)

	F	**W**	**A**	**E**
18	—	—	—	...BW4bxFP
19	PxB	R2b	NW1bxP	NF3a
20	K3b	R1bxN	RxR+	RF3c+
21	K4bxP	KxR	PE4a	RF4cxR
22	NxWK	Captured;	P2d	NF2c+
23	K4c	Frozen	PE4b	RW4bxFP
24	NW3c	Pieces	K1b	RW2b
25	KE4d		Q2c	NW4c+

	F	**W**	**A**	**E**
26	KE4cxP		PE3a	NF4c+
27	KA2d		PE3b	RF2c
28	NF4d		QE4b	RF2b
29	NE3c		PE2b+	Resigns

See commentary on moves 1–6 in opening play example 3(a), Fire of Fire, page 140.

After move 6, all pieces have reached middle-game play. Water immediately attacks with its Knight, but it is not a move that has much follow-through, since Air just casually moves its Rook back to 4a. Earth and Fire concentrate on positioning their pieces. Fire and Air forces advance on move 7. Water ignores Fire's threat, but Earth must retreat. Earth looks bottled up and could lose its Rook if it does not move fast. Water is prevented from moving to PA4d, which would block the Air Bishop, because of the threat to the Water Rook by a Fire pawn advance in move 9. However, due to the Air Bishop's threat to the Earth Rook, the Water Knight must capture the Air Bishop in move 10. Fire has underestimated the Water Rook's move and now cannot move an advanced pawn to capture a Water pawn because it will expose the Fire Knight. In move 9, Fire should have gone NW4c instead of PW4b, as this would have enabled it to carry through its Earth Rook capture.

Air and Fire have a double play in their moves; however, a simple EP2c would have prevented the Air Rook from storming across the board after the Bishop/Night/pawn exchange to line up the Earth King's pawn. Air therefore chooses not to capture the Water Knight with its pawn, causing a doubled pawn, and leaves the capture to the Fire Bishop. In the meantime, Earth makes an opening for its Rook. On move 11, Water links its outside pawn up with an Earth pawn to block the Fire Bishop's line of movement, and so the Fire Bishop is threatened in move 12.

Air uses its Queen very well by positioning its pawns so that the Queen covers two back pawns by a fork. WP3d was a bad move because it immediately exposed the Water Queen. The Queen was protected only by P1b, which could not be moved because it would expose the Water King to the Air Rook. So

Air   Water

AK	AQ		AR			WP	WK
				AN	WP		
	AP		AP	WP	FN	WR	
AP		AP			FR	FP	
		EP					FP
ER				EB			
		EP	EN	EP		FK	
EK	EP						

Earth   Fire

FIGURE 41—MOVE 18 IN EXAMPLE 2, EARTH TO MOVE

always remember not to place additional pressure on a pinned piece or pawn. The Water Knight must go to 2a; otherwise it would give Fire time to advance its Knight.

In move 13, Earth's move proves crucial to Water. Was Q4a right? By move 14, the tables have turned. Both the Fire and Air Rooks must run, and the Air King is in check. The Fire Bishop must capture the Earth Queen. The Water pawn then captures the Fire Bishop, leaving a Water pawn strategically placed, preventing the move AN2d and limiting the Air King's escape squares. Fire could have hindered this earlier by moving its Rook to F3c, but moving F3c after EN2d is foolish. Water is limited by move 16; any move could be costly. Fire is also limited, so move 17 could also be costly for Fire. However, Fire sees the opportunity to check Water, thereby hindering any forward

Air   Water

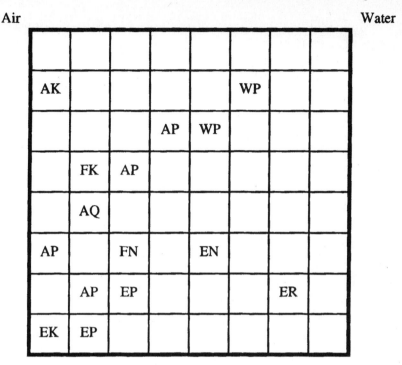

Earth   Fire

FIGURE 42—FINAL POSITION IN EXAMPLE 2(A)

pawn movement. The Air Knight maneuvers, capturing a Water pawn on the way, so that three pieces are eventually threatening the pinned Water pawn that protects the Water King.

Earth has to sacrifice a Bishop to buy time for Water, then tries to check the Fire King. This enables the Water King to capture the Air Rook (Kings can move into check if already in check) and the advantage is again turned, costing Air and Fire both Rooks. But is the cost worth it for the loss of the Water King? With the King's capture, Water is out of the game, and all Water pieces still standing on the board remain there as frozen pieces. Earth moves to force the Fire King into a drawn game, because if only two players were playing, Air would not get Fire's moves and the Fire King would remain on the board as a frozen piece. However, Fire is a bit too clever to lose its last piece and uses its King aggressively.

Moves 24–29 see Fire and Air very carefully closing ranks on the Earth King. If Earth had concentrated more on the Fire Knight and capturing Air pawns, rather than making futile checks to the Fire King, there might have been a difference in the endgame. But with Air having a full complement of pawns advancing on the Earth King, a victory is inevitable. If Earth had brought its Rook and Knight back to its King's defense and advanced the pawns to the other side of the board for exchange, the game could have been made difficult for Air and Fire.

Example 2b
If Earth moves NF3a in move 18 instead of BW4b.

	F	W	A	E
18	—	—	—	…NF3a
19	NW1bxP	RxN	RxR+	B2d
20	RW2cxP?	K1bxAR	NxWK++	RF2c+
21	K3b	Captured	NW2d	RF1c
22	K2a		NW4c	K2b
23	PW3b		PE4a	K1c
24	PW2b		P2d	BF4c+
25	K2b		NxB	RxN
26	PW1b#		PE4b	NF2c?
27	QW3b		PE3a	P2d
28	K1b		Q2c	K2c
29	QF2d		P4d	P1c
30	QF4bxP+		PF4d	RxQ+
31	K2cxN		PF2a	RW4d
32	RF3c		PE1a	RW4a
33	RE3c+		PE3b	K1d
34	RE4cxP		QE4b	RW1a+A
35	RE3c		K1b	RW1b+F
36	K1c		PE2b	RW2b+A
37	RE1cxP+		K2c	KF4b
38	RE2c		QE2dxP?	K3d
39	RE3c+		QE4b	KF4d
40	RF4c		K2d	KA4d
41	PW4a		QA2c	Retires

Instead of sacrificing the Earth Bishop, the Earth Knight moves forward and limits the Fire King's free squares. Fire ignores this and follows through on the attack on Water. The Water Rook captures the Fire Knight, and the Air Rook follows through, capturing the Water Rook and checking the Water King. The Earth Bishop makes way for the Earth Rook. Fire must be careful here because Earth looks as if it will be able to buy more time, as seen in move 20, where Water moves into check and exercises Rule 8.6. Fire is unable to capture the Water King because its own King will be in check on the next move. This would have given the Water King time, but because of the positions of the Fire pawns, the Water King will still have been lost. The Water King therefore captures a Rook on the way out to lessen the odds against Earth. The remaining Water pawn becomes a frozen piece.

Fire did not watch its back while in the heat of battle, and in move 22 it looks as if Fire will lose a pawn—or even its King, unless it moves K2a, which it does. The Air Knight then comes to the rescue and forks a Fire pawn and the F4c square to prevent an Earth Bishop check. The Earth King moves to a safer position pending an Air pawn advance.

By move 24, Earth's pieces are limited, so Earth checks with its Bishop in the hope that the Air Knight will retaliate, thus effecting an exchange. If the Air Knight does not respond, the Earth King will be lost.

In move 25 (see fig. 43 on next page), the Earth Rook captures the Air Knight (which captured the Earth Bishop) instead of the capture being made by the Earth Knight. Otherwise, the Earth Rook would be vulnerable to the Fire King. Move 26 promotes a Fire pawn to a Queen (two pawns were left, so the Queen's pawn must be exchanged for a Queen).

Earth attempts to position the King so as to capture an advancing Air pawn in order to prevent its promotion. As no pawn promotion can occur until one of the four Air pawns has been lost, Air must first tempt Earth into capturing a pawn. Earth ignores this, but this may be a mistake. By move 30, Fire has built up pressure on the Earth pawn on F4b. The exchange that could follow would decide the game in Fire and Air's favor

Air   Water

AK	AQ						
					FR	FP	
			AP	WP			
	AP	AP					
AP		EP					FP
			ER				
		EP		EP		FK	
	EP	EK			EN		

Earth   Fire

FIGURE 43—MOVE 25, EXAMPLE 2(B), EARTH TO MOVE

if Earth retaliates. Air also adds a pawn threat to the Earth Rook, which also forces Earth's decision.

Earth lost an opportunity in move 26 to capture the Fire Queen: it could have checked the Fire King with its Rook instead of moving the Knight. On move 31, the Fire King captures the Earth Knight. The forces are too great for Earth now, so it is only a matter of time. The Fire Rook moves across the board to close in on the Earth King . In move 32, an Air pawn reaches the opposite side of the board but cannot be exchanged because four pawns are still on the board. Earth attempts to move its Rook out and attack the Air King.

As you will have seen in this example, pawn moves in the endgame can be effective. In move 32, the Fire Rook can either make or break the game. By move 40, Earth is still trying to

Air   Water

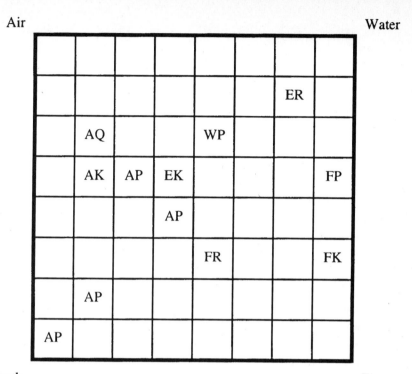

Earth   Fire

FIGURE 44—FINAL POSITIONS IN EXAMPLE 2(B)

gain a foothold, with Fire and Air hard in the chase. Earth finds cover from the Air pawns. With very few moves available to Fire in move 41, Fire pushes its pawn forward. After the Air Queen moves behind its King to prevent an Earth Rook check, Earth retires, seeing no way to beat Fire and Air.

Example 3
Fire Board, Air of Fire setting, playing widdershins.

This is an example of Rule 11.3, of how a player can capture his ally's King (see move 3) to save the opening game, thereby being in control of the allied pieces and only having to worry about defending one King. If the King had not been captured in this way, the opponent would have captured the Air King and thus frozen all Air pieces at the beginning of the game.

	F	W	A	E
1	P2c	Q2c	P2c	QA1c+
2	N4c	QA4bxP	K2b	N4c
3	BA2bxK	QxB	BxQ	QA3axN
4	P3c	N4c	BxQ	NxN
5	QxN	NxQ	P1c	P2c
6	P3d	PxP	Q4c	P4c
7	PxP	P3c	R1a	B3c
8	R2c	NA4d	BW3d	B2d
9	P4c	NW2d	P2d	P1c
10	P1c	R4a	PA4b?	P1d
11	K2b	RA3d	R1b	RA1d
12	P4d	P2c	BF2d?	K2b
13	PW4c	P3d	BF3c	BW3a
14	P1d	B2b	R1a	K1c
15	K1c	RA3bxP	BW4a	P2d
16	RE3bxP	RA3a	R1b	PF4a
17	RF2c	NA3c	R2b	RA1cxP
18	PW3c	B1c	QxB	BxQ
19	RE3c+	NE4bxP*	R2d	K2b
20	RE3b+	RA3c?	BE1d	K1c
21	RE3c+	RA2c	RF4a+	KxB
22	RE4cxP	K2b	RW4c	RE3a+
23	K2b?	K3b	RW4b+	BW3a
24	PW4d	K2a	RF2d?	PF4b
25	RE4d+	NA3c	RF3b	PF3a+
26	K1b?	NxFR	RF2d	KF4a
27	PW4a	NF3c+	RF2c	R4a
28	K1c	RE4b	RxN	PxR
29	Retires			

A fast-moving game with move 3 displaying an ally King capture and the opponents' Queen sacrifices to obtain two more pieces of value. By move 5, Air and Fire have lost their Knights, Earth and Water being left with one. Earth and Water are one piece and a pawn up. Fire pushes forward with its pawns to open up its Rook line and moves its Air forces forward. The

Air   Water

AR						WP	WK WB
		AP				WP	
AP	AP		AQ	AB	WP		WR
			WN				
		EP			FP		
	EP			FP		FR	
ER		EP	EB				FP
EK	EP						FK

Earth   Fire

FIGURE 45—MOVE 9, EXAMPLE 3, WATER TO MOVE

maneuver of Fire locks the Water Bishop in, as a P2c move would eventually expose the Water King's protecting pawn to two Rooks. By move 8, the pace has not slowed down. The Water Knight is forced away from F3c and chooses square A4d to protect the Earth Bishop and attack the Air pawn on 4b. However, Air lines itself up for a Water King attack. If the Water King goes to 2a, Air's next move must be BW1bxP+. If Water moves P1c, the Air Queen will capture a pawn: WPxQ ARxP+ WK2a ABW1b+. If Water moves P2c, Air will move QW1c+; the Water King must then move to 2b, and then the Air Bishop to W4c+. If the Water Rook moves to 3b, then Air may take the Rook with its Bishop, but to obtain an actual King capture quickly, the Fire Rook must capture the Water Rook. Water chooses to move its Knight to 2d, covering P1b. Is the Water Bishop able to move from the corner square? Not so. Such a move will open the line up to the Fire Rook, since the Air Bishop will only capture the pawn knowing P1c cannot move to expose the Water King.

By move 10, Water is so well placed it does not know where to move. Therefore, the only free piece is moved, the Rook, lining it up with the Water Knight. The advancing Air pawn should have captured the Earth pawn in move 9, which would have opened up Earth's lines. By move 15, Air lets its P3b be captured in order to place its Rook on the top rank again. The Air Bishop moves in. Meanwhile, Earth sneaks up behind Fire. The Fire Rook takes the opportunity to capture a loose Earth pawn. Since the Water defense is a little too strong, Fire and Air change their concentration from Water to Earth in move 17 and move to the attack.

As you will see, between move 17 and 21 there has been a shuffle as to who has the advantage. Fire and Air come on strong, but Water and Earth always seem to find a way out. In move 21, Water exercises the rule that, once in check, a King can move into check if it is likely to help its game. In this case, it does, because Earth checks the Fire King and holds up a Fire move follow-through to capture the Water King. This temporarily saves the Water King, but the pressure is kept up on it. Fire erred in moving its King back.

In move 24, the Earth pawn pushes forward; it could be detrimental to Fire. Fire could try once again to attack WP1b, but a simple P1c would counteract that with an Earth Bishop cover. With only one Air piece left, the Air Rook must move even if it is in a good position. Thus, with fewer active pieces than Water and Earth, Fire and Air are finding a difficult time of it, although they are doing very well to keep up the attack. The tide turns, however, and the Water Knight threatens the Fire Rook at the same time as the Earth Rook delivers check to the Fire King. The Fire Rook is lost. The careful move forward of Earth pawns eventually trapped the Fire King. After a few more moves, Fire retires, seeing the situation as hopeless. In move 19, the Water Knight move could have been fatal to the Earth if the Air Rook had taken the Knight, thus completely trapping the Earth King and leaving Water in a hopeless position.

If Fire had played Fire and Air forces differently in this game and not carelessly lost so many pieces, the game would have gone a much different way. Try this one out for yourself.

Example 4
Air Board, Earth of Air setting, playing deosil, two players operating pieces.

	A	W	F	E
1	P3c	P3c	P3c	P3c
2	P4c	B3b	P4c	B3b
3	B3b	N1c	Q1c	P4c
4	N1c	NA4b	B3b	P3d?
5	QW3d	B2c?	QW4c	N3c
6	QF2d	B3d?	QA4bxN	P4d
7	QxB	P1c	PE4dxP	BW3dxQ
8	NE4b	P1d	QA2d	P2c
9	P4d	Q1c	B4c	K2b
10	P1c	P4c	N1c	P1c*
11	BF3d	PA4a	QE3dxP	PxQ*
12	NE3dxP+	PA3a	BE1cxP+	K3b
13	P2c	QA4c	R2a	QxB
14	BxQ	QA2cxP	NF3b	R2a
15	P1d	P2c	P1c	NF4b
16	BW4b	K2b	RE1b+	K2c
17	PE4a	QE4dxP	RF4a	NF2c+
18	R1d	QF3bxN	K2a	KxAN
19	PE3a	QF1d	RE1d+	KF4b
20	RE4a	QW3a	RE1c	NW4a
21	PE4d	QF3d	K1a	KF3b
22	BxQ	P2d	K1b	NxB
23	K2a	R1b	R2a	BE3b
24	RA1d	K2c	P2c	NE3d
25	K3b	P4d	R2b+	KF3a
26	R2d	PA2a	RxR	BxR
27	RA2axP	RxR	P1d	NE4b
28	KxR	PA4b	P2d	BW3d

	A	**W**	**F**	**E**
29	K3b	PA4d	K1c	KF3b
30	PxP	K2d	P3d	BxP
31	K2c	P3d	PW4c	BE3b
32	K2d	PA4c	PW4a	NA4d
33	PE3d	PF3b	K1d	KF3c
34	PE2d	PA2b	PW4b	KF3d
35	PE2a	PA3c+	PW3c+	BxP
36	KE4a?	KA4b	PW2c	NF4c
37	KE4b	PA1b#	PW1c#	BW2c
38	KA3d	KA3b	QW3c+	KW4c
39	KE4b	NA2d	QW1c	BW1d
40	KE3b	PA2c	PW3a	KW3b
41	KE2b	PA1c#	Resign	—
42	Resign			

All players chose a P3c opening to provide an opening for their Bishops. By moves 5 and 6, the Fire and Air Queens put some pressure on Water. Water loses its Knight with no exchange and would lose its Bishop the same way if Earth did not move P4d. Air must capture the Water Bishop; otherwise the Water Bishop will capture the Queen and cause Fire to have a doubled pawn when Fire counterattacks. This combination of moves shows how the Queens, when working together, become an effective attacking force. Here Fire and Air obtain a Bishop, Knight and pawn for the exchange of a Queen. Now Earth and Water must not recklessly make any exchanges except to gain pieces. If Water had moved N1c instead of B3d in move 6, or P1c instead of B2c, Water would have come out of the combination of moves a lot happier.

On moves 9 to 10, all sides jostle for position and advance their pieces and pawns. Air keeps overlooking a floating Water pawn on W1d. Move 11 sees a buildup on Earth by Fire and Air, drawing towards a check. Water and Earth's moves at this point could be crucial to Earth's game, but Earth keeps missing the obvious. WP4d would only evoke a combination that would endanger the Water King, so Water decides to continue its advance on Air. Fire needs one more piece on EP1c to make an effective attack, but its Queen is trapped, which is a handicap. Fire sacrifices its Queen to open up Earth's pawns. Earth takes the bait.

On move 12, the Air Knight, which is seen to be hanging, checks the Earth King while taking a pawn and ends up positioned so that it can capture the pinned Earth pawn on 1c. That is all Fire needs to commence its attack on Earth. Meanwhile, Water sneaks up on Air, limiting Air's King and Rook moves. By moves 14 and 15, the Fire Knight links in with the Air Knight, but the King capture is not easy. Move 15 finds Fire with no attack follow-through, so Fire takes the opportunity to strengthen its own King defense. Air turns its attention back to Water, a weak pawn, plus opening up the Fire Rook line. The Water King moves forward to protect its pawn. The Earth Knight prepares for a possible fork by the Fire Rook and King.

These are examples of how players can use free moves to establish their defenses and deal with more than one opponent at once, which can be essential. Fire's hanging pawn on E4d is too difficult to protect, so Fire ignores its opponent's threat. This was a mistake, as becomes evident in moves 17–18. Fire and Air lose both Knights. As you can see, players must look forward to the possible repercussions of their own combinations.

The Fire King is unable to move to any square, but since the Rook is still in play, no stalemate occurs. Air forces the Water Queen off the F1d square, opening up further movement for the Fire King. At this stage, Water and Earth have regained their losses and are up two pieces, so Fire and Air cannot afford the loss of a piece.

By move 21, the Earth King is maneuvered across the board to get into the protection of Water's ranks, but first it must move through Fire. To have gone diagonally across the board would have left the King vulnerable. With respect to Rooks and opponent Kings, it is sometimes better to get up close to them in order to outsmart them. Water and Earth also set up a combination of moves that capture the Air Bishop with the sacrifice of the Water Queen. In endgame play, a Queen has little value

Air   Water

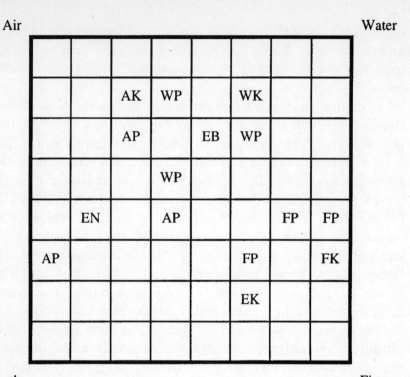

Earth   Fire

FIGURE 46—EXAMPLE 4, POSITIONS AT MOVE 29

when it is the only one left. If the Air Bishop ignored the bait, the Water King would move forward and capture the Bishop without an exchange.

On move 24, Fire foils the Earth and Water move on P2b. If Fire's move on move 25 is P3d, the pawn could be taken by the Earth King, resulting in a discovered check to the Fire King. However, the Earth King can still move to 3c to enable the discovered check. Then, in Earth's following move, it would move NF3b+, and so on. But Fire instead chooses to check the Earth King with a fork to the Earth Rook, thereby capturing the Earth Rook even though it is covered by the Earth Bishop. Air brings its Rook forward and likewise exchanges a Rook for a Rook. It appears that Fire and Air are gambling that their superior number of pawns still on the board will change the odds in

Air   Water

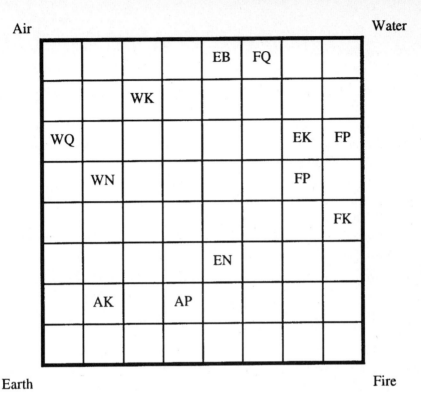

Earth   Fire

FIGURE 47—EXAMPLE 4, FINAL POSITIONS

the endgame. However, the Earth Bishop and Earth Knight work very hard to change those odds. The Earth Knight is placed in a quadruple fork so that the Air pawns cannot move without being captured and the Water pawn is protected from the Air King. The Earth King would have been better off to move to 3c instead of 3a in move 25, capturing a Fire pawn in the process.

The Air Knight moves to chase the Earth Knight and the Earth King chases behind the Fire pawns. The Water King stays close to its back pawn. At this stage, the placement of each piece and pawn could win or lose the game, so players must not get careless. The Fire pawns and King are moving along in good formation. The Air King makes a futile attempt to capture the Earth Knight, but then gets the opportunity to capture a Water pawn and threaten the Earth Knight—but it ignores this in move 36.

Air sacrifices a pawn to get a privileged pawn, but Water beats Air to a pawn promotion and obtains a Knight. The Earth King makes it very difficult for the Fire King to keep covering its pawns. The Earth Knight covers the square that the Air pawn must move to. Fire promotes a pawn to a Queen, which in move 38 tries to force the Earth King back. But the Earth King moves forward and the Earth Bishop lines up with square W4a to prevent the Fire King from moving forward with its pawns. The Air King does not seem to know where he is going, resulting in wasted moves. Remember, try to make every move count.

The Earth Knight, Water Knight and Earth Bishop positions block the Air King from moving toward its pawn or the Fire pieces. By move 38, Earth must move, and in doing so may give Fire time to obtain a promoted pawn. Earth moves wisely and traps Fire with the Earth King. On move 41, the Water pawn finally makes a promotion to a Queen. The odds seem too great for Air and Fire now, so they resign.

The Earth King was used very well in halting Fire in its march. This is an example of how effective the Kings can be if used carefully.

Part III

Book of Water

Divination

Enochian Chess
Divination

Introduction

If you are new to the concept of the esoteric sciences, you may be saying, "What is divination?" In simple terms, divination is looking in a probable direction and telling past, present or future happenings and/or results of that direction. Divination is generally event-oriented; however, it also has a person-oriented aspect. This approach gives an idea of emotional or psychological responses likely to take place in response to a relationship or event. It can describe people and events quite clearly at times, but the manner in which it describes them depends on the method of divination used and the interpretation of the diviner based on his or her sphere of experience.

Your next question may be, "How can it see into the future, or how does it work?" In answer to this I can only say, "It just does," as no fully adequate technical explanation has yet been found.[1] Others may say, "it taps into the universal current of what is and what is to be," but how can functions that leave room for pure chance tell the truth? The answer to this is that they don't. They only show a probable course as seen at the point of divination that the querent has previously/currently placed him or herself in. This course is likely to continue in that direction until some conscious interference, either by the querent or by some unexpected, unknown, outside force, changes it.

In the course of a day, an individual may change his or her probable direction several times if under stress to do so. If the external stress is greater than the elements underlying the impetus of the course taken, or the individual's Will, he or she will change direction. If the stress is not greater but is nevertheless enough to have an influence, direction still may be changed, showing a new probability, but with the same ultimate result. The difference is the manner in which the result is obtained.

I think current-day quantum physics is beginning to explain the concepts of divination and invisible energies which gurus, adepts, occultists, diviners, etc., have used and understood for centuries. In fact, there will always be people who will say, "Divination does not work; its all superstition," or, in great disbelief, "You don't believe in *that,* do you?" It would be quite a mindblowing shock to these people to find out that this world of mysticism and divination is already just beginning to be explained by physicists through quantum mechanics. In fact, it might be a shock to some of the physicists themselves.

Quantum mechanics deals with making allowances for probabilities and the prediction of probabilities within the confines of an experiment. Quantum mechanics has not yet advanced to the stage of being able to actually predict what will happen. It will predict only the probable result, or potential.[2] The main problem

---

1. In his study of the subject, which he termed "synchronicity," Carl Jung considered that divination was formed by restricting nature and making it produce an answer through the effort of the diviner.

2. A tendency for something—a quantum version of the Aristotelian philosophical concept of *potentia.*

may be that they are still trying to compartmentalize and measure from a three-dimensional view something that is multidimensional. However, if everything can be totally and accurately predicted as if there were one possible course and one course only, which Newtonian physics would lead us to believe, the true destiny of the world would have been well mapped out by now. I do not believe that this is so. Divination can only predict what will happen along a probable course of events, and that probable course is only one among many probabilities.

New physics tells us that the world may not be what it appears to be, and that it is much more than perceived. Ah! At last we are getting some sense out of our scientists! That's what the mystics have been trying to say for centuries. This is the same advice I must give to those using Enochian chess for divining. Enochian chess is a multidimensional system, and trying to perceive the full story from any combination of moves or an entire divination game is nearly impossible, because it has to be translated into our three-dimensional perceptions. Be happy with peeling one or two layers of this onion. It should yield enough information to provide a deep understanding of any situation.

One other word of advice: Do not take everything literally. After all, any form of divination can only show a probable course with a probable or potential result. If you want to view the other probabilities, just divine, divine and divine again. All you have to do is rephrase your question each time, adding ,"if I did this" or "if I took this route" etc.

Throughout most Orders, papers will be found that refer to various aspects of divination work ranging from Tarot cards to the I Ching (e.g., as in Aleister Crowley's "A∴A∴"). All these methods are just as effective as the Enochian chess game as far as the end results are concerned. The divination game of Enochian chess can, however, give a full working as to how an answer to a question stands in the scheme of things. It provides —very much like astrology—an insight into outside and internal influences, and the particular nature of such. But additionally it shows the complex movements of archetypes and their interactions with each other.

Enochian chess divination has been found to be a far-reaching system that requires that the expertise of the diviner must include knowledge of the Tarot, geomancy, esoteric psychology, the elements and astrology. The Enochian system itself reaches into the depths of the Universe, and this is what the diviner must do. One assimilates an enormous amount of data into the psyche during divination play—an amount of which only a portion can be tapped in the final analysis, because a great deal takes place with the players on the unconscious as well as the conscious level. This is of course in essence the pattern of all magical works: to receive the impetus, then act it out, sending the original emanation back up through the planes to its source.

MacGregor Mathers, in his papers on Enochian chess, tried to show us this when he used the Zodiac and the elements applied to the chess squares in divination matters. I have done the same, and I hope the following summarized information will provide a suitable guideline from which you can work.

The divination game of Enochian chess, as devised by Mathers and Westcott, was played in such a way that the first player was the querent and considered the Prime Mover, or the owner of the Ptah piece. This Prime Mover chose the element board for the divination game, then the angle of the board he/she was to operate, and finally the square of that angle where the Ptah piece was to be placed to signify the Ptah Square. To make such a choice, the Prime Mover had to understand the symbols and esoteric meanings of the Enochian Tablets so as to choose an Enochian pyramid square (chess square) that had associations with the actual question being divined. The answer to the question was then determined through chess play. Eliphas Levi says in his *Key to the Mysteries:*

> The game of chess, attributed to Palamedes, has no other origin than the Tarot, and one finds there the same combinations and the same symbols; the king, the queen, the knight, the soldier, the fool, the tower, and houses representing numbers. In old times, chess-players sought upon their chess-board the solution of philosophical and religious problems, and argued

silently with each other in manœuvring the hieroglyphic characters across the numbers. Our vulgar game of goose, revived
from the old Grecian game, and also attributed to Palamedes,
is nothing but a chess-board with motionless figures and numbers movable by means of dice.

Whether or not the Tarot was the origin of chess is beside
the point, but the fact is that chess has been used for divination
in one form or another since its inception from Chaturanga. The
Tarot of course is well noted for its divinatory process, and it is
almost inevitable that the chess pieces and the Tarot would be
eventually linked together in one form or another. However,
within the framework of the Golden Dawn, it was done with
real style. When all of this is mixed with an astrological framework, the tools to deciphering the outcome of the divinatory
game are excellent.

The players' moves were decided by the throw of a die,
which in turn determined which piece would be moved. Once a
player had established which piece was to be moved, the player
then had free choice as to how and where it was moved. Each
player followed in rotation, deosil, until the Prime Mover was
next to move. This was considered one round of the game. Play
continued (sometimes incorporating many rounds of the game)
until such time as the querent's King had reached the Ptah
Square and remained there for one round of the game, or was
captured.

The original Y manuscripts stated that the dice number
attributions to the chess pieces were governed by the "powers of
the squares on the Sephirothic Crosses." Therefore, when playing different piece settings, the numeric attributions of the
chess pieces would change. For example, in the Air of Air setting, a throw of 4 moves a castle, a 2 moves a Knight, a 3 moves
a Queen and a 5 moves a Bishop. In an Earth of Air setting, a 4
brings the Bishop into play, a 2 moves a Queen, a 3 moves a
Knight and 5 would bring a Castle into play. A throw of 1
always operates a King and a 6 any one of the pawns. Regardie,
however, reasoned in *The Golden Dawn* that it would be easier

to maintain one numeric attribution for the pieces in all settings. He showed that Kether, being the Crown and the first
square of the Cross, should be 1 and associated with the King.
But as the King is blocked from moving in the early part of the
game, a pawn move would also be optional on a throw of 1.
A throw of 2 corresponded to Chokmah and the Knight, 3 to
Binah and the Bishop, 4 to Chesed and the Queen, 5 to Geburah
and the Rook and 6 to the pawns. Because of the convenience of
this method, I have included it in the following rules.

From my own experience, I have found that it is best for the
players to experience a divination game without rationalizing,
merely playing the game and recording the moves. The actual
analysis can be made after the game is played by re-enacting
the play from your record sheet. In this way the players are not
tempted to consciously influence the casting of the die, or actual moves of the pieces, through knowledge of the actual effects
being shown by the game. For this reason, I do not have the
attributions of each square marked on my own chessboard. If
you play the game often enough, it is quite easy to identify each
square and its influence and understand on a more intuitive
level how the pieces are acting thereon. Intellectualizing can
occur after the divining forces have played out their story.

When I spoke to Regardie in his 1983 visit to New Zealand, I
had the opportunity of setting up my chess set. We discussed the
advantage of the unmarked squares versus the marked squares,
and he agreed with my approach. This concept also encourages
players to work a lot harder and results in their understanding
the system better, not only intellectually but psychically.

In the following text I have provided a fuller divinatory and
esoteric meaning to the chess pieces, including the Ptah piece,
but first the divination rules and method of play must be stud-
ied. Following the rules are guidelines as to choosing the Ptah
Square and methods by which one can analyze the results of divination play, together with reference material that may aid your
analyses. However, although reference material is suggested, it
is assumed that you have some knowledge of astrology, Tarot,
geomancy etc., or have some form of reference to the same.

Astrological symbols are a universal language whereby much information can be understood through the use of a few symbols. These astrological symbols have been used as glyphs through which the Enochian system radiates in much the same way as planets and signs radiate through the houses of an astrological chart. But it must be remembered that Enochian chess is not astrology; it merely uses the symbolic language of astrology, by association, to describe vibrations and happenings that arise on the chessboards during a divination game.

The same concept is also applied to the geomantic influence in the squares. These represent the vibrations of the Earth and must not be confused with the Zodiac. A geomantic vibration penetrated or influenced in some way by a celestial energy causes the geomantic energy to vibrate to a pitch that is in affinity with the celestial energy. Neither governs the other; they are only catalysts of each other.

With the expansive qualities being introduced to Enochian chess, I feel that some comment should be made on the theory of one of these concepts: four-dimensional Enochian chess. Over the years, this theory has been discussed in relation to the Enochian game. It must be considered that, on a game level, there is nothing wrong with using the four boards at once. From an esoteric concept, such as divination games, I would not recommend it. Firstly, in divination, nature is restricted (to a board) so that it is virtually forced to produce an answer. By the use of a single board, the utmost restriction is placed on the divination game, where archetypes, as chess pieces, are restricted and thus compelled to "cough up" the answers. It has been argued by some that, in using the four boards, the scope of divination play is increased, but this is not the case. First each elemental corner can equally represent each board in microcosm, and the chess pieces are the archetypal forms therein. Second, the accuracy of the game is in doubt because the answer becomes more general. The more restriction there is, the more accurate the answer. Third, from the esoteric point of view, each Enochian board represents a different hierarchy or structure, and by blending them to overlap in game play, confusion can occur. Four boards can be used individually but not simultaneously.

Enochian Chess
Divination

Official Rules

Continuing from Official Rules (pages 87–100):

13. General game play rules 1 to 12.3 are acknowledged as Official Divination Rules for game play unless contradicted by the following

14. Querent

    14.1 The querent is the player who requires a question to be answered by the Enochian chess divination play. There can only be one querent. The other three players assist the querent in finding an answer to the question by virtue of their roles as players.

    14.2 The querent places the Ptah piece on a chosen square in a chosen angle of a chosen elemental chessboard, which represents the question. (Guidelines on how to choose the Ptah Square are found in the following chapter.)

14.3 The querent operates the chess pieces belonging to the angle of the board on which the Ptah piece is placed.

14.4 The querent always starts the play; i.e., the querent is the first player (Prime Mover).

15. The Ptah

15.1 The Ptah is an all-white chess piece used only in divination games. It has no other function than to signify the square representing the querent's question.

15.2 The square upon which the Ptah piece is placed is called the "Ptah Square."

15.3 The Ptah piece is not moved from the square throughout the game, nor can it be attacked or captured.

15.4 The Ptah Square can be moved on or over by other pieces. To all intents and purposes, the Ptah piece does not exist except as a visible marker of the Ptah Square. Other pieces can be placed on the square occupied by the Ptah.

16. Objective

16.1 During the course of the game, with the pieces to be moved dictated by the throw of a die, the querent, with the aid of his ally, must move his or her King to the Ptah Square and stay there for one round of the game; i.e., until the querent's next turn to move.

16.2 The querent and ally are protectors of the Ptah Square.

16.3 The two players who are in opposition to the querent and ally must attempt to cover the Ptah Square so that the querent's King cannot safely attain it. In so doing, the opposition creates as many obstacles as possible during the normal course of play.

17. Determining Moves

17.1 Each player's moves are decided by the throw of a die, the highest number of the die determining the move. (The die is numbered 1–6, one number on each flat surface, and each number determines that a particular chess piece is to be moved.)

17.2 If 1 is thrown, a King is moved. If the King cannot move because all adjacent squares are occupied, a pawn is moved instead.

If 2 is thrown, a Knight is moved.

If 3 is thrown, a Bishop is moved.

If 4 is thrown, a Queen is moved.

If 5 is thrown, a Rook is moved.

If 6 is thrown, a pawn is moved.

17.3 If a number is thrown for a piece that has no unoccupied square to move to, that move is considered "No Move" and is recorded as such or by a dash on the recording sheet.

(a) A "No Move" does not allow a player to make a second throw of the die in that turn. The player surrenders that turn and does not move any chess piece.

(b) A "No Move" also occurs when a number is thrown that represents a chess piece that has previously been captured.

17.4 If a number is thrown for a piece that has only an unsafe square or squares to move to, that piece must nevertheless move. (An unsafe square is where a piece may be under threat of capture. This is allowed, because the oppositions' throw of the die may not determine that a threatening piece will move.)

18. The King

18.1 If the querent's King is captured, the ally can try to obtain an opposing King to effect an exchange, if the odds are sufficiently favorable.

18.2 A King or any of its pieces can move while the King is in check, according to what is defined by the die throw.

18.3 A King can move into check even if it is not already in check. This rule is in accordance with rule 17.4, and overrides rule 8.11.

18.4 The King of the angle that the querent plays is the only King that must obtain the Ptah Square and attempt to stay there for one round of the game.

19. Outcome of the Game

19.1 If the querent's King obtains the Ptah Square and stays there unchecked for one round of the game, the question is then said to be successful; i.e., the answer is positive.

   (a) If the King stays on the Ptah Square during an all-out attack, the question is successful under strong opposing conditions.

   (b) If the querent's King is checked while on the Ptah Square, the game must continue until the King can remain on the Ptah Square, unchecked and uncaptured, for one round of the game, to obtain a successful result.

19.2 If the querent's King does not attain the Ptah Square either through being captured or by any other means, the question is considered unsuccessful; i.e., the answer is negative.

19.3 Whether the querent's King reaches the Ptah Square or not, the game can still be analyzed by the movements of the pieces over the board during game play. This gives the diviner an idea of the interacting forces concerning the question, how it attains its outcome and what opposes or supports it.

19.4 If both the querent's King and its ally King are captured, the game is at an end.

Setting Up
Your Board
for a
Divination Game

The "Ptah Square" is a square on which the Ptah chess piece sits during a divination game. This square represents a question supplied by a querent (one of the players), which is answered by the outcome of the Enochian chess divination game.

To set up your board for a divination game, a Ptah Square must first be decided upon. This decision depends entirely on the "nature" of the divination question. This "nature" can be interpreted through the vibrational nature of the four elements, Earth, Air, Water and Fire, and combinations thereof. This of course is very convenient, because it coincides quite well with the nature of the Enochian chessboards. One can in turn isolate which elemental board is in affinity with the divinatory question, then the angle of that board, the chess pieces with which the querent must operate and finally a square upon which the Ptah piece is placed.

Described below is an easy and concise method of choosing your chessboard, angle, piece setting, and Ptah Square for your divination game.

1. Choose the element board most in affinity with your question: Fire, Water, Air or Earth.

2. Choose the elemental angle of your element board that is in affinity with your question. By now you will be looking at an element within an element.

3. Choose the square in the angle of the element board which was chosen in points 1 and 2 above by virtue of its Zodiac/house influence.

4. Place your Ptah on the square chosen in point 3.

5. The game play setting in which your pieces will be placed will be that of the angle and board chosen in points 1 and 2.

The following correspondences should provide suitable guidelines for performing steps 1 to 5.

The Elemental Boards
Choosing the Board and Angle for the Ptah

Fire Board
The World of Atziluth—The Primal Creative Urge

To understand the nature of the Fire Board, you must understand the Fire element, its actions and its spiritual and physical nature.

The Hebrew letter "Yod" in Tetragrammaton, is the first, the initiator; therefore one could say that a characteristic of the Fire element is the initiation of events, the beginning of matters. As heat and energy, the Fire Board is concerned with drive, anything that requires action, sports, war, arguments, sex, self-motivation, enthusiasm, excitability, the dynamic core of psychic energy, inspiration, life in its spark or seed. It also shows expressions such as power, desires, strength, expression of freedom, courage, meeting challenges, competition. The Fire Board would relate to questions on a deep spiritual level.

Fire Angle of Fire Board—Atziluth of Atziluth

The pure essence of Fire. The first seed of matter, inspiration and initiation. Catalyzing events. Pure heat, energy and drive. New projects, matters of the spirit, to win, war, spiritual love, power, authority. For matters of spiritual growth and new experience.

Associated are the planet Mars, the Zodiacal sign of Aries, the Fire element, the geomantic figure Puer, the Tarot card The Emperor and the geomantic ruler Bartzabel.

Water Angle of Fire Board—Briah of Atziluth

An answer to a "true" dream may be formed from this angle. It alludes to strong competitiveness, to win or gain, business affairs on a hidden level, on questions of fortune but not financial, entertainment, performing arts, music, creative inspiration, teaching, birth, the life force. On matters relating to hidden talents, secrets, children of the Soul, creation, to externalize what is within.

Associated are the Sun, the Zodiacal sign Leo, the Watery part of the Fire element, the geomantic figure Fortuna Major, the Tarot card Strength and the geomantic ruler Sorath.

Air Angle of Fire Board—Yetzirah of Atziluth

Questions concerning religion in its divine essence, spiritual gain and insight, travel and communication of mind and spirit, absorbing, receiving, comprehending. Philosophy, higher teaching, business communication, long distance communication, science and technology in its pure form, space travel. World peace concerns, political relationships between nations, and matters that need to be received and absorbed clearly for success.

Associated are the planet Jupiter, the Zodiacal sign Sagittarius, the Airy part of the Fire element, the geomantic figure Acquisitio, the Tarot card Temperance and the geomantic ruler Hismael.

Earth Angle of Fire Board—Assiah of Atziluth

The threshold (to the Water element), going out, for endeavors that you wish to flow spontaneously, for self-motivation in creativity, on matters of personal identity, for the manifestation of a nonmaterial project, religion in its mystical sense. For matters changing to another area of development, transformation, upheaval—violent or otherwise, world events affecting the consciousness of mankind individually or en masse, concerning leaving something, Karma.

Associated are the planet Pluto, the element of Earth in the Earthy part of Fire, the geomantic figure Cauda Draconis, the Tarot card Judgment and the geomantic rulers Bartzabel and Zazel.

Water Board
The World of Briah—The Creative World

The Hebrew letter "Heh" in Tetragrammaton refers to the Mother, feminine in nature, the receiver from "Yod." In all essence, representative of the great waters of the universe; the astral body, Azoth.

The Water element is in tune with many nuances and subtleties. The Water Board is representative of awareness of the power of the unconscious mind, rules subconscious motivation, the subliminal and an attunement with the deeper dimensions of life. Although the Water element may be calm on the surface, there may be storms brewing underneath.

This element corresponds to the gaining of consciousness through a slow and sure realization of the Soul's deepest yearnings. Subjects covered are emotions, relationships on emotional levels, love, yearnings, healing, protection, organizations, anything requiring creative expression or formation, spiritual groups, psychic concerns.

Fire Angle of Water Board—Atziluth of Briah

Matters concerning people, groups, congregations, psychic concerns, transformation, extremes in emotional concerns, spiritual love. The privacy of oneself and home, emotional and spiritual nourishment. Evocation and invocation, ceremonial initiation. Finding answers around difficulties, family concerns, and clearing up confusing issues.

Associated are the Moon, the Zodiacal sign Cancer, the Fiery part of the Water element, the geomantic figure Populus, the Tarot card The Chariot and the geomantic ruler Chasmodai.

Water Angle of Water Board—Briah of Briah

Concerning matters of suffering, and where a sacrifice takes place before the Soul can grow. Where relief from suffering is needed. Answers provided to difficult times. Concerning death, the afterlife. To find out the undercurrent of matters, the hidden, secret thoughts. Spiritual regeneration, the occult, the power of the Spirit in the affairs of the World. Where conclusions must be sought on matters above. Human rights. Very emotional matters.

Associated are the planet Mars, the Zodiacal sign Scorpio, the Water element, the geomantic figure Rubeus, the Tarot card Death and the geomantic ruler Bartzabel.

Air Angle of Water Board—Yetzirah of Briah

Future matters where the outcome depends on logic and reasoning guiding emotion. Expansion of the intellect and intuitive understanding, for inner awareness, to find the value of a matter and to discover your enemies. Concerning one's psychological health. For sensitive matters, understanding others' attitudes or reactions. Advanced medical science and metaphysics, retreats. Locating the cause of matters. Travel over water. Sources of misfortune, but generally joy, health and present or future to come.

Associated are the planet Jupiter, the Zodiacal sign Pisces, the Airy part of the Water element, the geomantic figure Laetitia, the Tarot card The Moon and the geomantic ruler Hismael.

Earth Angle of Water Board—Assiah of Briah

The threshold to the Air element. For changes in decisions and emotions. To find direction, for gain, greed, the power of the unconscious mind. Concerning unconscious emotions driven by material need, the nourishing of the psyche for growth. To journey for personal (not material) gain on an emotional level. Maintaining resources, insights to emotional burdens, and on matters of security. Where matters are not what they seem.

Associated are the planet Neptune, the Earthy part of the Water element, the geomantic figure Via, the Tarot card The Hanged Man and the geomantic ruler Chasmodai.

Air Board
The World of Yetzirah—The Formative World

In Tetragrammaton the Hebrew letter "Vau" takes the cosmic energy and actualizes it into intelligible form. Archetypal ideas form, specialized in creative patterns which then become expression. The element of Air is associated with breath, life prana. Its realm is of archetypal ideas behind the veil of the physical world. Energy is focused on specific ideas that are materialized in the Earth element. Creation is brought forward into idea. This element emphasizes theory, logic, abstract thoughts, matters of the mind, expression of art, studies, writing, publishing, travel, sickness, death, communication on tangible levels, matters of trouble.

Fire Angle of Air Board—Atziluth of Yetzirah
The harmonizing of polarities is concerned here with matters that need balance or impartiality. Matters concerning Will and effort. Putting desires into constructive thought and seeing the outcome thereof. Beginning of ideas, contracts, diplomats and intermediaries, combustible situations. Sudden trips, intensive communication. This angle is good in demands relating to women/debauchery. Divorces, lawsuits and public disputes.

Associated are the planet Venus, the Zodiacal sign Libra, the Fiery part of the Air element, the geomantic figure Puella, the Tarot card Justice and the geomantic ruler Kedemel.

Water Angle of Air Board—Briah of Yetzirah
This angle alludes to matters of socialism, societies, rebellions, disputes, reformation, the shedding of the old for the new. Where reason rules emotion. Where control is required. Some-

times concerning death, sadness and grief, condemnation, perversion. Stormy situations. From another perspective this angle depicts fortifying international friendships. Friends, companions, aeronautics, politics, service.

Associated are the planet Saturn, the Zodiacal sign Aquarius, the Watery part of the Air element, the geomantic figure Tristitia, the Tarot card The Star and the geomantic ruler Zazel.

Air Angle of Air Board—Yetzirah of Yetzirah

Matters needing continuous motion of thought and tremendous intellectual energy. For states of insanity, instability. For communication, negotiations, debates, studies, philosophy, relatives, the abstract. Advertising, ideas and their outcome, postal organizations, anything needing change, neighbors, short journeys, messages, news.

Associated are the planet Mercury, the Zodiacal sign Gemini, the geomantic figure Albus, the Tarot card The Lovers and the geomantic ruler Taphthartharath.

Earth Angle of Air Board—Assiah of Yetzirah

The threshold to the Earth element. This is the intellect at its best and controlled aspect. Leadership, diplomats, speculation, agreements, contracts made concrete, books, publications, business journeys, psychology, media, acting out ideas. Good for any matter where a person wishes to proceed quickly but safely. Teaching, universities and other teaching institutions, where change is necessary to reform. For the commencement of concrete ideas, the awakening.

Associated are the planet Uranus, the Earthy part of Air, the geomantic figure Fortuna Minor, the Tarot card The Fool and the geomantic ruler Sorath.

Earth Board
The World of Assiah—The World of Action and Matter

This element shows the "here and now" reality of the material world. "Heh final" of Tetragrammaton represents the Earth element, concrete manifestation which again gives birth to the "Yod" force. It is the passive and receptive; its strength is endurance and persistence. Matters concerning building structures, the land/agriculture, our physical bodies, anything material and not concerning the unseen world. Reproduction, stability, recreation, possessions, wealth, poverty, greed.

Fire Angle of Earth Board—Atziluth of Assiah

For matters that require great physical energy, struggle for attainment, to obtain power and authority, ceremonies, governments, professions/career, ambition, economy, employers, engineering etc. Earthquakes, volcanos, passion, sexuality, competitive sports, fighting, crime, penalties, prisons. Corporate organizations, companies, directors, rulers. Animals, labor, mines, construction/building. Business ventures and their success or failure. Exploration.

Associated are the planet Saturn, the Zodiacal sign Capricorn, the Fiery part of the Earth element, the geomantic figure Carcer, the Tarot card The Devil and the geomantic ruler Zazel.

Water Angle of Earth Board—Briah of Assiah

Concerning growth of a matter, loss of goods or where one is cut off from something or someone—finding the answer of getting the loss back. Concerning art, creative endeavors, the actual physical end result of one's artistic/creative efforts. Finance, banking, possessions, investments, farming, jewelry, loans, musical instruments, possessive emotions. Storage architecture, excavations, irrigation, crops, the home, family unit, beautifying anything, interior decoration, gardens, drugs/medicine.

Associated are the planet Venus, the Zodiacal sign Taurus, the Watery part of the Earth element, the geomantic figure Amissio, the Tarot card Strength and the geomantic ruler Sorath.

Air Angle of Earth Board—Yetzirah of Assiah

For matters of conjunction, union, recovery, health, physical ailments, operations, alternative healing, communication on the physical level, travel over land. Writing, studies, agriculture, employees, training, armed forces, chemicals, doctors, psychiatry, libraries, organizing labor, assembly of groups/crowds, conjunction of anything, renewing, computers, analysis, vocations, finding employment, education, demonstrations, seminars, workshops, sales persons, commerce.

Associated are the planet Mercury, the Zodiacal sign Virgo, the Airy part of the Earth element, the geomantic figure Conjunctio, the Tarot card The Hermit and the geomantic ruler Taphthartharath.

Earth Angle of Earth Board—Assiah of Assiah

All matters of the most earthy and physical nature. Buildings, constructions, machinery, industries, material gain and belongings, entering into a venture, threshold of anything, good for gain, to endure and persist in a project, involvement in the practical world.

Associated are the planet Earth, the Earth element, the geomantic figure Caput Draconis, the Tarot card The World and the geomantic rulers Hismael and Kedemel.

The Squares

Choosing the Ptah Square

The squares of each Enochian chessboard have associated attributes, as shown in Part I of this book. However, for convenience, we will refer to them by their fixed Zodiac and astrological house[1] association so that each square may be identified quickly and easily. Nevertheless, the full attributions of each square must not be neglected in your final analysis of a divination game. The diagrams on the following pages show the Zodiac sign (symbol) and house (number) attributions to the chessboards. These diagrams will be helpful when you require a quick reference to the squares during piece movement in a divination game.

---

1. Astrological houses signify the 12 divisions of a daily cycle created by the Earth's rotation on its axis each day. Each house has one of the 12 signs of the Zodiac attributed to it, and it is through these attributions that we are working. These 12 houses represent an area of influence or activity in which one can operate.

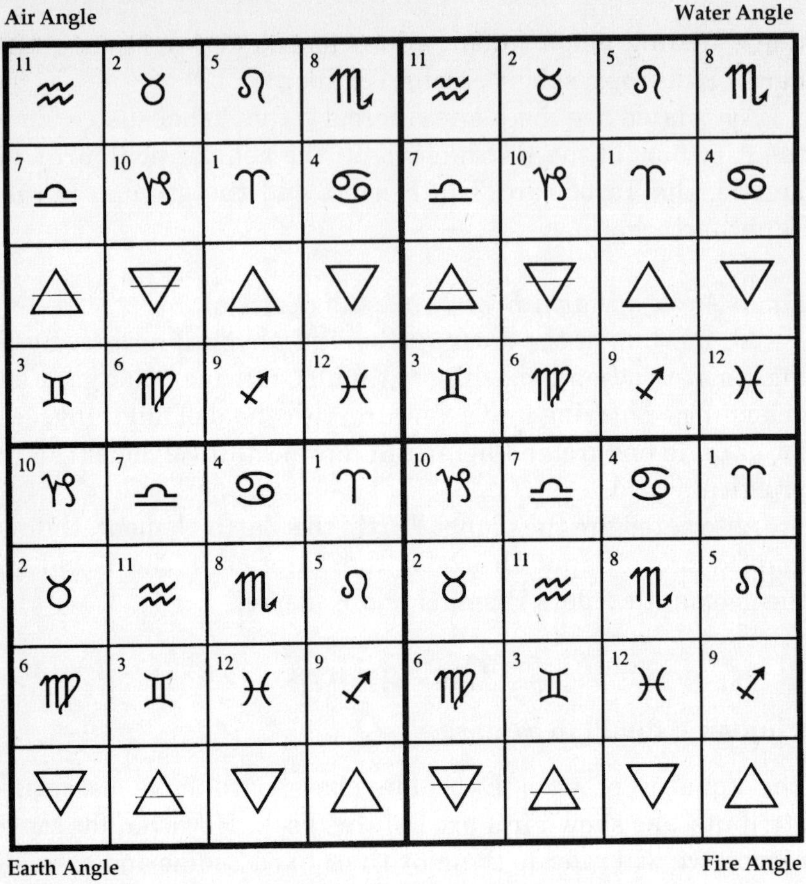

Air Angle   Water Angle

Earth Angle   Fire Angle

FIGURE 48—HOUSE AND ZODIAC ATTRIBUTIONS TO THE FIRE
AND EARTH ENOCHIAN CHESSBOARDS

To choose the Ptah Square, you must choose a square to which your question relates. By this time you would have already decided on the board that will be used and the angle that the querent is to play. The Ptah piece must sit in a square of this angle.

The following descriptions of the houses from the diagrams should provide a guideline to choosing your Ptah Square.

Where symbols of the elements (as opposed to astrological signs) appear in the diagrams, there is no house association. The diviner would choose an element square for the Ptah only

Air Angle   **Water Angle**

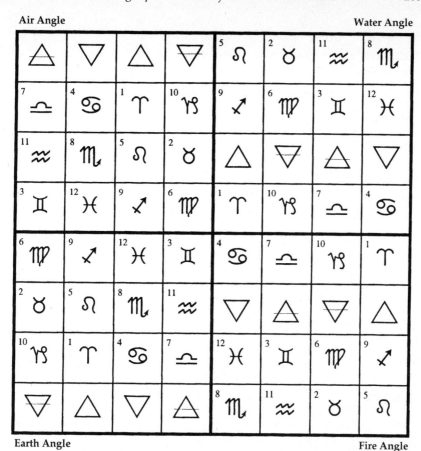

Earth Angle   **Fire Angle**

FIGURE 49—HOUSE AND ZODIAC ATTRIBUTIONS TO THE WATER
AND AIR ENOCHIAN CHESSBOARDS

when no house could be attributed. This might occur in situations when the question was on too grand a scale to apply personally, as do the houses.

First House (1)—The beginning of a matter, childhood environment, concerning the personality, physical body whether of an individual, country or population; e.g., general character of a race or community, or the condition it will be in. Life and health of the querent, effects of any action on the querent's life. Self-awareness, response of individual to outside stimuli.

Second House (2)—Financial conditions individually or nationally, possessions, investments, property, stock exchange, banks, commercial affairs and trade, losses and gains, loans. The intent and fortune of those assisting the querent in any difficulty is revealed.

Third House (3)—Brothers, sisters, neighbors, short journeys, writing, communication, books, transport, relationships, intellect (conscious thought), logic, environment of family, forms of communication, transport, stocks and bonds, nearby countries, changes and removals of business, advisability of undertaking any enterprise, documents to be signed, messages and news from far away.

Fourth House (4)—For a man, the mother. For a woman, the father. Houses, lands, agriculture, weather, mines, inherited tendencies, estates, the end of a matter, environment, home, private life, emotional makeup, public buildings. Politics of the opposition. People against authority. Questions concerning the latter part or end of life and its circumstances.

Fifth House (5)—Pregnancy, children of mind and body, pleasure, feasts, speculations, courtship, enterprises, creativeness, instinctive affections, pets, playmates, loves and hates, sexual relationships that are in the open, sports, gambling, forms of amusement, theaters, educational facilities, public morals, ambassadors and formal social functions.

Sixth House (6)—Work and toil, service and labor, employees, and relationships thereof, subordinates, sickness, aunts, uncles. The Army, Navy, and their machines of war. Public health, civil service, working classes generally—strikes if afflicted. The integrity of those you work with. Concerning those who depend upon you, livestock, farmers, the querent's health and virtues of those consulted on health.

Seventh House (7)—Partnerships personal and social, known enemies, the "other party" in negotiations, legal affairs, contracts and agreements, workings of karma, commerce, representatives and public relations. Marriage relationships and divorce. Encounters with lawbreakers. The place you move to when changing residence. International relationships, arbitrations, wars, foreign trade.

Eighth House (8)—Deaths, suicides, wills, pain, anxiety, estates of the deceased, mortality, death of the old and birth of the new, crime, property of another, settlements, impulses, moods, hidden sexual activities, the occult, mystical experiences, the nonphysical. Privy councils, financial relations with foreign countries, your partner's property, joint partnership, the strength of public enemies,

Ninth House (9)—Religion, matters of the church, philosophy, higher education; e.g., colleges, universities. Long travels, the legal profession, relatives by law, concerns of the higher mind, mental exploration, research, metaphysics, foreign countries, divination ideals, civilization and its values—social morals, commerce in general. The meanings of visions and dreams, the accumulation of knowledge.

Tenth House (10)—For a woman, the querent's mother; for a man, the querent's father. The outcome of your efforts to gain public recognition, rank, honor, trade or profession, authority, employment, ambition, business/career success, law of cause and effect, organization, discipline, government, power structures. Causes by which you may become disgraced. Pensions, king, queen, president, prime minister, national trade, national integrity, celebrities, aristocracy, credit and power.

Eleventh House (11)—Friends, hopes, wishes, clubs, societies, groups, aspirations, openness, creative group expression on a higher mental and intuitive level, humanity, fulfillment. Stepchildren, income from business, social alliances, your attitude towards people, Parliaments, House of Commons, the Senate and House of Representatives, legislation, states, towns and county governments, international friendships. Personal social connections and their effect. The uppermost desires of the querent and possible fulfillment. Those that counsel.

Twelfth House (12)—Imprisonment, assassination and suicide, sorrows, fears, punishments, secret enemies and how successful their schemes, unseen dangers, restriction, disappointments, loss, self-sacrifice, forsaking worldly things for spiritual, health of your partner, lengthy illnesses, psychological health, growth of society, the past, understanding, hospitals and institutions, care for unfortunates, retreats, spies. Secret societies, occult religions, karmic responsibilities, the unconscious.

Once you have chosen your square, you are now in a position to place your Ptah on this square, and prepare for play.

Piece Positions

The game-play setting in which your pieces are placed should, by all accounts, be that of the angle from which you play. However, there are rare occasions when one of the other settings applicable to the board you are playing may be in greater affinity with your question, to complete the associations to the question.

Examples of chosen boards, angles and Ptah squares:

A querent is concerned for her brother's happiness:

Q: Is my brother happy in his present situation?

A: Water Board, Air Angle, Gemini (Third House) square, Air of Water play setting.

A querent is embarking on a business venture:

Q: Will my project that I am initiating flourish?

A: Earth Board, Fire Angle, Capricorn (Tenth House) square, Fire of Earth play setting.

Q: How will my employees' working relationship go with my new business venture?

A: Earth Board, Air Angle, Virgo (Sixth House) square, Air of Earth play setting.

Ptah

The Ptah piece is silent and unmoving. In Egyptian mythology Ptah was considered one of the greatest of all the old gods, and his worship in one form or another goes back to the earliest part of the dynastic periods.

The name Ptah has often been explained as "the opener." He was a god of life and creation, later associated with the arts and handicrafts. The master architect of stones and metals, Ptah was believed to fashion our new bodies in the underworld. The Ptah was called "father of fathers, power of powers, father of beginnings and creator of the egg(s) of the Sun and Moon, Lord of Maat, King of the two lands, the god of the beautiful face in Thebes, who created his own image, who fashioned his own body, who hath established Maat throughout the two lands."[1] As a god-form, he was a symbol of creation directed into matter and an

---

1. E. A. Wallis Budge, *The Gods of the Egyptians,* vol. 1.

aspect or emanation from Atum (or the celestial Ra), the source of becoming. So Ptah gave the breath of life to all things and was considered the force which "brings into existence" all species.

In the form of the figure used in my own Enochian chess set, the Ptah is seated on a throne and holds a knife in his right hand and a 12-petaled daisy in the left. The knife was used in performing the ceremony of "opening the mouth" of the gods. The 12 petals represent time (the Zodiac), because Ptah is also related to Cronos (time). The headgear relates to Maat, showing the equilibrium in the balance of forces, the decision maker. Life and afterlife oaths were sworn to Ptah.

The Ptah god-form represents the divine essence of the Tablet of Union, both the corporeal and incorporeal forms. Its nature is to bind certain forces relating to the question on the chessboard, and by this action is representative of the two aspects of the Enochian Tablets. Colored white for the purposes of the chess game, it signifies beyond the spirit and the divine. The Ptah must not be confused with the spirit forces and actions of the Kings, for by their very existence they create the Ptah piece in much the same way an electromagnetic field produces a current by polarity. In short, the Ptah is a higher form of the Kings, but because of its station, which is more spiritual, it is not utilized in this plane of existence. Hence the Ptah remains motionless. Theoretically, the Ptah is invisible, and the pieces on the board pass over or on the square upon which it sits as if it did not exist.

The Ptah is a representative of the question and marks the square to which the querent's King must attain. Apart from this use in game play, when it is placed on an angle on a particular square, the Ptah becomes the higher genius of the King of that angle. The King in his earthly state must strive to be reunited with his basic essence, the Ptah, with whom he must create a strong link to prove his connection with Spirit.

The reason that the querent's King must remain on the Ptah square with the Ptah for one round of the game is that the King must not only unite with the Ptah, but go through the elements in stages before that union is complete. As a piece in each elemental corner is activated during this critical round of the game, so a different level has been achieved by the King (querent). Here also you can see the most critical point of the divination reading. The actions during this one last round of the game, though classed as elemental, are really an element of Spirit.

Divinatory
Meanings
of the
Chess Pieces

When playing and analyzing your divination game, the chess pieces play a major role. They are the forces in action which signify the pattern and outcome of a matter by virtue of their archetypes and movement across the chessboard. As they move across the pyramid squares, forces are activated according to the virtue of each square and the chess piece thereon. To the chess pieces are given various associations, and by virtue of these associations one can begin to understand the type of vibration each piece generates.

The Enochian chess pieces can be viewed on different levels of influence as regards their symbolic associations. On one level they can be seen Kabbalistically as operators in the four Kabbalistic Worlds as were the chessboards and their angles. For example:

The World of Atziluth—The Fire Set and the four Worlds
therein:
    Fire Knight—Atziluth of Atziluth—Yod of Yod force
    Fire Queen—Briah of Atziluth—Heh of Yod force
    Fire Bishop—Yetzirah of Atziluth—Vau of Yod force
    Fire Rook—Assiah of Atziluth—Heh final of Yod force

And so this would go throughout the four Worlds for the other
elemental sets: Water set for Briah, Air set for Yetzirah and Earth
set for Assiah. From this you can see patterns of Worlds within
Worlds within more Worlds. The Kings are the representatives of
Kether (Spirit) in each Kabbalistic World, and the pawns are the
vice-gerents of each set of the four elemental pieces, They are the
moving elements of these Worlds, the subtle forces. The pawns
also represent the minor elemental portions of these Worlds, but
more especially of their quadrant in the board being operated on.
    On another level, the chess pieces, like the boards, have Tarot
associations. However, instead of the Tarot Trumps, the court
cards (Royal Arcana) and the Aces are applied to the individual
pieces, which form archetypes. Here the diviner can see archetypal movements over the pyramid squares that can represent individuals and their influence on the divination question. Within
each chess piece is its elemental association as well, and the sub-
elemental parts of elements within these pieces correspond to the
court cards. Table IV shows the associations to the chess pieces.

TABLE IV—ROYAL ARCANA AND ELEMENTAL ASSOCIATIONS OF
THE ENOCHIAN CHESS PIECES

Fire Set		
Piece	**Court Card**	**Sub-Element**
King	Ace of Wands	Spirit of Fire
Knight	Knight of Wands	Fire of Fire
Queen	Queen of Wands	Water of Fire
Bishop	Prince/King of Wands	Air of Fire
Rook	Princess of Wands	Earth of Fire

TABLE IV—ROYAL ARCANA AND ELEMENTAL ASSOCIATIONS OF THE ENOCHIAN CHESS PIECES (*CONTINUED*)

Water Set		
Piece	**Court Card**	**Sub-Element**
King	Ace of Cups	Spirit of Water
Knight	Knight of Cups	Fire of Water
Queen	Queen of Cups	Water of Water
Bishop	Prince/King of Cups	Air of Water
Rook	Princess of Cups	Earth of Water

Air Set		
Piece	**Court Card**	**Sub-Element**
King	Ace of Swords	Spirit of Air
Knight	Knight of Swords	Fire of Air
Queen	Queen of Swords	Water of Air
Bishop	Prince/King of Swords	Air of Air
Rook	Princess of Swords	Earth of Air

Earth Set		
Piece	**Court Card**	**Sub-Element**
King	Ace of Disks	Spirit of Earth
Knight	Knight of Disks	Fire of Earth
Queen	Queen of Disks	Water of Earth
Bishop	Prince/King of Disks	Air of Earth
Rook	Princess of Disks	Earth of Earth

If, however, you were looking at one pantheon per board, the same associations would apply because, even though one elemental pantheon would govern each angle, each set would still represent the elements of each angle as identified by the colors of their thrones/bases.

A further level of association with the chess pieces are the planetary forces. Here the diviner can see planetary movements over the pyramid squares. This would show planets moving into houses and Zodiac signs. From an astrological viewpoint, complete stories can be formed from this. Table V below gives the planetary associations that I deem appropriate as a result of research and practice; however, you may choose to form your own opinion.

The divination section of the Enochian chess game has an emphasis on astrology, and to understand the full functions of the divination game you should really study astrology or have at least a basic knowledge of its essence. Without it, you would be handicapped in using the chess game for divination. Within our own temple, any members who are taught the divination aspects of the Enochian chess game must have first reached a level where they are very proficient in astrology. I seriously suggest that, if you wish to study the divinatory part of the game more deeply, you should study basic astrological meanings and the movements of the planets through the various astrological houses. Although the entire divination game is not totally astrological in nature, the framework in which it operates is.

TABLE V—TABLE OF PLANETARY ASSOCIATIONS TO THE ENOCHIAN CHESS PIECES

If Querent Plays	Fire King	Water King	Air King	Earth King
Fire set	Sun	Neptune	Uranus	Pluto
Water set	Pluto	Sun	Uranus	Neptune
Air set	Pluto	Neptune	Sun	Uranus
Earth set	Pluto	Neptune	Uranus	Sun
Chess Pieces	**Fire**	**Water**	**Air**	**Earth**
Queens	Moon	Moon	Moon	Moon
Knights	Mars	Mars	Jupiter	Jupiter
Bishops	Chiron	Mercury	Mercury	Chiron
Rooks	Saturn	Venus	Venus	Saturn
Pawns	Fire, Air, Earth	Water, Air, Earth	Air, Fire, Water	Earth, Fire, Water

The querent's King always represents the Sun (the querent him or herself) and the other three Kings take on the three outer, slower planets. Throughout the foregoing table you will see the Earth element taking on a different planet each time, as all of these planets have an influence on Earth/matter.

The pawns are extensions of the pieces to which they are vice-gerents, and their associations have been discussed earlier in this book (in "Constructing the Chess Pieces"). Through their elemental influence, however, they can represent movements in time along the earth plane, and aspects of the psyche. They could also be attributed to asteroids.

As regards the human physical appearances corresponding to the chess pieces, experience has proven that there is no set appearance per piece, only a generalized view as given in the Golden Dawn Tarot court cards. However, this becomes more heavily modified as a piece works through different elemental sections of the boards, which results in a lack of consistency in the physical appearance signified by any individual chess piece. I have found that the chess pieces represent individuals by personality, not only as described below but by their elemental attributions, sometimes giving a particular appearance or character. If you look carefully at your friends, you will be able to see what combination of elements they represent most. For example, a woman who is generous, loving and rather mystical in appearance or character, but too passive and reflective in nature, would be represented by the Water Queen, the Watery part of Water. Sometimes I have found the elemental combinations allude to a combination of a person's Sun sign and rising sign, or sometimes one of these with the Moon sign.[1]

The operation of the chess pieces on the chessboards can be positive or negative. It all depends on the circumstances described during any individual moment of game play. Therefore, only a general description can be given below on each of the chess pieces.

---

1. These are astrological terms for planetary and first house cusp positions.

The Kings

A King "answereth to the action of the Spirit." Wherever they move, they initiate a fresh current, but in a balanced movement which first starts as a mute force (throned upon water) then finishes as:

> . . . life manifested and throned upon the earth. And herein is a mystery of the Lord Aeshoori when enthroned between Isis and Nephthys, thus representing the beginning and end of the action of Him in whom end and beginning are not, but rather concealment and then manifestation. Herein is a great mystery of life, for His Thrones are not in the two active elements, seeing that these latter are his horse and chariot of transition in the passage from concealment into manifestation. This piece, then, is the symboliser of the action of the potencies of the crosses on the Servient Squares.[2]

The Enochian chess pieces represent the "Word" Yeheshuah (YHShVH). The central letter in the middle of the letters of Tetragrammaton is the Hebrew letter "Shin" and is represented by the Kings. Since Shin represents the hidden force of Spirit behind the whole name YHVH,[3] its true title is Yeheshuah. As such, Spirit as Shin can be placed behind any of the four holy names, likened to the four Kings, just as another piece, itself represented by a letter of Tetragrammaton, always shares the Throne Square with the King at the beginning of the game.

In Egyptian mythology, the King alludes to the Osiris myth, and Zeus in Greek mythology.[4]

---

2. "Notes on Rosicrucian Chess" by S.L. MacGregor Mathers.

3. For a full discourse on this name, see the Kabbalistic book *Shaar Ruach Ha Kodesh* (The Gate of the Holy Spirit) by Chaim Vital, part of which is given in *Meditation and Kabbalah* by Aryeh Kaplan (Weiser, 1982), p. 222.

4. You are advised to do your own research into the mythologies associated with the chess pieces; this is a far too lengthy and complex a subject to be included in this book.

King of the Fire Pantheon: Chnupis Kneph

The unmanifested force of Divine Will penetrating manifestation as a positive/masculine energy. An uncontrolled force in operation that can be likened to fate in action. Therefore in divination the Fire King shows forces beyond one's control entering into a situation—creative energy. The type of situation it enters is described by the square the King moves into and its relationship to the surrounding chess pieces. The force can be violent or gentle and depicts transmutation.

King of the Water Pantheon: Ptah Ra Pan-Lses

A generative force pouring forth from the Waters of Creation manifesting from the Great Mother as the immortal spiritual nature of mankind, a passive/feminine energy. The Water King represents the unconscious mind. As it moves over the squares, it shows the areas where conscious realization, love and wisdom are needed, where waste must be purged, and where there is or must be fluent soul/emotional expression. It shows areas of fertility and the dominance of Spirit over Matter.

King of the Air Pantheon: Socharis

The power of manifesting forces being directed to either good or evil—a masculine force. The King of Swords shows where ignorance must be dispelled and spiritual energy invoked to manifest Truth. As a divinatory piece the King therefore moves to where there is affliction which must be eliminated, punishment be met and justice be affirmed. It is the power of thought and represents an irresistible force that cannot be stopped without the powers of the unmanifest behind you. It shows that the higher intellect can pierce the planes of understanding and wisdom.

King of the Earth Pantheon: Osiris

The unmanifest becoming manifest as a union of Spirit and Matter. Feminine force. As a divinatory piece the Earth King ministers to the development of the matter and shows what can be brought forth through material manifestation. It represents both heaven and earth, life and death. Limitations of matter are depicted, however, and through its movements and relationships with the other chess pieces a blueprint of the cosmic knowledge of a situation can be seen. In divination the Earth King, like all the Kings, is neither good nor bad; it all depends on the querent's intentions, or the intentions of the forces or those that oppose the querent.

The Knights

This piece represents the action of Fire and is the Yod force. As Hoor is the avenger of Aeshoori, the Knight is the Revealer of the Strength of Spirit. Its force is seen potent and terrible, opening the locked doors of matter which reveal the treasure within. "Therefore hath all life its beginnings in a fire Celestial."

As an archetype, the Knight is the warrior, hero, avenger and rescuer. As the Yod force, it is the Father and the initiator—the commencement of material forces. Swift, violent, short in effect but long in affect. The Egyptian myths of Horus and his many aspects are good examples of this archetype. For example, the Roman god Mars, the Greek god Ares, and many other sons of the Sun represented by a symbolic birth, a period of youth and exile and then as a young warrior. As an avenger the Knight is also a protector and therefore has a dual role in the divination game.

Knight of the Fire Pantheon: Ra

The divinatory meaning here is too much energy or force in a matter, but only shortened force; there is no staying power. This can lead to destruction or creation; for example, instigating new enterprises, projects, etc., or sudden endings, dangerous situations. This Knight is a catalyst to circumstances wherever it is moved and whatever piece it threatens. As an archetype, he is an innovator, but tends to act too hastily, or burns himself out from too much effort and energy, therefore overly active and restless. Problems can occur when dealing with others due to self-centeredness and unrestrained desire to act directly. Abrupt and aggressive, given to exaggeration, very passionate, overconfident and self-indulgent. As a Mars force, his actions on the boards allude to a Mars effect such as combativeness, executive abilities, energy and sex, physical activities, accidents, quarrels, courage or daring.

Knight of the Water Pantheon: Sebek

Careful discrimination takes place when this Knight enters into play, and the quality of things is examined. Rationality is now used and knowledge is transferred; however, if negatively positioned, this piece shows limitation and communication breakdown. Desires can become greater than ability, or be contained too much below the surface. The square position of this Knight will show what is being hidden in a person's thoughts, or where a situation or a person is impressionable and may react too strongly to external impetus rather than his or her own drive. The archetype is one of emotional feelings without true control, responding more to desire. Positively aspected, this Knight will show illumination of thoughts and ideas, and an understanding of cause and effect. There is strength and outer protection; therefore it may show a person who can shield you from difficulty. The Water Knight is a Mars force that works more in an undercurrent effect rather than on the surface like the Fire Knight.

Knight of the Air Pantheon: Socharis

This is an archetype that gives orders and directions, a quick mind, fleetness of purpose. As a thinker and planner he can be the architect of many things; however, to actually get anything done reinforcements must be brought in. He can be a teacher, a good listener and give an objective opinion about things. He can brood too much, which brings storminess in nature and can bring harshness to a situation. He represents travel and movement. If this piece is left to sit too long in one place, it shows problems in the area that the square depicts. There must be short, swift bursts of energy in a matter to keep the impetus up; otherwise a situation or person will crumble. Distinction is made as to what is good, and in sympathy with the question, and what must be judged and swiftly dealt with. The Air Knight represents communication being made and future events shaped or planned. Wherever he is placed on a board, matters of swiftness are depicted. He is a Jupiter force, showing new vistas and opportunities, speculation and travel. Well positioned, cheerfulness and good hopes. If negatively positioned the Air Knight shows risks taken, waste of energy or material goods.

Knight of the Earth Pantheon: Horus

Nourishment and abundance, fertility and wealth are depicted here. If positively positioned the Earth Knight shows growth, regeneration and prosperity, but this is only while there is purpose and direction to the Knight's moves or position; otherwise a situation may be considered sterile, static or inert. He shows where there is potential and hope. The archetype is one who wants more of everything, a "well-to-do" person, or one who has attained a lot through hard work. Sometimes extravagant, exaggerating and overconfident, but very practical. A warm character who can be very giving under the right circumstances. The Earth Knight's effect on the house (square) he may be placed in is not as quick as that of the other Knights, but it is still a catalyst, and things do happen because he is a prime mover of things to come. His effect is longer lasting, with a powerful momentum. The Earth Knight is a Jupiter force of a beneficial material nature.

The Queens

This is the Heh force in Tetragrammaton, that of a receptive/feminine nature. In mythology she is referred to as the mature woman, the fertile and maternal figure. Some archetypal associations are the Egyptian myths of Isis, Hathor, Nuit and many other counterparts of these goddesses. In other mythologies her counterparts would be Hera and Hecate. So many goddesses come under the archetype of the Queen. Although some were considered virginal, most of the goddesses applied to the Enochian chess queen were mother archetypes. A threefold aspect must be considered here: the maiden, mother and crone. Many were one and the same but were separated as aspects of the one. In the identity of mother and daughter, the eternally child-bearing mother manifests herself as an eternal being.

The chess Queen is associated with the Moon. The Moon is the Queen Mother of the heavens. She is known by many names in different civilizations (Isis, Virgin Mary, Diana of Ephesus, Shu, etc). As Luna, or Lucina, she presided over childbirth and life, and as Hecate she was the goddess of death. She ruled in the underworld over magic and enchantments, and in heaven she was the chaste Diana, the Queen of Night. In Babylon the Moon was worshiped as the god Sin, and by the Jews as Jehovah.

From this you can see that the Moon was generally taken as feminine, but occasionally has been referred to as a cause in itself, and spoken of as male, or as an androgyne, or a triple power in itself. For example, Diana the Moon-goddess was sometimes called "three formed": Diana the shy, Diana (Artemis) on Earth and Proserpine (Persephone) in the world of the dead. The crescent Moon was connected with her, as it was with the Chaldean Astarte and the Egyptian Isis. The Hindus had a myth of the Moon being the parent of Mercury.

In Enochian chess divination, the Queen's movements are like the undulating waves of the sea, and a cherisher of Life. As mentioned above, she can represent either a young or old woman; however, the general association would be a woman over 30 (unless the individual's appearance and character proves otherwise in nature) or one who has had children.

She is represented by the Moon, which shows reaction on the basis of subconscious disposition. Movements over a chessboard would allude to day-to-day matters, mental and emotional karmic patterns which either inhibit or help us in our attempts of adjustment and expression in life. Wherever she is placed shows a spontaneous reaction to a matter, emotional ups and downs. She also symbolizes the image of oneself and how one may see one's dealings with the public. Therefore a stressed position would show disharmony in everyday dealings, whereas a fortunate positioning shows harmony. Positioned where another piece is threatened would show stress being placed on the threatened piece. Fertility and childbirth are also represented by the Queen.

In the Fire element, the Queen shows quick and often impulsive action to a situation; in the Water element reactions are based on emotional intensity; in the Air element instinctive action without thought is depicted; and in the Earth element a steady type of calm reaction to a given situation.

Queen of the Fire Pantheon: Sati-Ashtoreth

This Queen represents persistent energy, calm authority, kindness, generosity and a capacity for friendship and love, but at her own initiation. There is much pride, charm and social ease with popularity. Adversely positioned, she shows impatience, brooding, gullibility, and one who harbors revenge. She shows a sharp tongue and cruel wit. She may tend to intoxication during periods of melancholy.

Moving over the squares, this chess piece shows situations that are incomplete or are adjusting and adapting, successful achievement, and balance and harmony being within one's power. There may be initial obstacles, but success after disorder. General impulsiveness to situations without pre-thought if you allow matters to influence you on a subconscious level.

Queen of the Water Pantheon: Thoueris

The image for this archetype is of beauty and purity with infinite subtlety. A highly imaginative person who is artistic. Very intuitive, receptive and transmissive of surrounding influences. Adversely positioned she is a dreamer, and so reflective of outside influences or other people's thoughts that none can see through her to the truth. Sometimes perverseness and distortion of facts. Very moody, however, psychic ability, and some-times prophetic.

As the Water Queen is moved over a board, she shows success and benefits in day-to-day affairs, talk and social enjoyment. If adversely aspected or aspecting another piece, she shows you must check your actions to avoid danger in matters, and advises one to be careful and patient and to beware of trickery and deceit. There may be difficulty in growth or movement. A waiting period is shown, but if this Queen is weakly positioned, it may show the lack of incentive to get moving and change matters.

Queen of the Air Pantheon: Knousou Pekht

This is an archetype with the power of transmission, an intelli-gent and complex person with attention to detail and accuracy. A keen observer, graceful and skilled at balancing situations, therefore versatile. Adversely positioned, she is cruel, sly, half truths and quiet slander, superficial beauty and attractiveness aids in deceit.

In her movements over a board, she shows how one can take hold of matters and turn them to one's advantage. There is always a struggle, but there is plenty of ability for great under-takings if one wills it. Sometimes ambitions are greater than abilities. The untrustworthy must be avoided, so work to improve a situation and oneself, which will attract success. Then potential will be fulfilled. This piece shows breakthroughs and situations being dealt with before they become too danger-ous. Badly aspecting other pieces, she may show someone lay-ing down the law to others concerning a situation, and dealing with arrogance.

Queen of the Earth Pantheon: Isis

This archetype shows one with quiet qualities, a "down-to-earth" person, compassionate and a lover of luxury who usually collects possessions. She gives great affection and is very for-giving, hardworking and sensible. Usually domesticated and not intellectually inclined. Adversely positioned, there can be debauch, spendthriftiness, general extravagance, narrowness in sight and abuse of alcohol or drugs. She could be too materialistic, dull and/or foolish.

When the Earth Queen is moved over a board, she shows areas or situations where there is attraction, stimulation, cooperation and merging of separate parts, relationships between people and gatherings. She shows that there is enough success in a matter to continue and that all is being nourished for growth. After a struggle, one is succeeding. Adversely, it is not a good time for movement. Wait for a more appropriate time for change.

The Bishops

In mythology the Bishops represent counterparts of the Knights. They took the role as the second brother—usually a god-form of light, but sometimes the jealous and the destroyer who plots against his father or brother. The Mercurial aspect of this god-form depicts the messenger, like Hermes of the Greeks or the Roman god Mercury. These gods had the gift of prophecy. The Bishop represents a keen and swift wind, is ascribed to Aroueris as an Egyptian god-form and represents the swift vehicle of Spirit. The four Bishops are all variations of Aroueris, as shown by their Egyptian god-names, although they are all but aspects of Horus and Osiris.

The Bishop represents the Vau force. The Son of the Mother and Father who realizes the balance of the scales. He then marries the daughter in Malkuth, which is also known as Kalah the Bride, and the cycle starts again as the Son and Daughter become Father and Mother. He is straight and airy but is obstructed by any solid object and must go around. He represents intellect and communication. The Yetziratic World of Formation. A planner and thinker who tries to initiate matter. In a divination game, the Bishop can act for or counteract your plans, depending on his position on the board. He is the first and sometimes last resort in matters.

The Planets associated with the Bishop are Mercury and Chiron. The Mercury influence shows relationships, writing, travel, the mind and intellect, changes of thought and occupation, studies and examinations. Sometimes irritations and vexations, problems with transport and dealings with relatives. The Chiron influence shows timing of events, foreseeing outcomes, teaching, guardians, or mentor, medical science, the healer. A loner and sometimes a maverick or pioneer. Creativeness and showing a better way, a guide or link to something.

Bishop of the Fire Pantheon: Toum

This is an individual who is eager for action and who has strength and drive to carry effort through. When this piece is placed in a fighting situation, it shows aggression being pulled along by a lot of strength and energy. A definite direction is being applied, as this is not a scattered force. The situation can be volatile, however, so it must be directed by Will. Expanding horizons are depicted and plans are carefully applied.

The danger here is not being able to settle on anything in a situation that requires a decision. Positively aspected, this Bishop shows strength and decisiveness. Matters which are distinguished according to their nature. There is independent thought and reason. Negatively aspected, you will see a force that cannot be stopped, which influences everything around it and ignores all stops. In business, he shows a forward movement with little that can hold him back. He also depicts travel, but only with a purpose.

Bishop of the Water Pantheon: Hapimoun

This Bishop shows superficiality coming into a situation. Something which cannot be trusted. Something is being kept secret. In a situation, hidden depths have not yet been reached or penetrated. There is continual voyaging and unrest, travel. This is a transitional state in all matters where the surface is just being skimmed, and one from harmony and balance to penetration and transformation. As an individual, you will be dealing with someone who has control over emotion and who can act objectively. However, such controlled emotions are not resolved and dam up, at times causing an overflow. This is an individual who applies himself to a task with plenty of drive, but he uses any means to obtain the desired result without consideration for others. Action is a means to release emotions. Positively aspected, he is objective and willing to look for causes of problems and then get rid of them. He who can take good counsel.

Bishop of the Air Pantheon: Shu Zoan

When moving across the chessboard, this Bishop shows areas of no restriction, where whim is followed. Energy may be wasted and answers may become elusive. It can show one's mind racing too fast. As an individual, the Air Bishop shows the thinker and planner who handles matters skillfully. Vast plans are brought into action; however, this person can be very abstract and is in danger of losing sight of the goal. Negatively placed, the reality of a situation can be disassociated from, especially when dealing with peoples' emotions. Usually this person will be traveling or handling matters alone. Energies can be scattered in too many directions, matters happen too fast and confusion can set in. Too many people are having their say, which confuses matters even further. There is indecision, and one ends up not getting anywhere but running in circles. Positively aspected, caution is applied together with a willingness to try on all accounts. Old values are broken for new concepts to follow.

Bishop of the Earth Pantheon: Aroueris

Wherever this Bishop is placed positively, one will see prosperity and growth. Matters operate slowly but surely. It rules seasonal changes, fertility and matters of development. Everything must be timed if one wishes success. Matters materialize and all efforts and theory take root as the final formula is put into place. Therefore the material result of all one's efforts are beginning to show. As an individual, it is someone who seeks comforts with some effort. He takes everything in his stride, one day at a time. Both intellectual and physical effort is applied to anything that is desired. He is generous and loving. Negatively, he is greedy and too materialistic, making an excuse for everything. When moving across the board, the Earth Bishop shows situations of gain, movement, shifting from one place to another taking all your possessions. In the business world, everything is obtained through progression.

The Rooks

In Tetragrammaton, the Rooks are "Heh final," the Daughter that married the Son. She is the feminine part and represents a full cycle of development in preparation for entering a new cycle. In mythology she is depicted as the Amazon warrior queen or princess, and starts off as the virgin goddess; for example, the myths of Diana, Athene, Artemis of Ephesus, Aphrodite, Nike, Nephthys, etc. At some stage throughout some myths, this goddess loses her virginity. In some cases she becomes the harlot and in others the Mother. She is ordinarily barren but sometimes fruitful. Some myths show her entering the underworld where she becomes for part of each year a goddess of the dead.

This chess piece represents a pondering, formidable Earth force, and is the completed action of Spirit in Matter. Wherever she is moved, matters crystallize, become more apparent. Temptation of matter, whether sexual or material, is always near. The Rook shows ideas put into concrete action, or matters under construction when positively aspected. When negatively aspected, ideas or matters under collapse. The Rooks are "time pieces."

The planetary influences for the Rook are Saturn and Venus. The Venus influence shows relationships of a sexual nature, pleasure, holidays, enjoyment, social life and social adjustments, music and the arts, matters of beauty and materialism. The Saturn influence shows conservativeness, consolidation of affairs and resources. If badly positioned, disappointment and loss, ill health, responsibilities and burden, duration of time. There is a strong sense of duty from individuals and dealings with land, possessions, estates, etc.

Rook of the Fire Pantheon: Anouke

This is a very powerful personality who is fully able to back up her wants and commands. She is strong-willed and forceful. She is generally able to control her emotions, although ready to fight if challenged. If the ultimate goal will benefit her, she will conform to conditions around her. She can create or destroy, depending on her position on the board. Negatively aspected, she tends to be wanton and a bit loose with her virtues. She makes up her own mind on matters, and if told what to do will go in the reverse direction. When this Fire Rook is moved to different squares on a board, it shows situations where sudden concrete action is taken after a period of stillness. This action is sometimes impulsive and sometimes calculated, depending on the previous movements on the board. Strong effects are felt in the areas of life depicted by the squares to which she is moved.

Rook of the Water Pantheon: Shooen

This individual is soft but determined in nature, although rather dreamy. However, her tremendous strength of purpose can turn her dreams into reality. Most of her actions are emotionally charged, so emotional involvement is rarely avoided. Her beliefs and convictions are strong, though she usually acts in harmony with the times. There is no forgiveness for those who cross her, and she can set up quite a campaign against her enemies. She likes to share her experiences, and her expression is to create.

In divinatory matters, dreams and ideas are being crystallized. People are being nourished and educated, and the battle of life is being won. Turmoil and chaos may be around, but it is not bothering a matter, and a new life force is developing to a situation. If positively aspected, nothing will sway the querent from a task. If this Rook is situated in a position where she is not influencing any situation, it shows that too much time is spent on entertainment and self-indulgence.

Rook of the Air Pantheon: Tharpeshest Jefine Pasht

This is an individual with a practical grasp of a situation who needs to express herself through an abstract, quasi-intellectual manner. However, material matters sometimes do not move as fast as the mind's conception of plans; therefore, she can get very frustrated when everything moves slowly. Patience needs to be learned. Negatively aspected, she shows no compassion for others and only intellectualizes situations. If she has not experienced it, she will not understand it.

In divinatory matters, social and communal integration is shown, together with the expression of the culture of those around one. Ideas are materialized. The people are benefited rather than the individual. Goals must be worked for. Negatively aspected, this piece shows where victory can be snatched away from others for selfish ends. In tense situations on the chessboard, she may be the bearer of exciting news.

Rook of the Earth Pantheon: Nephthys

A receptive, fertile situation is depicted here. The Earth Rook shows matters of finality which now must open up and be receptive to a new cycle. Therefore we see here a situation of absorption to those of fixed expression and pursuits, because a revision of ideals and situations must take place. The old must be discarded. The squares where the Rook is placed show where consciousness and awareness are necessary. Journeys may be disrupted.

This is the beginning of a matter and yet the end of a matter. Concerning growth, it shows the potential to be great, but it depends entirely on the individual. Good luck is depicted; however, it can be the reverse if the Rook is adversely aspected by another chess piece. A situation or person can be relied upon, and new concepts are consistently being put into effect. Negatively aspected, one might encounter others who are hungry for power, who are ready to sacrifice anything that gets in their way.

As an individual, she is one who gets on with things and accomplishes things rather than spending time thinking about them. Kind and generous, but encourages materialism.

Analyzing a Divination Game

First draw up a recording sheet; then commence your game. Record every move made on your sheet, but do not concern yourself with analyzing the game during the initial divination game play. By analyzing while playing, an overconcentration of the intellectual processes on your game occurs, and this interferes with the unseen forces which guide your divination play and intuition. Once the game is over, you can then analyze it by re-enacting the chess moves from your recorded sheet.

According to what your needs may be, you may analyze an Enochian chess divination game in full, in summary or with a short answer. A short analysis caters to a "yes or no" type of question. This is where you see whether the King obtains the Ptah Square or not, and if so, under what duress does it remain there. For example, if the King reaches the Ptah and stays there for one round of the game, the answer is "successful." If the King does not reach the Ptah, the answer is "unsuccessful."

If the King reaches the Ptah but has strong or minor opposition while staying on the Ptah Square for one round of the game, the question is successful but with difficulty. By observing what type of opposition there is to the Ptah Square at the end of the game, you will be able to see the circumstances of any difficulty, and whether the success is partial, brief or lasting.

A summary analysis skims over the whole game play, summarizing the overall influences without detail, and gives an end result. It may dwell on one or two pertinent points of importance described by the game.

A full analysis is made by studying the effects of all moves made from the first to the last move. In the information given below, the emphasis is on reading the results of your divination game from the perspective of a full analysis.

During your game, you will find that the querent's ally's pieces show a force in favor of the querent, whereas the opponents' forces are against the interests of the querent. Attacking forces will show how the elements treat the querent, or the matter in concern. The ally's actions describe how much support is given. The pieces which the querent operates are aspects of him/herself. When an answer is obtained, the querent can then see the outcome, the force resisting the outcome and how the resisting forces will go about their attack. This can be very helpful when planning a future venture.

A great many things must be considered in your analysis to form a full picture.

Piece Movement and How the Pieces Relate to the Question

Viewing the pieces as archetypes/personalities will help when a question refers to human relationships. If for example the Fire Knight blocks a King from the Ptah, this may mean a man of fiery temperament obstructing you. In a macrocosmic perspective, the Knight could represent a government or country fitting the Knight's elemental nature and that causes the obstruction.

The pawns may stand for people of a lesser influence, or groups of people, being manipulated by the respective archetype described by any piece influencing them. This of course could be the reverse where the group of people influence the individual. The pawns, however, generally show happenings and influences rather than personalities, and their nature is the nature of the piece to which they are vice-gerent.

A chess piece, when moving from one angle of the chessboard to another angle, retains its essential character. Any changes that do take place are the elemental affects on that personality; for example, a change of thought, action, direction or emotion. The chess pieces are also found to be weakened or strengthened in different elements; therefore, this would occur when they are played on the different elemental boards and when they move into the various angles during play. This means that a piece weakened by an angle it moves into will have a weaker influence on any piece or square it may influence. If it is moved into an element that gives it added strength, then its effect will be great on the surrounding pieces and squares. Observe also when a buildup of pieces takes place in a particular element. For example, a concentration of pieces in the Fire Angle of a board will show a very heated situation in which everything will be moving a lot faster. Table VI (page 240) shows the strengths and weaknesses of the chess pieces in the elemental boards and angles.

The planetary influence of a piece must also be taken into consideration. You must observe what pieces a piece may threaten because this shows what planets aspect each other. Observe the square upon which a piece is placed because this shows a planet in a Zodiacal sign and house. Table VII shows the strengths and weaknesses of the pieces as planets in the Zodiac (on the chess squares).

Table VI, on the following page, is based on "The Concourse of Forces" as given in Regardie's *Golden Dawn*.

Table VI—Elemental Strengths and Weaknesses of the Chess Pieces in the Chessboards and Angles

Chess Piece	Strongest Angle	Strong Angle	Angle in Detriment	Weakest Angle
Fire King	Fire of Fire	Its own	Air Board	Water Board
Water King	Water of Water	element	Earth Board	Fire Board
Air King	Air of Air	angle on	Fire Board	Earth Board
Earth King	Earth of Earth	any board	Water Board	Air Board
Fire Queen	Water of Fire	Fire of Water	Earth of Air	Air of Earth
Water Queen	Water of Water	Air of Water	Earth of Earth	Fire of Fire
Air Queen	Water of Air	Air of Water	Earth of Fire	Fire of Earth
Earth Queen	Water of Earth	Air of Earth	Earth of Water	Fire of Air
Fire Knight	Fire of Fire	Fire of Air	Air of Air	Water of Water
Water Knight	Water of Fire	Fire of Water	Earth of Air	Air of Earth
Air Knight	Air of Fire	Earth of Fire	Fire of Air	Earth of Water
Earth Knight	Earth of Fire	Fire of Earth	Water of Air	Air of Water
Fire Bishop	Fire of Air	Earth of Air	Air of Fire	Water of Earth
Water Bishop	Water of Air	Air of Water	Earth of Fire	Fire of Earth
Air Bishop	Air of Air	Water of Air	Fire of Fire	Earth of Earth
Earth Bishop	Earth of Air	Fire of Air	Water of Fire	Air of Earth
Fire Rook	Fire of Earth	Earth of Fire	Air of Water	Water of Air
Water Rook	Water of Earth	Air of Earth	Earth of Water	Fire of Air
Air Rook	Air of Earth	Water of Earth	Fire of Water	Earth of Air
Earth Rook	Earth of Earth	Fire of Earth	Water of Water	Air of Air
All Pawns	Own angle	Ally angle	Opposite angle	Side angle

The Fire King is strongly attracted to the Leo square, the Water King to the Scorpio square, the Air King to the Aquarius square and the Earth King to the Taurus square.

TABLE VII—PLANETARY STRENGTHS AND AFFINITIES

Planet	Sign of Rulership	Sign of Exaltation	Quadruplicity	Sign of Detriment	Sign of Fall
Sun	Leo	Aries	Fixed	Aquarius	Libra
Moon	Cancer	Taurus	Cardinal	Capricorn	Scorpio
Mercury	Gemini	Virgo	Mutable	Sagittarius	Pisces
Venus	Taurus and Libra	Pisces	Fixed	Scorpio and Aries	Virgo
Mars	Aries	Capricorn	Cardinal	Libra	Cancer
Jupiter	Sagittarius	Cancer	Mutable	Gemini	Capricorn
Saturn	Capricorn	Libra	Fixed	Cancer	Aries
Chiron	Virgo	Sagittarius	Cardinal	Pisces	Gemini
Uranus	Aquarius	Scorpio	Mutable	Leo	Taurus
Neptune	Pisces	Sagittarius	Mutable	Virgo	Gemini
Pluto	Scorpio	Leo	Fixed	Taurus	Aquarius

TABLE VIII—OPERATION OF PLANETS IN HOUSES

Sun	One's perception of life	Consciously directed
Moon	Reactions based on subconscious	
Mercury	Communications and thinking	
Venus	Expressions, feelings	
Mars	Assertion, desires	
Jupiter	One seeks to grow, trust	States of being
Saturn	Establishment, preservation	
Chiron	Transcending	
Uranus	Generational attitudes	Collective unconscious transpersonal
Neptune	Attuning to forces of change	
Pluto	External and internal	

The planets represent specific principles of energy exchange between the individual square and the universal supply of all energy. Each planet therefore reveals not only a type of outgoing energy and an urge toward expression of a certain kind, but it also reveals a specific need for activity and fulfillment that must be fed along a particular vibratory wavelength. This vibratory wavelength is used as a catalyst to the vibration of the Zodiac sign and other attributions of the square. From this the makeup and function of the Servient Square become more clear.

Planets in the Elements

Mercury in:
 Earth—Through action, practical needs.
 Air—Abstract thoughts.
 Water—Influenced by deepest yearnings and subconscious predispositions.
 Fire—Influenced by aspirations, positive thinking.

Venus in:

Earth—Tangible commitments.

Air—Sharing expressed in words.

Water—Emotional feeding and sympathetic, steady responsiveness of sensitivity and vulnerability.

Fire—Grand gestures.

Mars in:

Earth—Expression of will and assertive power through concrete achievement.

Air—Expression of idea.

Water—Harnessed emotional power, assertion towards unconscious desires.

Fire—Direct physical action.

Moon in:

Earth—Reaction grounded, steady, matter of fact way.

Air—Reacts by thinking first then acts according to evaluation, expression of thoughts to feel right.

Water—Reaction colored by emotional intensity.

Fire—Reaction with enthusiasm and direct action; leap before look.

Chiron in:

Earth—Finding means for accomplishment.

Air—Anticipation of the future. Restless to the constraints of the present.

Water—Mystical quest, devotion to a matter.

Fire—Independence and self-sufficiency.

Saturn in:

Earth—Stabilizing efficiency.

Air—Stabilizing of understanding.

Water—Overly sensitive, emotional repression.

Fire—Stabilizing identity.

Jupiter in:

Earth—Spontaneous flow of practical application.

Air—Spontaneous flow of mental application.

Water—Spontaneous flow of emotion and intuition.

Fire—Spontaneous flow of energy.

The Sun in any element is energy which feeds the basic sense of purpose.

Uranus in any element shows individualistic freedom, independence, originality.

Neptune in any element shows the intangible having an effect, and freedom from ego-self.

Pluto in any element shows transformation.

The Squares and Their Influences

As you are aware at this point, each square on the Enochian chessboard has symbols associated with it, and these symbols have specific meanings. These symbols are in fact representative of the influences and forces put into action when the chess pieces are moved onto the squares. Therefore, you must observe how the pieces react in the squares. In doing this, you will be seeing planets and archetypes in the Zodiac and houses, so you will be looking at:

1. The Zodiacal influence of the square to the situation being divined. (See Table IX on the opposite page.)

2. The area of life under influence, depicted by the house, as given in the earlier chapter on finding the Ptah Square.

3. Combinations of these influences between chess pieces and how their specific energies activate the squares.

TABLE IX—ZODIACAL INFLUENCES

Sign	Influence (in general)
Aries	Enthusiasm, energetic, proud, excitable, hasty, expedient, aggressive, courage, independent, competitive, self-willed, frank, outspoken, organizer, leader, fearless and aspiring, clever. The destiny of this sign is to Truth.
Taurus	Lethargy, self-indulgence, domestic, patient, steadfast, conservative, brooding, stubborn, discriminating, trustworthy, acquisitiveness, secret, cosmic law, practical, capable. The destiny of this sign is to Obedience.
Gemini	Humane, changeable, eloquent, sensitive, dextrous, inventive, democratic, analytical, superficial, restlessness, mental tension, reasoning, nervousness, communicative, impulsive, diffusive. The destiny of this sign is to Motive.
Cancer	Impressionable, psychic, imaginative, intuitive, domestic, self-sacrificing, versatile, reserved, artistic, sensitive, maternal, fanciful, romantic, highly emotional, tenacity, seek to be individualized, self-possessed and self-reliant. The destiny of this sign is to Power.
Leo	Ambitious, optimistic, challenging, generosity, affectionate, idealistic, vain, illusory, autocratic, forceful, highly magnetic, ruling, love, impulsive to desire, firm, self-controlling, earnest. The destiny of this sign is to Harmony.
Virgo	Studious, ingenious, dextrous, methodical, skeptical, analytical, self-centered, service to others, melancholy, petty, recuperative, critical, materialistic, discriminative, retiring, ingenious, adaptable. The destiny of this sign is to Discrimination.

TABLE IX—ZODIACAL INFLUENCES (*CONTINUED*)

Sign	Influence (in general)
Libra	Egotism, changeable, romantic, imitative, tactful, fond of show, materialistic, jealousy, persuasive, seeks equilibrium, intuitive, amenable, inspirational and perceptive, compassionate. The destiny of this sign is to Balance.
Scorpio	Altruistic, penetrating, temperamental, sarcastic, imaginative, revengeful, secretive, emotional extremes, scientific, uncompromising, sensuality, judgmental, dignified, affable, courteous, determined, reserved, tenacious. The destiny of this sign is to Regeneration.
Sagittarius	Progressive, frank, philosophic, ambition, adventurous, jovial, amiable, idealistic, impersonal, petulant, irritable, exacting, pursuing higher thoughts, ideals, frank, honest, prophetic, liberty, impressionable. The destiny of this sign is Law.
Capricorn	Inhibition, unforgiving, cold, concentrative, domineering, thinker, fatalistic, moody, calculating, industrious, arduous, self-conscious, avaricious, deceptive, calm, contemplation. The destiny of this sign is Service.
Aquarius	Intellectual, independent, profound, vivacious, gentle, changeable, unconventional, temperamental, worrying, honest, integrity, studious, thoughtful, imaginative, discriminative. The destiny of this sign is Humanity.
Pisces	Repressed, sensitive, impressionable, devoted, melancholic, introspective, lacking confidence, emotional, chameleon, self-esteem or approbation, sensationalist, traveler, medium, fastidious, psychic. The destiny of this sign is Spirituality.

There are also the geomantic vibrations that are put into action when the chess pieces move over the chessboard. The geomantic influence will show the more earthly, mundane result to the matter being divined.

In the diagrams of the chessboards (figs. 32–35 on pages 22–25), you see in each square a geomantic symbol associated with that square. You will also note that each angle of each board repeats the 16 geomantic figures. Table X (pages 248–9) shows the geomantic figures and gives the names applied to them and their associations.[1] In Table XI (pages 250–265), the basic influence of these figures in each of the elemental angles of all four Enochian chessboards is shown. The meanings given in this table are only general influences and are to be reversed, balanced or emphasized, depending on the circumstances of the piece influencing the square in question.

---

1. For more detailed study on this subject, read *The Oracle of Geomancy* by Stephen Skinner, *Divination by Geomancy* by Stephen Skinner, *A Practical Guide to Geomantic Divination* by Israel Regardie and *The Golden Dawn,* vol. 4, bk. 8, by Israel Regardie.

TABLE X—GEOMANTIC FIGURES AND ASSOCIATIONS

Figure	Name	Meaning	Element	Planet	Zodiac Sign
	Puer	Boy	Fire	Mars	Aries
	Amissio	Loss	Earth	Venus	Taurus
	Albus	White	Air	Mercury	Gemini
	Populus	People	Water	Moon	Cancer
	Fortuna Major	Greater fortune	Fire	Sun	Leo
	Conjunctio	Conjunction	Earth	Mercury	Virgo
	Puella	Girl	Air	Venus	Libra
	Rubeus	Red	Water	Mars	Scorpio

TABLE X—GEOMANTIC FIGURES AND ASSOCIATIONS (*continued*)

Figure	Name	Meaning	Element	Planet	Zodiac Sign
(geomantic figure)	Acquisitio	Acquisition	Fire	Jupiter	Sagittarius
(geomantic figure)	Carcer	Prison	Earth	Saturn	Capricorn
(geomantic figure)	Tristitia	Sadness	Air	Saturn	Aquarius
(geomantic figure)	Laetitia	Joy	Water	Jupiter	Pisces
(geomantic figure)	Cauda Draconis	Tail of the dragon	Fire	Saturn and Mars	Cauda draconis
(geomantic figure)	Caput Draconis	Head of the dragon	Earth	Venus and Jupiter	Caput draconis
(geomantic figure)	Fortuna minor	Lesser fortune	Fire	Sun	Leo
(geomantic figure)	Via	Way	Water	Moon	Cancer

TABLE XI—GEOMANTIC INFLUENCES IN THE ELEMENTAL ANGLES
OF THE ENOCHIAN CHESSBOARDS

Fire Board, Fire Angle	
Via	The love is great, but will cause great jealousy.
Acquisitio	A sincere love from an upright heart.
Puella	This person/situation is whimsical and changeable.
Conjunctio	He or she wishes to be yours this moment.
Tristitia	Await the time and you will find the results great.
Albus	You can trust this person's actions to be true to his or her heart.
Caput Draconis	The person loves you sincerely.
Fortuna Major	The person has a great love for you but wishes to conceal it.
Fortuna Minor	You had better decline any offer, for it is neither constant nor true.
Cauda Draconis	This action comes from an upright and sincere heart.
Rubeus	Decline a situation which may be your destruction.
Laetitia	You love/regard a person who does not speak well of you.
Carcer	Their love/motive is false to you.
Puer	This is true and constant; forsake it not.
Amissio	Avoid this situation.
Populus	This is from the heart and will continue until death.

TABLE XI—GEOMANTIC INFLUENCES IN THE ELEMENTAL ANGLES
OF THE ENOCHIAN CHESSBOARDS (*CONTINUED*)

Fire Board, Water Angle	
Via	What you wish for, you will shortly obtain.
Acquisitio	Whatever your desires are, for the present decline them.
Puella	If you are not extravagant, your efforts will be rewarded.
Conjunctio	You may have distress if you do not alter your attitude or intentions.
Tristitia	You may obtain your wishes by means of a friend.
Albus	Your efforts are in vain. Time to wait.
Caput Draconis	No.
Fortuna Major	Yes.
Fortuna Minor	The direction to go will not be obstructed.
Cauda Draconis	Change your tactics and you will do well.
Rubeus	Success.
Laetitia	You will quickly obtain what you want.
Carcer	Be happy with what you have achieved.
Puer	This is not the time to expect success.
Amissio	Requests will be granted.
Populus	It is someone else's turn for success.

TABLE XI—GEOMANTIC INFLUENCES IN THE ELEMENTAL ANGLES
OF THE ENOCHIAN CHESSBOARDS *(CONTINUED)*

Fire Board, Air Angle	
Via	You will obtain better luck elsewhere.
Acquisitio	Remain among your friends and you will do well.
Puella	There is gain in foreign areas.
Conjunctio	Remain with what you know and you will avoid difficulties.
Tristitia	It is safe to move on and make your intentions known.
Albus	Stay with those of like mind and there will be no opposition.
Caput Draconis	Travel out and enjoy yourself.
Fortuna Major	Success in ventures and relationships.
Fortuna Minor	If you plan ahead you will succeed as you desire.
Cauda Draconis	While traveling watch out for evil people.
Rubeus	A stranger may enhance your fortune.
Laetitia	Draw upon your current resources, rely only upon those you know and trust.
Carcer	You can dwell abroad with comfort and happiness.
Puer	This is not a time to move forward or make new contacts.
Amissio	Be prepared for changes and people changing their tactics.
Populus	Travel in groups. It is a majority decision.

TABLE XI—GEOMANTIC INFLUENCES IN THE ELEMENTAL ANGLES
OF THE ENOCHIAN CHESSBOARDS *(CONTINUED)*

Fire Board, Earth Angle	
Via	You will meet an attractive person.
Acquisitio	A prosperous partner/acquaintance influences the situation.
Puella	A virtuous person may be influenced.
Conjunctio	Marriage and respectability.
Tristitia	There is wealth in a situation.
Albus	This person/situation may be of help but is very volatile.
Caput Draconis	It is profitable to enter into a matter.
Fortuna Major	Success is to be expected.
Fortuna Minor	Only partial success.
Cauda Draconis	There is honesty but no wealth.
Rubeus	This situation/person could be self-destructing.
Laetitia	A worthy undertaking and good fortune.
Carcer	With integrity you may succeed.
Puer	There is a union with an equal.
Amissio	An uncomfortable union.
Populus	There is difficulty in co-operation from others.

TABLE XI—GEOMANTIC INFLUENCES IN THE ELEMENTAL ANGLES OF THE ENOCHIAN CHESSBOARDS (CONTINUED)

Water Board, Fire Angle	
Via	What has gone will not return as soon as expected.
Acquisitio	There is no return.
Puella	An unexpected happening.
Conjunctio	Circumstances delay a situation.
Tristitia	Answers come bringing joy.
Albus	There is absence of an essential item/person, preventing a full result.
Caput Draconis	An abundance of help is given.
Fortuna Major	Success will depend on one's conduct.
Fortuna Minor	Matters come about slowly.
Cauda Draconis	This is a no-win situation.
Rubeus	Watch for illness, as it may delay.
Laetitia	Stranger(s) will come and influence the end result.
Carcer	There is joy in order.
Puer	There is another love elsewhere.
Amissio	Unforeseen circumstances cause a delay.
Populus	Gatherings of friends.

Table XI—Geomantic Influences in the Elemental Angles of the Enochian Chessboards (*Continued*)

Water Board, Water Angle	
Via	Happiness between people.
Acquisitio	Trouble and sorrow.
Puella	Someone may do you a favor.
Conjunctio	There is plenty for everyone. There may be a wedding.
Tristitia	To accomplish your pursuits, you must first clear the obstacles.
Albus	There are others who will endeavor to obstruct you.
Caput Draconis	Be prepared for sadness and danger.
Fortuna Major	You will soon be away from the influence of your enemies.
Fortuna Minor	There is a change for the better.
Cauda Draconis	Misfortune threatens you, but it can be prevented.
Rubeus	You may be out of your depth. Watch for deceit.
Laetitia	You will get money.
Carcer	There may be sexual involvement.
Puer	Sorrow will depart.
Amissio	Matters begin to grow and improve.
Populus	Be very careful and matters may go wrong.

TABLE XI—GEOMANTIC INFLUENCES IN THE ELEMENTAL ANGLES
OF THE ENOCHIAN CHESSBOARDS *(CONTINUED)*

Water Board, Air Angle	
Via	The situation may improve, but only for a short while.
Acquisitio	Circumstances are doubtful.
Puella	There is lasting recovery.
Conjunctio	Be prepared for the worst.
Tristitia	Prepare for change while you can.
Albus	Matters of the Spirit become of importance.
Caput Draconis	Good health is expected.
Fortuna Major	It is doubtful as to whether one's health/situation will recover.
Fortuna Minor	There is now no danger.
Cauda Draconis	It is time to enter into an activity that will improve your health.
Rubeus	Forces beyond our control are at work.
Laetitia	Relief from difficulties.
Carcer	Religious convictions.
Puer	A situation will be finished or left.
Amissio	Time to make improvements.
Populus	Support from others is necessary.

TABLE XI—GEOMANTIC INFLUENCES IN THE ELEMENTAL ANGLES
OF THE ENOCHIAN CHESSBOARDS *(CONTINUED)*

Water Board, Earth Angle	
Via	Commence your travels, as others will attend to matters as you wish.
Acquisitio	Too many things need doing first.
Puella	You will be prosperous on a journey.
Conjunctio	Unless you can be assisted, you might not succeed.
Tristitia	Any move now will be an advancement.
Albus	Your answer comes from within.
Caput Draconis	Be confident and you will proceed safely.
Fortuna Major	Home and security become of importance.
Fortuna Minor	Make your intentions known and take a step forward.
Cauda Draconis	Turn down any offers for now.
Rubeus	There is protection in your travels.
Laetitia	Your efforts are in vain.
Carcer	Be prudent in your endeavors and you will prosper.
Puer	Watch out for danger from another.
Amissio	Proceed with caution.
Populus	There may be a short journey.

TABLE XI—GEOMANTIC INFLUENCES IN THE ELEMENTAL ANGLES
OF THE ENOCHIAN CHESSBOARDS (*CONTINUED*)

Air Board, Fire Angle	
Via	There is a son, wealth and honor.
Acquisitio	There is a daughter.
Puella	This person/situation will endure.
Conjunctio	Two people may influence the situation.
Tristitia	This is time to be forward and not backward.
Albus	Although attractive, this person is annoying.
Caput Draconis	Going out to learn—education.
Fortuna Major	Pay attention to these circumstances; if overlooked there may be trouble.
Fortuna Minor	Your children will be dutiful.
Cauda Draconis	This person will honor and respect you.
Rubeus	You will have what you want.
Laetitia	This situation is weak and may not last.
Carcer	The situation is healthy and contained.
Puer	Refine your manner.
Amissio	Reproduction.
Populus	Children.

TABLE XI—GEOMANTIC INFLUENCES IN THE ELEMENTAL ANGLES
OF THE ENOCHIAN CHESSBOARDS *(CONTINUED)*

Air Board, Water Angle	
Via	Others may beat you to the mark.
Acquisitio	Everything comes at once; you will need help.
Puella	It is meant for you to be happy and successful.
Conjunctio	There is no luck. Success only through effort.
Tristitia	You are being held back from success at present.
Albus	Trust in destiny.
Caput Draconis	Your expectations are vain.
Fortuna Major	Be careful; your fortune may be changed into misfortune.
Fortuna Minor	Keep trying; you will succeed.
Cauda Draconis	You may meet sorrow and trouble.
Rubeus	It will work out better than expected.
Laetitia	Success.
Carcer	Difficult times are leaving.
Puer	Depend on your merit and integrity.
Amissio	Success is coming, be patient.
Populus	Misfortune through others.

TABLE XI—GEOMANTIC INFLUENCES IN THE ELEMENTAL ANGLES OF THE ENOCHIAN CHESSBOARDS (CONTINUED)

Air Board, Air Angle	
Via	This person exceeds all others in every respect.
Acquisitio	The one close to you pretends.
Puella	There is sincerity between people.
Conjunctio	Plan everything carefully and don't rely on others.
Tristitia	This person can be relied on.
Albus	Watch your back.
Caput Draconis	This person is sincere while there is gain for him or her.
Fortuna Major	Secret enemy.
Fortuna Minor	Valuable friend.
Cauda Draconis	There is inconsistency and deceit.
Rubeus	Brothers in arms.
Laetitia	There is ruthlessness in business.
Carcer	Ideas must be put into perspective.
Puer	There are double meanings to everything.
Amissio	Respect this situation; it operates according to true will.
Populus	Cause for sorrow if you are completely trusting.

TABLE XI—GEOMANTIC INFLUENCES IN THE ELEMENTAL ANGLES
OF THE ENOCHIAN CHESSBOARDS (*CONTINUED*)

Air Board, Earth Angle	
Via	This day will bring increase of happiness.
Acquisitio	This day is not very lucky.
Puella	You will be safe if careful.
Conjunctio	Think for everyone else to avoid misfortune, as they are not thinking clearly.
Tristitia	Prepare everything carefully.
Albus	Do not act now; draw up your plans first.
Caput Draconis	Beware—there is opposition.
Fortuna Major	Change your plans for today to avoid bad luck.
Fortuna Minor	It may be difficult to escape problems today.
Cauda Draconis	Cheer up; matters are getting better.
Rubeus	Avoid arguments.
Laetitia	Be reconciled; your circumstances will shortly mend.
Carcer	In spite of obstacles, you should do well.
Puer	It will all work in your favor.
Amissio	Success is almost near.
Populus	Gatherings of people can bring misfortune.

TABLE XI—GEOMANTIC INFLUENCES IN THE ELEMENTAL ANGLES
OF THE ENOCHIAN CHESSBOARDS *(CONTINUED)*

Earth Board, Fire Angle	
Via	Release from restriction.
Acquisitio	Releasing the hold of others over you.
Puella	Suffer now, honor later.
Conjunctio	Death of a matter—sorrow.
Tristitia	With great struggle there is a small gain.
Albus	There may be no freedom in this matter.
Caput Draconis	Breaking free.
Fortuna Major	Sorrow and anxiety are great, and answers are uncertain.
Fortuna Minor	Liberty and freedom.
Cauda Draconis	The sacrifice may be too great this time.
Rubeus	After a long ordeal there will be success.
Laetitia	Answers come soon.
Carcer	A prisoner.
Puer	Another may limit your movements.
Amissio	There are those who will show compassion.
Populus	The people will have a say in this matter.

TABLE XI—GEOMANTIC INFLUENCES IN THE ELEMENTAL ANGLES
OF THE ENOCHIAN CHESSBOARDS (*CONTINUED*)

Earth Board, Water Angle	
Via	By perseverance, you will recover the situation.
Acquisitio	Bear your loss with fortitude.
Puella	You property or possessions may be lost.
Conjunctio	You may recover stolen property through the efforts of another.
Tristitia	Those who have done wrong will be punished.
Albus	Although you may lose, the other party may suffer the most.
Caput Draconis	Property is found; there is gain.
Fortuna Major	The odds against you are too great.
Fortuna Minor	These odds can be overcome.
Cauda Draconis	The end of a matter.
Rubeus	Work alone in this matter.
Laetitia	Wait.
Carcer	The authorities intervene.
Puer	Do not expect to regain the past.
Amissio	You may succeed, but this will be through trouble and expense.
Populus	An organization or group of people has an influence.

TABLE XI—GEOMANTIC INFLUENCES IN THE ELEMENTAL ANGLES
OF THE ENOCHIAN CHESSBOARDS (*CONTINUED*)

Earth Board, Air Angle	
Via	Through careful thought you can find some answers.
Acquisitio	Relationships may not work.
Puella	Prosperity.
Conjunctio	It is not time for gain.
Tristitia	Do not delay—happiness.
Albus	It is time to move fast to achieve results.
Caput Draconis	By entering into an agreement, your happiness will be ensured.
Fortuna Major	This may be more than you can handle.
Fortuna Minor	All will work out well.
Cauda Draconis	Do not enter into any agreement, as it will not last.
Rubeus	This is a union which will add to your welfare.
Laetitia	This situation may bring poverty. Be discrete.
Carcer	Your peace may be destroyed.
Puer	Work alone; you need your freedom.
Amissio	If you wish to be happy, do not marry this person.
Populus	This course of direction will not answer your expectations.

TABLE XI—GEOMANTIC INFLUENCES IN THE ELEMENTAL ANGLES
OF THE ENOCHIAN CHESSBOARDS (*CONTINUED*)

Earth Board, Earth Angle	
Via	Great gain.
Acquisitio	Doubling your success.
Puella	What you seek you will receive.
Conjunctio	Great fortune is coming; be patient.
Tristitia	Loss.
Albus	Decline any offers and you will be okay.
Caput Draconis	Be faithful.
Fortuna Major	Time to put more work into a matter.
Fortuna Minor	Success will be trivial.
Cauda Draconis	Tie up loose ends first.
Rubeus	Unexpected gain.
Laetitia	Someone may cheat you.
Carcer	Be happy; prosperity is assured.
Puer	Deal fairly with others and they will repay your efforts.
Amissio	Providence will support good causes.
Populus	Be wise and careful. If it is for the gain of the people, it will be successful.

In addition to the foregoing influences in the squares, you must not forget the Tarot and elemental associations, although these would be the last things to consider. The other associations tend to cover the general meanings that the Tarot and elements can provide.

Divining the Timing of Events

To foretell how long a matter will take place, depicted by a divination game, is very difficult. The following methods may be of help.

1. The elements: Fire = very swift, Air = swift, Water = moderate speed, Earth = slow.

2. The triplicities: The Cardinal signs (Aries, Cancer, Libra and Capricorn) show matters moving rapidly with great power—hours or days. The Fixed signs (Taurus, Scorpio, Aquarius and Leo) show matters that endure—months or years. The Mutable signs (Gemini, Virgo, Sagittarius and Pisces) show fluctuation in times, not so quick but not enduring—days to weeks.

3. You can time when attacking forces will be weakest or strongest according to current celestial planetary transits, concentrating on the astrological symbols.

4. No-move dice throws as in Rule 17.3.

5. Relate the planetary movement to the querent's natal horoscope and plot the movement through the natal houses. Although an actual planet may be in a sign for many days, months or years, the signs move through the houses every two hours throughout a day (24-hour period). In view of this, one could calculate when a sign that holds a particular planet passes through a specific house on a specific day. I would not advise that this method be attempted by those not adept at astrology.

Direct, Indirect Action

Direct action is obvious, as when you see a piece move and directly threaten, defend or capture another piece. Indirect action is seen when a piece is the instigator or collaborator in causing difficulty to an opponent but does not itself bring out the direct action. These actions on the chessboards are also reflected in daily life, in situations affecting the querent or his or her question.

Significator

It is reasonably clear at this point that the querent's King and the Ptah Square and Ptah are significators in their own right. The King is representative of the most spiritual aspect of the querent, dealing with the querent's self-awareness, or just awareness. It is the Sun of the querent and is the power of creative self-expression.

The Ptah Square has already been discussed, so I will not go any further into that subject, other than to say that the combination of the querent's King and the Ptah Square in the last round of play gives a "nowness" to each new moment. It is a way in which one actively merges with life in the outer and inner worlds, and an aspect of personal destiny.

In all readings, however, there must be one other chess piece that will act as a Significator and represent the querent or question "in the material." Any action of or to that piece should be observed by the diviner as an incident of great importance. In fact, the Significator is of next most importance after the querent's King.

The Significator can be found in many ways, all of which you should be able to identify through the previous reference text and tables; that is, by:

1. The planetary nature of the divination question

2. Archetype/personality of querent, if querent is to play a major role in the events

3. Archetype/personality of the person concerned in the divination

4. Planetary ruler of the person's ascendent (from his or her horoscope)

5. Planetary ruler of the house/sign to which the question relates

6. Chess piece most representative of the matter in hand

Chess Piece Relationships and Movements

Throughout the game, chess pieces will be influencing each other either beneficially or negatively. These relationships become important points in your divination analysis, for these relationships describe the type of dynamism or harmony in the matter concerned.

Ideal relationships are energy releasing and form maintaining. Such effects between chess pieces create a synthesis of complementary energy. Let us look at some of these.

Take the energy release of a dynamic relationship, for example. This occurs when allied pieces cover (protect) each other and both (or one, that of the querent) is placed in a cardinal-sign square. This would signify, modified by the nature of the pieces and squares involved, restlessness, tremendous urges towards action, starting new activities and/or pursuing a definite direction. If this relationship is between one of the querent's pieces (or one of his or her ally's pieces) that sits in a cardinal square and an opponent piece on another square, and neither captures the other, it would depict a crisis or issue being faced but not resolved. How the pieces move after that moment shows how the matter will be dealt with.

If one of the querent's or ally's pieces is on a fixed sign and shows some form of a protecting or threatening relationship with another friendly piece, this would describe deeply ingrained habit patterns, extremely concentrated power or stubborn willfulness. If the relationship is with an opponent's piece, however, it would show energy beginning to flow, opening up a wide range of capabilities, and determination that may bring matters to a conclusion.

Mutable signs would show energy release through mental channels, with the input of other factors to a situation, and a need for change and new things.

Where a piece blocks another from movement, restrictions are placed on a matter. Where blocks are purposeful to protect a piece, it alludes to the nature of its actual action.

When a chess piece is captured and taken off the board, you must observe the type of piece that is captured together with what piece captured it, what strength the piece held before its capture and any effects caused by removing the captured piece from the board. For example, if your ally removed an opponent piece, you would understand in your divination that some help is being given. If your ally loses its piece through capture in its attempt to help you, your help is being eliminated. If your own pieces are caught where, if the throw of die had been different, help could have come, it may show that people or circumstances turned against you, or that the forces in a situation lose the power to work to your advantage.

A King capture of any King except that of the querent shows the removal of powerful forces that may have been for or against the querent. If the querent's King is captured, the querent would have been unsuccessful in his or her efforts, or perhaps changed his or her mind. The results are all very dependent upon what is happening in the game.

Circumstances are realized when a piece captures another but does not get captured itself, usually in the querent's favor if a querent or ally piece is the captor.

When a querent or ally piece captures an opponent piece, landing on the square whereupon the opponent sits, it shows the culmination of a point or matter within the divination, or the removal of a factor. It may show a new move or factor entering a situation. New impulses are carried out in previous activities. The importance or unimportance of the factor would depend on the context of the whole game.

If any opponent piece captures a querent's piece or an ally's piece, a situation arises where there is an inability to compromise, a painful reaction to criticism or a case of revealed vulnerability. The reaction thereof, and to what, would depend on the pieces and squares involved. It is a very tense situation when a piece threatens a capture but finds that its target is protected by one or more pieces.

A risky venture or questionable behavior pattern is recognized when a piece willfully moves into danger of being captured. But, if forced to move into such a position, the situation is not risky or questionable. Factors beyond one's control do not work in favor of the querent. It shows dissatisfaction, unease, a time to meet and assimilate experiences.

If a querent's or ally's piece moves into a position where it threatens another piece but finds itself also threatened by that piece, or by another piece, it shows the querent (or the divined matter) moving into areas without foresight or where there is a lack of control. If the opponents find themselves in any difficulty, the reverse occurs, where the situation turns in favor of the querent: it shows opposing elements making mistakes or having weaknesses.

Where the game play flows with ease and without conflict, hope is built for conditions; beneficial influences and spontaneous activity are shown. Where the game play flows with ease but with some conflict or obstruction, it shows the formation of matters wherein advantage can be taken of environmental opportunities for growth and development. This can also happen when a piece or pieces of the same element moves into squares that cover a threatened ally, or a piece of the same element. This is a relationship of creativity.

Pieces withdrawing from a difficult matter where they are the aggressors show willful removal of force. Where they are the victims, it shows a timely retreat or maneuver. Where it was an advancing piece or a piece strategically placed that withdrew, it shows delays in a matter, or matters which must be considered more carefully before any action takes place.

As you can see from the examples above, the reading of circumstances is very easy, because they can be likened to the actual events on the chessboard during divination play.

In the divination game, from a planetary perspective, the above also applies. A piece that threatens or acts as the aggressor is usually representative of the planet affecting matters as a dominating influence, and the associations of the square it occupies are therefore also applied.

When houses such as the first, second, third, tenth, eleventh and twelfth predominate, you will see more personal and self-determined activities. When the fourth, fifth, sixth, seventh, eighth and ninth houses predominate, you will find activities may be influenced by others in some way.

Queen moves usually show definite events, especially when a Queen moves from one element to another. The elemental angles will also have an influence on your divination game. Fire shows matters of action, and Water shows reflection, emotion and reaction. Air shows planning, relationships and changes, while Earth shows awareness of immediate concerns, work and the practical formation of matters.

Table VII (page 241) shows the planetary strengths and weaknesses. Look at the piece that is influenced by the sign of the square where your piece sits, whether rulership, exaltation, detriment or fall. If the first piece affects the sign of the other piece in any manner, you will be able to tell how much influence your piece has in a situation. If the affecting piece rules or is exalted in the sign, your chess piece sits in good relationship with the other piece and the effect is harmonious and strong. If in detriment or fall, the effect is harmonious but weak. If, however, the relationship is threatening, the strength or weakness of the situation can be determined by the planetary influence of the sign of the square which your piece occupies. Your own piece's influence on that sign must also be taken into consideration.

For example, using the planetary and Zodiacal associations: a Mars piece in a Capricorn square threatened by a Saturn piece shows that caution and reserve will be overruled in a matter. This is because Mars is exalted in Capricorn and Saturn rules Capricorn, which brings more strength to the situation and therefore a greater struggle. It would also show, if for example Saturn were in an Aries square, a tendency for two people to quarrel.

Divination
Example

Q uestion: Will Russia revert to a type of democracy by or before the year 2005?[1]

Board used: Air Board
Play setting: Water of Air
Ptah Square: Capricorn—W4c
Game played: 23 Nov 1989

(Where there is a number followed by a dash, this shows the die number thrown but indicates "No Move.")

---

1. This game was played November 23, 1989. During the three years this book was at the publisher, events have overtaken the question: the independence of the Soviet Union satellite countries, the unification of Germany, and the ousting of Gorbachev as leader in Russia. Considering the attempted coup in 1993, the chess divination game as given here has been analyzing prophetically.

	W	F	E	A
1	N3c	N3c	P3c	3—
2	3—	P1c	NA3d	P4c
3	P1c	P4c	P2c	N3c
4	NF4d	R4a	P1c	P3dxEN
5	NA3dxAP	Q3a	P2d	P1c
6	B1b	P4d	R3b	B1b
7	K2a	P2c	Q3a	K2a
8	P3c	P1d	PF4axFR	P2c
9	K3b	Q1c	2—	N4a
10	B3d	Q3a	B1b	Q3c
11	BA3axAR	B1b	R2b	5—
12	NF4dxP	5—	PF3bxP	P2d
13	R2a	NW4bxP	RF4b	QE4c
14	BF2d	K2b	RF4a	QF4dxWN+
15	K4c: Ptah	NW2axR	P3d	NW2c

The answer appears to be "successful," but in view of the fact that pieces, both ally and opposition, still advanced and threatened and captured other pieces, one could assume that Russia will not fully achieve such a result within the time frame given. They will still be coping with friction and having to work on what was spoiled. Drawing to the end of this time span, a strong emphasis was placed in the game on Pisces and the 12th house: possible assassinations, unseen dangers, the populace looking to spiritual matters and religion, matters of the growth of society as a whole being of prime concern and hidden enemies; i.e., the "underground."

In the last moves, the Saturn influence in Aquarius (Earth Rook's pawn on E3d) is under tension from a Fire Moon influence in Aquarius (Fire Queen's pawn). Because these are pawns, you would look at the masses rather than individuals, and with the Aquarius influence, fulfillment of society's ideals, political and otherwise, come to the foreground. This all happens very slowly as government reform (Capricorn and 10th house), structure, service and labor is attended to, along with the health and well-being of the people (Air's last move of the Knight into a Virgo square, 6th house, from the Air Angle to the Water Angle).

The game moved relatively fast, however, with few "No Moves" to show time delays over the decade and a half. With this, one can assume that the final move of this game happens before the given date.[2]

Judging by the way the pieces are positioned at the end of the game, there will still be many restrictions imposed on the people and the country. Air's last move of Jupiter into Virgo, from Air to Water, showed erratic use of the armed forces. Or perhaps it may be describing the Jovian tendency to expansiveness conflicting with the Virgo influence of concentration on the part, and detail. This conflict may result in either overdoing matters or some improper treatment of some aspect of the matter. Employment may be unstable at this point due to people having more freedom to choose. Many may drift from one job to another. Disagreements may erupt. It appears that Russia will not be out of trouble yet.

From a general but nonrestrictive view, the Fire Angle represents the Kremlin and possibly the armed forces. The Air Angle represents the Communist Party, or perhaps allied forces of some kind. The Water Angle may represent the people, and authorities favoring the change, while the Earth Angle represents the economy and those in favor of the changeover who may be outside influences. Observe the Earth Bishop's pawn and how it penetrates the Kremlin, opening up for the Earth Rook and also eliminating some minor would-be opposition.

Most of the encounters throughout the game were handled directly and seemed very final. This could allude to the handling of satellite Eastern Bloc countries that will continue to turn away from Communism.

The Significator (the Water Knight) may represent Gorbachev, who played a direct role in solving problems effectively in his communications with the people (pawns). As shown a few months after this game was played, he tried to obtain a multiparty democracy, which was voted in. However, at the time of this writing, this multiparty democracy in Russia was yet to be proved as a working structure. Also, Gorbachev is removed before the final result by

---

2. This had in fact started to take place only months after my analysis of the game when the single-party system was voted out.

the Air Queen. The Queen also checks the Water King in that move, so this move and the loss of the Water Knight jeopardizes Russia's move into democracy. Taking into account the Queen's symbology, she could represent more than one possibility. One thing is for sure, though: the Air Queen has great significance. In a later divination game I played concerning Gorbachev, that same piece eliminated the querent's King, which in that particular case represented Gorbachev himself. That elimination stopped the game, showing that Gorbachev would not live or remain in power long enough to see the full results of his work.

Moves 5 and 8 show significant gains in some parts of Russia, perhaps satellite countries moving out of Communism. These moves could be showing gradual political changes in the satellite countries in the late 1980s to mid 1990s. Take for example East Germany's exploits, which may be described in the first few moves of the game. Throughout the game, it is clearly evident that the "people" seem to be controlling or taking a more active part in their country's politics.

At the time of writing this analysis, there had been conflicts between the Azerbaijans and Armenians. These, perhaps, are described by move 4, where the people take aggressive action (Mars moves from Water to the Fire Angle) for protection of their land and homes (Cancer square). The religious difficulties are shown by the Earth move of Chiron's pawn into a Libra square, putting it under a direct threat from Fire/Saturn's pawn in Scorpio. The Fire and Air moves show the Kremlin's reaction (Moon in Aquarius), where it sympathizes with the needs of humanity but in an impersonal manner. The Moon in Aquarius influence also shows the need of the people for freedom at any cost. Azerbaijan, by the way, is under the rule of Aquarius.

To give a fuller analysis of this particular divination question, I would have to be very familiar with Russia's internal politics, which I do not claim to be. Therefore, I will leave it up to the reader to look into this and compare what has happened since the writing of this text with the results of the divination game.

This of course poses an important point. To do a thorough analysis of an Enochian chess divination game, one would have to have a deep understanding of the subject matter of the "question"; for example, the subject of internal politics as above.

Part IV

Book of Fire

Training of the Adept

And in
the Beginning

In the Order of the Golden Dawn, once an initiate is put through the 5=6 grade, he or she will have become a member of the R.R. et A.C. and will be considered an adept. By this time, the adept will have been totally exposed to the Enochian Tablets and Tablet of Union and is ready to work with and learn Enochian magic. Within the system of Enochian magic is the magical system of Enochian chess. Up to this point in this book, you have learned the technical use of the Enochian chess game, tactically and for divination. These are the first two stages with which the adept must become familiar before any magical use of the chessboards and pieces can be discussed.

In this section I will discuss some points about using the Enochian chess sets and boards in an adept's training of the 5=6 grade of the R.R. et A.C., in addition to game play and divination. You will appreciate that what you are given here is in fact the methodology of magic and of Enochian chess. The real impetus and concepts must come from the individual, and rather than impose my own magical philosophy on this particular area I would seriously suggest some experimentation along the lines of the magical framework to which you are attuned.

Although I have written this book from a Golden Dawn perspective, I would actively encourage you to apply and experiment with your own inner concepts in this section of Enochian chess. If you are a beginner, I suggest you read this section but do not practice anything given until you have had a good grounding in occult sciences.

One of the first things an adept is advised when being introduced to Enochian chess is about the effects that playing with the fully colored boards and chess pieces (god-forms) may have on individuals. Over years of game play, I found that the Enochian chessboards affected individual players in different ways. For example, one player might be weak in playing the Air chess pieces but strong with the Fire and Water pieces and average with the Earth pieces. Another player might be strong in Fire, Air and Water but weak playing the Earth pieces. Various combinations arose in weaknesses and strengths playing one, two or more elements, no matter how experienced a player was. When an experienced player played the element angle that he or she was weak in against an inexperienced player who played the element angle that he or she was strong in, it was usually the inexperienced player that put the experienced player into difficulty.

After some thought, and inquiry into each individual's natal astrological chart, I found that their element weaknesses and strengths that were shown in Enochian chess game play paralleled their weakness and strengths in their natal charts. Take for example one who has no planets or major angles in Earth signs in her chart. This person would have great difficulty playing the Earth pieces no matter how good she was as a player. As another example, a person who was weak in the Air and Water elements in his birth chart: his efforts in playing the Air and Water Angles were weak compared to his method of play with the Fire and Earth Angles.

I experimented with this concept with the help of those individuals who played regular Enochian chess games in our Temple, by encouraging them to frequently play the element in which they were weakest whenever we got together for our regular chess games. I also included myself in this experiment. After a period of time, each individual became stronger in play until that person's skill in playing the weakest element matched his or her skill when playing the strongest element.

Now, naturally, you are going to say at this point, "Of course they would get better; don't we all after enough practice?" The difference here is, although we all become better players, those that did not force themselves as frequently as the others to play their weakest element, still had difficulty in playing that particular element as effectively as they played the other elements, irrespective of how experienced they had become in game play.

This strengthening also showed itself in each individual's daily life activities and psychological make-up, consciously and unconsciously. This was observed in their own experiences and by those around them. All influences appeared quite beneficial in a manner according to the particular element involved for each individual.

Playing Enochian chess, as seen above, does have a subconscious effect on the players. It is like a state of moving Zen, for in it you hit different levels of consciousness that can be likened to states of satori in Zen Buddhism.

The element boards have an even stronger influence on the players, so you can use the boards in the manner described above to strengthen an individual. Take for example those who lack a balance of Water in their natal chart compared to the other elements. The Water Board will be chosen, and the individual will be given the opportunity at different sessions to play each element on the Water Board. Where a weakness shows, he or she will repeat with that element until he or she feels stronger and more balanced.

For example, a weakness may show in the way a person operates the chess pieces. The pieces may always become bottled up and block each other, or they may be scattered all over the board, etc. A like weakness may also show in daily life, and if the individual finds better control throughout daily life, the strengthening will have taken effect. Remember, however, it is only considered a weakness (or, for want of a better word, irregularity) when a player plays obviously out of character with the set of pieces of a particular element or on a particular board.

I must warn you at this point that, if you have had a particularly emotional upset in your day, or one from the past that you have not resolved and find yourself brooding upon, do not play on the Water Board. You may find yourself out of control emotionally. The same advice applies to anything excessive, in activity, emotion or mentality/psychology. Do not play on any element board that emphasizes such a state. The chessboards emphasize; they do not de-emphasize. Choose a board that will counter the excess.

For example, if your mind is racing and will not settle, choose the Earth Board, not the Air Board. If you are depressed, choose the Fire Board, not the Water Board. If you are upset and cannot reason a matter out, choose the Air Board, not the Water or Fire Boards. Apply the same principle with the angle you play. In severe cases it is best not to get out your Enochian chess set at all. Leave it until you are calm and have more peace of mind. The colors of these boards play very subtly on one's psyche, and it is very easy to further unbalance an already vulnerable state of being.

Enochian chess should be perfectly safe under normal conditions and if used with respect and care. When you are not working specifically on an inherent irregularity, do not become attached to one particular element, choosing only that element to play. Give yourself constant variety, playing all elements. The Earth Board is the only element board that is suitable to play on constantly. To do the same on the Air, Fire or Water Boards would, in the long term, cause an imbalance.

There was one instance in my experience when a player preferred the Air Board and preferred to play either the Air or Fire Angle. He was already overbalanced in favor of the Air element in his make-up, as shown in his natal chart. It did not take him long to become temporarily quite psychotic. This sort of thing can be rectified by a game or two on the Earth Board (which in this instance was the course taken), or keep the individual away from Enochian chess and the Enochian Tablets altogether for a while until normality returns. Even in mild cases, psychological help may be necessary. My suggestion is to use all of the latter methods. First rebalance the individual with the appropriate element, then remove contact with the Enochian system for a while, and if necessary seek help from a professional or someone who knows what they are doing.

Do not forget that a fully colored Enochian chessboard is not a mere chessboard. It is a board from which a very powerful magical current of energy is produced, and this vital difference can have a major effect on an individual's psyche. Even if there were no magical emphasis whatsoever, and the individuals were playing on the colored chessboards, the effect of the multi-colored squares on a person's subconscious would still be considerable. Coupled with the magical current coming through the Tablets, one can generate a great deal of energy in a game.

Within the Inner Order of the Golden Dawn (the R.R. et A.C.), the trained adept is exposed to these Tablets during ritual. Thus he or she gradually gets used to harmonizing with the forces that come through the Tablets so that, when an Enochian chess game is played, the individual's aura is in empathy with the relevant board being played.

You are probably wondering at this stage what effect playing a chess game may have on an individual who has never used the Tablets before in his or her life. The answer here is twofold. Some people will feel no difference whatsoever, as their senses will close down and they will play the game merely as a chess game. Anything that takes place will take place on a subtle subconscious level. Other people will find that they open up to the energies of the chessboards and must therefore be very careful to control that energy. I do not think I have ever found the in-between category when playing Enochian chess. Over the years, I have played a number of games with people who have no connection with magic whatsoever, other than the love of the game, and they seem to fall only into the above two categories. However, I have found it best to operate on the safe side and only use the Earth Board for such people.

By now you will be aware of the different divinatory and esoteric systems of symbolism applied to the chessboards. There is another point of observation which must not be overlooked, and that is numerology. First, there is the numerological comparison to the Chinese system of prophecy, the *I Ching*. In the *I Ching* there are eight trigrams, comparable to the eight squares across and down each board. If you multiply eight times eight, you will get 64, which is the number of *I Ching* hexagrams made up by the eight trigrams. Sixty-four is also the number of squares on a chessboard.

Playing with numbers a bit further and using the Kabbalistic system of association with numbers from the Tree of Life:

Eight is the number of Mercury and Hod. Note that 8 x 8 = 64, which is the number of Isis. Also, 64 = 6 + 4 = 10 (Malkuth), and 1 + 0 = 1 (Kether). The number four seems to play a major role. Four is also the number of Jupiter and Chesed. There are four boards, four sets of chess pieces, four pawns per set, four main playing pieces per set and four Kings to a board, each governing an angle, making up four elemental angles per board. You can see that 4 x 4 x 4 = 64 x 4 = 256, which makes up the total pyramid squares in all the four element boards, and each pyramid square has four pyramid faces. As for 256: 2 = dual creation (Chokmah) of 5 = feminine power (Geburah) and 6 = Sun, masculine power (Tiphareth). Note that 2 + 5 + 6 = 13 = 1 + 3 = 4. Now 3 = Saturn and Binah, 4 = Man—construction. Four also is the equal division of a circle. A circle is 360 degrees. If you divide it up equally into four, you get 90-degree divisions: 90 = 9 + 0 = 9, and (360) 3 + 6 + 0 = 9, which is the number of Yesod and the Moon. Four 90-degree right angles construct a square (our boards). A square is four sided; 4 yields a numerical parity to perimeter and area when used as the dimension of the sides of a square: perimeter = 4 + 4 + 4 + 4 = 16 and area = 4 x 4 = 16. And 16 is the number of Osiris risen. Also, 6 + 1 = 7, the number of Venus, Netzach and Set, and 16 = 1, which is the light of Kether shining through 6. In one angle of a board there are 16 squares: four across and four down. In the numbers 4 and 16 is the building block of human predomination of thought and design.

The letters of Tetragrammaton (YHVH)[1] are used as the formula for the design of the chessboards. Out of these four letters there are 24 different permutations;[2] however, if one treats the H and the H'[3] as the same, there will then be only 12 permutations. Now the number 12 has always been a notable number and highly esteemed by most nations of antiquity. The 12 permutations were considered by the ancient Hebrew teachings to be the 12 Banners of YHVH and were associated with the 12 Biblical tribes of Israel, which in turn were attributed to the 12 signs of the Zodiac.

Out of the 12 permutations, only four are used for the formula of the Enochian Tablets because these four are the only permutations that go sequentially forwards and backwards without changing their pattern; i.e., between each masculine letter (Y and V), there is a feminine letter (H or H'). In the other permutations you will find combinations of feminine or masculine letters together and undivided by its opposite. The Zodiac signs attributed to these four permutations are the Cardinal signs of the Zodiac, and the four permutations appear four times, once on each of the element boards.

YHVH = Aries and the tribe of Gad, and is shown as the formula for the Fire of Earth, Fire of Fire, Fire of Water and Fire of Air Angles.

HVHY = Cancer and the tribe of Issachar, and is shown as the formula for the Water of Water, Water of Air, Earth of Earth and Earth of Fire Angles.

---

1. See the "Book of Berashith" in the *Zohar* for further information.

2. See *The Kabbalah Unveiled* by MacGregor Mathers.

3. The term H' describes the Hebrew letter "Heh final."

VHYH = Libra and the tribe of Asshur, and is shown as the formula for the Air of Air, Air of Water, Air of Earth and Air of Fire Angles.

HYHV = Capricorn and the tribe of Zebulun, and is shown as the formula for the Earth of Air, Earth of Water, Water of Earth and Water of Fire Angles.

If you treat the H and H' as different letters, you will end up with eight permutations in which the letters run sequentially, but you will still only have the four tribes associated, two combinations per tribe. The eight gives the eight different play settings. Eight as a number is noted as the "first cube of energy" and is considered an evenly even number representing "Universal Harmony." So one may assume at this point that each play setting is a cube of energy, or the first impetus of a game.

By studying the chessboards, you will see that out of the 16 angles of the four element boards, 12 angles are associated with the Zodiacal signs and the remaining four with the four elements. In addition, the element angle that is the same element as the board is the greater angle of that board. When looking back at the four permutations, you will see by reading them in the correct directions[4] that the greater angle of each board has the permutation attributed to that same element. Here one can see that Aries would rule the Fire Board, Cancer the Water Board, Libra the Air Board and Capricorn the Earth Board, irrespective of the Zodiac sign attributed to the actual angle.

These rulerships are merely token however, for each chess square (Servient Square) has its own rulerships and external influences which act thereon. To understand the Servient Squares in more depth, look back to the layout of the Enochian Tablets and the Calvary Crosses in each quarter of each Tablet. An influencing force on a Servient Square is observed through the relationship that the square has with the Calvary Cross of its quarter by column and rank.

---

4. See fig. 9, p. 28.

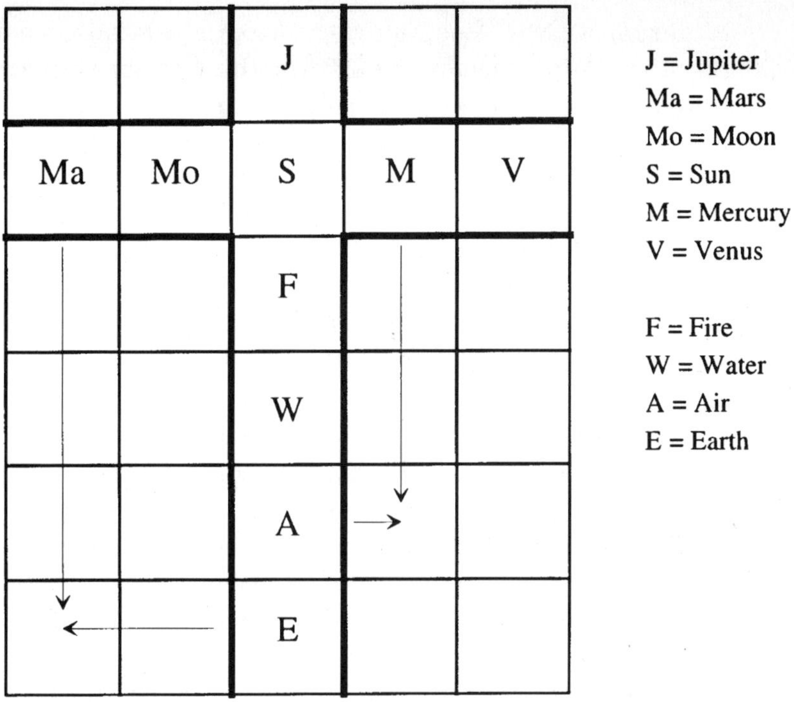

		J			
Ma	Mo	S	M	V	
		F			
		W			
		A	→		
←		E			

J = Jupiter
Ma = Mars
Mo = Moon
S = Sun
M = Mercury
V = Venus

F = Fire
W = Water
A = Air
E = Earth

FIGURE 50—INFLUENCING FORCES FROM CALVARY CROSS

The four planets involved are Mars, Moon, Mercury and Venus, and these planets represent specific principles of energy exchange between the individual squares and the elements from the column of the Calvary Cross. Since there are four elements, each planet has four possible vibrations that it can produce, but only one vibration per Servient Square under its dominion. Each planet will reveal a type of outgoing energy together with an urge toward expression of a certain kind, but it also reveals a specific need for activity and fulfillment which is fed along a particular vibratory wavelength.[5] The vibratory wavelength is used as a catalyst to the vibration of the Servient Square's Zodiacal sign and other attributions. From this the function of a Servient Square becomes more evident. Take for example figure 50 above.

5. I assume that you are now familiar with the vibratory influences of the planets and elements.

In this diagram we will focus on the bottom left-hand corner pyramid square. As you see by the arrows, this Servient Square is influenced by Mars and the element of Earth (Geburah and Earth element in Malkuth). If we were looking at the third square on the second rank, the influence would be Mercury and the Air element (Hod and Air element in Malkuth). The Sun in the center of the Cross has its influence through the Zodiac signs as attributed to the Servient Squares. Jupiter is an outer planet and not included as a force directly through the Servient Squares. It works indirectly through the Kerubic Squares. When analyzing a divination game, therefore, you should also take into account the Calvary Cross influence on the chessboards.

As a structure, the pyramid system of the Tablets is much like Eastern mandalas, though infinitely more complex. Being based on the quarternary (four elements), the pyramid formation and structure gives birth to the quinary by the truncated top (Spirit). This can relate in terms of Eastern philosophy to the five stages of human consciousness. An individual pyramid can relate to a part of the Universe in microcosm. With this in view, it is advised that you do not work with the "part" but first construct the "whole"; that is, the full set of Enochian Tablets should be constructed. Through the virtue of your effort in constructing them, you will be integrating yourself into the system through a systematic process of the nucleus of self.

The Enochian chessboards, though only part of the Tablets, can be used magically similarly to the Tablets. However, when working with the Enochian system, I would suggest only the following practices be used in conjunction with the chessboards. Any other method, for example pyramid workings, etc., should be worked with the Tablets.

1. Invocation—God-form assumption or deity association with the chess pieces. Invocation of the Angle of the Ptah, as this piece takes place of the "I," the innermost part of yourself.

2. Evocation of the god-forms and of the energy within the pyramid square that they preside over. Evocation of an external entity to help strengthen your perception during game play.

Before an adept can activate any of these methods, she[6] must first integrate in her psyche a binding of all the associations of the Enochian system—or, at least, of the particular element Tablet, its hierarchies and associations, which she will be working with. This is very important, for when using the chess boards magically, you will not be working just with the boards. You will be drawing from the whole Enochian system through the Tablets, even though the actual Tablets may not be visibly there. Pat Zalewski's *Golden Dawn Enochian Magic* should be of help here, together with books previously recommended.

---

6. For convenience, I use the feminine pronouns.

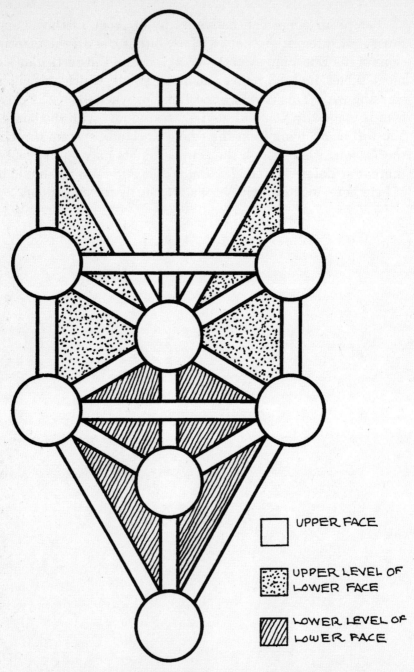

UPPER FACE

UPPER LEVEL OF
LOWER FACE

LOWER LEVEL OF
LOWER FACE

FIGURE 51—DIVISION OF FACES ON THE TREE OF LIFE

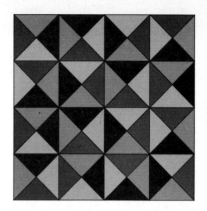

Four
Ego Types

If you take the Kabbalistic Tree of Life as a working glyph, you will see that the elemental divisions of the Enochian chessboards and chess pieces and pawns parallel the divisions of the four Worlds of the Tree of Life, and the subdivisions therein. This is done through the association of Fire with the World of Atziluth, Water with the World of Briah, Air with the World of Yetzirah and Earth with the World of Assiah.[1] Because we are dealing with the four elements, however, which are basically of the "world of matter," our main frame of reference in the following will be with the World of Assiah and its subdivisions.

First of all, break the "Tree" up into an upper face and a lower face. Then break the lower face into four upper triads that pivot on Tiphareth and four lower triads that pivot on Yesod, as shown in the diagram on the opposite page.

---

1. See Part III of this book.

The "triads" that I refer to are the triangular spaces between the Sephiroth as divided by the Paths (fig. 52). Looking first at the lower triads of the lower face: these all pivot on Yesod, which in this instance represents the ego, the everyday working psyche. The triads generating off Yesod, which represents the ego and its needs, are divided into the extroverted and introverted nature. Dealing first with the extrovert triads, the first triad is the Intellectual Triangle, which has a sanguine humor[2] and is made up from Malkuth, Yesod and Hod. This is the intellect that accumulates facts, communicates and patterns everything into what is logical and acceptable to the conscious mind, the thinker, planner, the detailer and examiner. Through Malkuth, it is influenced by material and external, mundane concerns. Through Hod, it is influenced to gather information and to be able to apply the intellect to a purpose. These are put to form by the subconscious perceptions formed by the ego through Yesod. This triad is associated with the Air element, to which I have associated the Bishop's Pawn (Air Pawn).

The second outward-looking triad is the Physical Triangle, which is made up from Malkuth, Yesod and Netzach. This triad is the function of the psycho-physical make-up. The power of Netzach gives an overlay of body type and physical/sexual desires and psychological influence on the physical. Things are seen in the form of activity through the perception of Yesod, and ego is expressed through what one can physically achieve. The theory formed by the intellectual triad is utilized in the physical triad. This is the triad of the five senses as given by Malkuth. The Earth element is associated here, together with the Rook's Pawn (Earth Pawn).

The two introverted triads are both connected to Tiphareth and are concerned with honesty, beauty and clarity, in an interrelationship of Yesod and Tiphareth.

---

2. The term "humor" is a medical term used by herbalists and medical practitioners of the early 19th century and earlier. It represented a physical and psychological type.

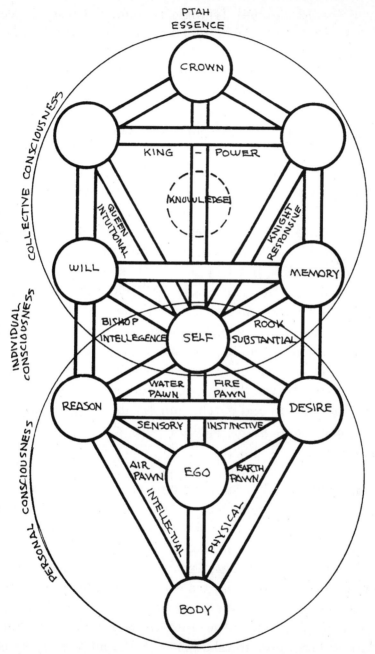

FIGURE 52—THE TRIAD TYPES AND CHESS
PIECES AND PAWNS APPLIED TO THE TREE OF LIFE

First, the Instinctual Triangle is made up from Yesod, Tiphareth and Netzach. The type evolved here is influenced by Tiphareth through natural balance, with the perception and imagination of Yesod, and the strength, drive and creativity of Netzach. This triad gives the ability to react to any deviation by putting it into balance. It initiates action and is a complement to the intellectual triad. Its instinctive behavior and initiative is what comes naturally during times when one does not have time to think about a response. This triad is associated with the element of Fire and the Knight's Pawn (Fire Pawn).

The final triad is the Sensory Triangle, which is made up from Yesod, Hod and Tiphareth. Hod's influence causes a gathering of information, but in this case it is on an inner intuitional level of data that is not tangible. Tiphareth enables it to relate this data clearly and with truth through Hod and Yesod. This triad is the one that picks up impressions and information, which would normally not have been absorbed through the intellect or physical body, and sifts them into clear impressions at terrific speeds. It acts like a radar and works in the realm of the sensors and psychic impressions. The Water element is associated here, together with the Queen's Pawn (Water Pawn).

Now let us briefly list the upper triads of the lower face which all pivot on Tiphareth, the pure expression of the Self. These are an evolved reflection of the lower triads and work in the realm of individual consciousness rather than personal consciousness as the lower triads do.

The first is the Intelligence Triangle, made up of Hod, Geburah and Tiphareth and associated with the Air element and the Bishop among the Enochian chess pieces. If you break up the word "intelligence," you will see that "in" is "from within"; "tell" is to "give information, to relate or reveal"; and "gen" is "to be born or to become." When you examine the Hebrew letters of the Paths that make up the triad, you will see combinations that also tell a story. For example Mem/Ayin/Lamed,[3] which means to divide into parts, and Mem/Lamed is to cut off. This phrase meant the circumcision that was inflicted on Adam (and supposedly to be done to all men) after the Fall. The Lamed/Ayin combination refers to licking up or swallowing down, with the Mem representing "from." So here, when studying the Kabbalah, the Tree and its influences through the Paths, the Sephiroth as shown in the lower triads and the meanings of the words given to each, one can begin to understand the inner meanings of the Enochian chess pieces. Through the utterances of the "Words," the powers can be revealed. You can see from this that the above would allude to the "Fall" or transition from one level of awareness to another: something is born from an intelligence and in doing so brings forth knowledge. Birth is usually severe but beautiful, hence the combination of Geburah and Tiphareth.

The second triad is the Responsive Triangle: Tiphareth, Chokmah and Chesed, associated with the Fire element and the Enochian chess Knight. The word "responsive" may be broken down thus: "res" gives "a thing or a point, a matter that is a cause or action"; "pons" comes from Latin, "a bridge"; and "response" is to answer or react to a stimulus. The combination of Hebrew letters from the connecting Paths is Yod/Heh/Vau, which is "to be" and is a natural generative force. Yod is the Logos and Heh the Primal Light, Vau is the united result of the two, therefore the response, or should I say the result of the reaction of the two. Looking at this another way, it gives a positive exclamation and encourages, grieves or threatens. Here we see the connecting link between above and below that must respond to stimulus and generate or transmit.

3. These consonants are written here to be read from left to right, but if they were written in Hebrew, the letters would be reversed and read from right to left. Therefore, for example, Mem Ayin Lamed would be written in Hebrew as Lamed Ayin Mem (מעל), Mem being the first letter of the combination.

The third triad is the Substantial Triangle: Netzach, Tiphareth and Chesed, associated with the Earth element and the Rook. In the word "substantial," "sub" is beneath or a stance or position. This seems quite appropriate, because the Rook is the Heh final of the Yod/Heh/Vau, and as shown in figure 52, it is placed below the Knight. This also fits in quite adequately from a Kabbalistic interpretation.[4] "Stance" is from the Latin *substantia* and means an essence, or from the Latin *substantare,* which is to be present or to exist, and "substant," which is "continuing substance." The Rook is an "earthy part of" piece and represents the substance of the element it is in. The combination of Hebrew letters derived from the Paths of this triangle is Nun/Yod/Kaph: this refers to a union or foundation/throne.

The fourth triad is the Intuitional Triangle: Tiphareth, Geburah and Binah, associated with the Water element and the Queen. The word "intuitional" may be broken down as: "in" = from inside, within; "intuit," which is to look on or consider; "tion," from; hence "intuition" means to regard or look at from. The Hebrew letter combination herein is Lamed/Cheth/Zain, which is to withdraw inside, but Zain/Cheth is to pluck— remember the apple in the Garden of Eden. Zain/Lamed is to "let go," and Cheth/Lamed is to make a hole or opening. This area receives the information from the Responsive Triangle, gestates it and gives birth to the Intelligence Triangle.

Finally we have the King of the chess set, which has been associated with the quaternary of the upper face, the Collective Unconsciousness. It is the power of the elements and is second only to the Ptah, the essence. The quaternary (four elements) gives birth to the quinary (Spirit). Power broken up gives "pow," which stands for the poll, the head or chief, and "er" = more of. Power comes from the Latin *posse,* which is "to be able."

If you look at the combination of Paths surrounding this area, you will find the Hebrew letters Beth, Aleph, Zain and

4. A detailed examination of the Kabbalah is beyond the scope of this book. The reader is referred to the *Zohar* (vols. I–V), *The Kabbalah Unveiled* by S.L. MacGregor Mathers, *The Holy Kabbalah* by A.E. Waite and *Kabbalah* by Charles Poncé.

Heh, with the Paths crossing over the area horizontally and vertically being Daleth and Gimel, respectively. Combinations of these give: Beth/Daleth = single, alone; Beth/Gimel = meat, or food which is broken off or apart; Gimel/Beth = supporting back or altar; Zain/Beth = a gulf, spring or issuing out; Daleth/Aleph/Beth = gold (philosophers stone); Gimel/Aleph/Heh = to increase or swell, grow higher; Beth/Aleph = to descend and Aleph/Beth = to come or go; Heh/Beth/Aleph = to be willing; Beth/Heh/Aleph = to love; Zain/Aleph = time or at that time; and Heh/Beth = empty space, a hollow.

A description of the above combinations could give: "And so from a single source the bread is broken apart so that it may pour forth from the altar (tabernacle) like a spring as gold so that all may increase and swell with the light through love, and at that time all may be willing to ascend just as the light descends through space and time."

Each of these major chess pieces when moved on a chessboard represents a shift in consciousness, or rather in the unconscious. The point here is that the chessboard in reflection and the pieces on it represent the world above as well as below. Therefore, by careful manipulation of the chess pieces, you can tap into the astral currents of the world above and thereby increase your own awareness and perception of what is happening in the present with respect to the natural laws that govern us. The chess pieces such as the King are merely reflections of these energies, but they are represented in archetypal forms. By manipulating these pieces, we tend to use this conception of energy when dealing with everyday life. So, when we reach out during meditation to the image one of these pieces represents, we can in fact draw from this energy through the archetype and manipulate it to our desired end.

The soul of mankind according to the *Zohar* was formed in the Garden of Eden by the four winds, and the activity within the Garden is said to coincide with the created physical form of the four elements. Here both upper and lower worlds unify in a single instance to create life itself. This concept is analogous to the statement given in the Emerald Tablet of Hermes Trismegistos:

In truth certainly and without doubt, whatever is below is like
that which is above, and whatever is above is like that which
is below, to accomplish the miracles of one thing. . . . it rises
from Earth to Heaven and comes down again from Heaven to
Earth, and thus acquires the power of the realities above and
the realities below. In this way you will acquire the glory of
the whole world, and all the darkness will leave you.

It will be seen now that many combinations are possible of
the above triads, but the main purpose is to ascend the lower
triads to the upper triads, to Tiphareth, then to continue to
ascend. Using the World of Assiah as a glyph and the Four
Worlds within, take each element set of chess pieces and pawns
and apply them each to each of these Worlds; i.e., Earth set to
Assiah of Assiah, Air set to Yetzirah of Assiah, Water set to
Briah of Assiah and Fire set to Atziluth of Assiah. It is here you
will see the many combinations of character types given by the
chess pieces. Note in figure 53 how the Worlds overlap, causing
the Yesod of one World to overlap Daath of the World below.

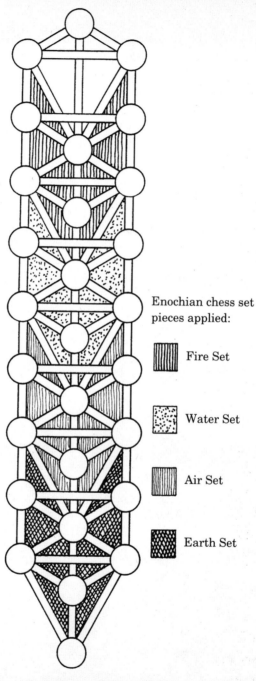

Enochian chess set
pieces applied:

Fire Set

Water Set

Air Set

Earth Set

FIGURE 53—JACOB'S LADDER:
THE FOUR WORLDS IN THE WORLD OF ASSIAH

Ritual Magic
and the
Chess Game

One of the most interesting and important documents in the Golden Dawn's Inner Order are the Z2 papers. Apart from the introduction, the Z2 is broken down into five parts under the Name of Yeheshuah (YHShVH, יהשוה), with each section prefixed by a Hebrew letter. As the Order papers state:

For to the Letter Yod ׳ and the element of Fire belong the works of Ceremonial Magic, as the evocations of the Spirits of the Elements . . .

Unto the First Heh ה the consecration and charging of Telesmata, and the production of Natural Phenomena, as storms, earthquakes . . .

Unto the Great Holy Letter Shin ש are allotted Three classes of works: spiritual development, transformations and invisibility.

Unto the Letter Vau ו Divination in all its branches; and the art of making the Link between the subject of the work and the process of divination.

And to the Final Heh ה the works and operations of the
Art of Alchemy, the order of its processes and Transmutation.

One can see that, by any standard, this formula is considerable and very technical. The basis for it is the 0=0 or initiation
ceremony of the Golden Dawn, which, in the Z2, has its component parts broken down into 24 steps. This ceremony was
adapted to the above formula for basically all matters of magic,
in one form or another.

Index for General Reference to
the Enterer Ceremony of the 0=0 Grade

A —The Ceremony itself. The place of the Temple.

B —The Hierophant.

C —The Officers.

D —The Candidate.

E —The Ceremony of Opening.

F —Hierophant states that he has received a Dispensation from
    Second Order, and commands Hegemon to prepare Candi-
    date. Candidate prepared. Speech of Hegemon.

G —Admission of Candidate. First barring by Kerux. First bap-
    tism of the Candidate with Water and Fire.

H —The Candidate is conducted to the foot of the Altar. Hiero-
    phant asks "Wherefore hast thou come, etc." Candidate
    replies "I seek the hidden Light, etc."

I —Candidate is asked whether he is willing to take the Oblig-
    ation. He assents; and is instructed now to kneel at the
    Altar.

J —Administration of the Obligation, and raising the Neophyte
    from the kneeling position.

K —Candidate is placed in the North. Oration of the Hiero-
    phant, "The Voice of my Higher Self, etc." Hierophant com-
    mands the mystic circumambulation in the Path of
    Darkness.

L —Procession. Candidate barred in South. Second Baptism of

Water and Fire. Speech of Hegemon. Allowing the Candi-date to proceed.

M—Hoodwink slipped up. Challenge of Hiereus. Speech of Hegemon. Speech of Hiereus. Candidate re-veiled and passed on.

N—Circumambulation. Barred in North. Third Baptism. Speech of Hegemon allowing Candidate to approach unto the Gate of the East.

O—Hoodwink slipped up for the second time, Hierophant chal-lenges. Hegemon answers for the Candidate. Speech of Hierophant. Candidate passes on.

P—Candidate led to West of Altar. Hierophant advances by the Path of Samekh. Officers form the Triangle. Prayer of Hierophant.

Q—Candidate rises. Hierophant addresses him, "Long hast thou dwelt in darkness. Quit the Night and seek the Day." Hoodwink finally removed, Scepters and Swords joined. "We receive thee, etc." Then the Mystic Words.

R—Hierophant indicates Lamp of Kerux. He commands that the Candidate be conducted to the East of the Altar. He orders Hiereus to bestow signs, etc. Hiereus places Candi-date between Pillars. Signs and words. He orders the fourth and final consecration to take place.

S—Hegemon removes rope and invests Candidate with his Insignia. Hiereus then ordains the Mystic Circumambula-tion in the Path of Light.

T—Hierophant lectures on the Symbols. Proclamation by Kerux.

U—Hierophant commands Hiereus to address Candidate.

V—Hierophant addresses Neophyte on subject of study.

W—Blood produced. Speech of Kerux. Hiereus' final caution.

X—The closing takes place.

The main section which concerns us at present is the Div-ination section. In spite of what is said about this part of the Z2 papers, about being "Divination in all its branches," as it stands it is in reality designed for the Tarot. When we first tried to apply it to the chess game it fell down badly. It could not be considered for the chess game unless some parts of it were rewritten. This was done, but it was written so that it still adhered to the general index of the 0=0 as given previously.

You may ask whether the use of ritual formula applied to the chess game is really necessary. Even if one could not summon any magical power, the psychological preparation of the game with this formula would be enough of a benefit to align one's mental processes for the divination game. By this, I mean that these various states or levels of consciousness which one enters during the ritual (closely allied with Zen states of satori) prepare your psyche for a better understanding of what it will assimilate during the game.

The following formula is modified for Enochian chess, yet still adheres to its original concept in the Z2.

Z2 Formula of Chess Divination
Under the Letter Vau

A —The Form of Divination.

B —The Diviner.

C —The Forces acting in the Divination.

D —The subject of the Divination.

E —The preparation of all things necessary, and the right understanding of the process, so as to formulate a connecting link between the process employed and the Macrocosm.

F —The Invocation of the Higher, arrangement of the scheme of divination and initiation of the forces thereof.

G —The choosing of the Elemental Board. First assertion of limits and correspondences.

H —The actual and careful formulation of the question; and consideration of all its correspondences and classifications when choosing the square for the Ptah piece.

I —Announcement aloud that all the correspondences taken are correct and perfect; the Diviner places his hand upon the Ptah piece. Sitting East, he prepares to invoke the forces required in the Divination.

J —Solemn invocation of the necessary spiritual forces to aid the Diviner in the Divination. Then let him say, "Arise before me clear as a mirror, O magical vision requisite for the accomplishment of this divination."

K—Accurately define the term of the question; putting down clearly in writing what is already *known,* what is *suspected* or *implied,* and what is sought to be known. And see that thou verify in the beginning of the judgment that part which is already known.

L —Recording of play moves and taking note of correspondences and their interrelationships.

M—The completion of the first round of play.

N —Same as section L.

O —The second round of game and up to, but not including, the first move of the King.

P —The first move of the Diviner's King towards the Ptah piece.

Q—The Diviner now completely and thoroughly formulates his whole judgment as well for the immediate future as for the development thereof, taking into account the knowledge and indications given him by the angelic form (if he is in direct astral contact with the force governing the divination play).

R —The King reaching the Ptah Square and remaining there for one round of the game gives a positive result. If the King does not reach the Ptah Square but the game nonetheless ends through King capture etc., there is a negative result to the question.

S —Final round of game play.

T —The Diviner then compares carefully the whole judgment and decisions arrived at with their conclusions, and delivers now plainly a succinct and consecutive judgment thereon.

U—The Diviner gives advice to the Consultant as to what use he shall make of the judgment.

V —The Diviner formulates clearly with what forces it may be necessary to work in order to combat the Evil, or fix the Good, promised by the Divination.

W—Lastly, remember that unto thee a divination shall be as a sacred work of the Divine Magic of Light, and not to be performed to pander unto thy curiosity regarding the secrets of another, and if by this means thou shalt arrive at a knowledge of another's secrets, thou shalt respect and not betray them.

Experimental Methodology

This section has been included for those who wish to go further into the magical arena with the chess game. It is based on a number of experiments we have been conducting. Although my studies are far from complete, I felt that comment on them should be made to give those who wish to experiment in this area information on some of our developments on the subject.

The first experimental area to be discussed is god-form assumption. While this is not a new concept with the Golden Dawn in itself, its adaptation to the chess game is. This experiment is usually conducted after the completion of a divination game, after it has been analyzed. For example, if the game has turned out to be negative, from the analysis certain key points of influence are noted that if handled differently may have turned the tide of the game to a positive victory. I have tended to term these key aspects "pivot points," for they are points of balance that can alter the game.

Taking a lead from Chinese sages who, when experimenting with the *I Ching* for divination, found that if they had a negative hexagram for an inquiry, they could then work their way back to the point or line where the negative influence began. This was done through a careful study of how the Chinese elements would interact with each other. At that point they would find out what would go wrong and look at a probable alternative action that the inquirer could take to avoid the negative result. They assumed that if, through foreknowledge of a probable destiny, they made a correct move at the right time, then the whole concept or outcome of the divination could be altered.

If this method works with the I Ching, it most certainly would work with Enochian chess divination, because the same fundamental principles apply. I have used this method quite often with the Tarot. If a probable direction looks negative, I divine further probable directions in accordance with particular alternative reactions or actions until I find a more suitable result. In this way one can have more control over one's life.

There is an important limitation to the chess game that must be considered when using this method. It can only apply to personal events, not to cases where entire countries are involved. To change the direction of countries would be beyond the ability of most adepts, but the method will work when applied to a personal situation over which you do have control.

This effort involves two areas of involvement. The first is to be ready to make the correct changes when the time in the situation occurs that parallels the pivot point. The next, and this must be done first, is to try to astrally alter the influence. Even the Chinese sages who did this with the I Ching insisted that a small ritual be performed to appease the ancient gods and tell them what one was about to do before one actually did it. This is done by assuming the astral form of the chess piece, which is placed over the correct chess square, and directing its energies through the power of the square.

There are two ritual methods to accomplish this. The first is by the Z2 formula of Transformation under the presidency of the letter Shin. The second is a shortened formula: The temple is set up in the 0=0 grade of Neophyte with the chess game up to the pivot point placed on the altar. The object of this exercise is to be able to neutralize the influence of the opposing astral currents, shown as the opposing chess pieces, by visually forming the god-form of the piece in question to direct the energy of the square to a desired end.

As mentioned earlier, this is still very much in the experimental stage and a great deal more experimentation needs to be done to confirm its effectiveness. However, at this point, the results look promising.

Z2 Formula of Transformation Under the Letter Shin

A —The Astral Form.

B —The Magician.

C —The Forces used to alter the Form.

D —The Form to be taken.

E —The Equation of the Symbolism in the Sphere of Sensation.

F —Invocation of the Higher. The definition of the Form required as a delineation of blind forces, and the awakening of the same by its proper formulation.

G —Formulating clearly to the mind the Form intended to be taken. The Restriction and Definition of this as a clear form and the actual baptism by Water and by Fire with the Order Name of the adept.

H —The Actual Invocation aloud of the form desired to be assumed to formulate before you, the statement of the Desire of the Operator and the reason thereof.

I —Announcement aloud that all is now ready for the operation of the Transformation of the Astral Body. The Magician mentally places the form as nearly as circumstances permit in the position of the Enterer, himself taking the place of the Hierophant, holding his Wand by the black portion ready to commence the Oration aloud.

J —Let him now repeat a powerful exorcism of the shape into which he desires to transform himself, using the Names, etc., belonging to the Plane, Planet, or other Eidolon, most in harmony with the shape desired. Then holding the Wand by the black End, and directing the flower over the head of the form, let him say, "In the name of the Lord of the Universe, Arise before me, O Form of _____, into which I have elected to transform myself. So that seeing me men may see the thing that they see not, and comprehend not the thing they behold."

K —The Magician saith, "Pass toward the North shrouded in darkness, O Form of _____, into which I have elected to transform myself." Then let him repeat the usual Oration from the Throne of the East. Then command the Mystic circumambulation.

L —Now bring the Form around to the South, arrest it, and for-mulate it there, standing between two great Pillars of Fire and Cloud. Purify it with Water and by Fire, by placing these elements on either side of the Form.

M—Passes to West, face Southeast, formulate the Form before thee, this time endeavoring to render it physically visible. Repeat speeches of Hiereus and Hegemon.

N—Same as L.

O—Same as M.

P —Pass to the East of Altar, formulating the Form as near in the position of the Neophyte as may be. Now address a solemn invocation and conjuration by Divine Names, etc., appropriate to render the form fitting for thy Transforma-tion therein.

Q—Remain East of Altar, address the Form "Child of Earth, etc.," endeavoring now to see it physically. Then at the words, "We receive Thee, etc." he draws the Form towards him so as to envelop him, being careful at the same time to invoke the Divine Light by the rehearsal of the Mystic Words.

R —Still keeping himself in the form of the Magician say, "Before all Magical Manifestation cometh the knowledge of the Divine Light." He then moves to the Pillars and gives Signs, etc., endeavoring with the whole force of his Will to feel himself *actually* and *physically* in the shape of the Form desired. And at this point he must see as if in a cloudy and misty manner the outline of the Form enshroud-ing him, though not yet completely and wholly visible. When this occurs, but not before, let him formulate himself as standing between the two vast Pillars of Fire and Cloud.

S —He now again endeavors to formulate the Form as if visibly enshrouding him; and still, astrally, retaining the Form, he thrice circumambulates the place of working.

T —Standing at the East, let him thoroughly formulate the shape, which should now appear manifest, and as if enshrouding him, even to his own vision; and then let him proclaim aloud, "Thus have I formulated unto myself this Transformation."

U—Let him now invoke all the Superior Names, etc., of the Plane appropriate to the Form that he may retain it under his proper control and guidance.

V—He states clearly to the Form what he intends to do with it.

W—Having obtained the desired effect, and gone about in the desired form, it is required that thou shouldst conjure the Powers of the Light to act against that shroud of Darkness and Mystery so as to disintegrate it, lest any force seek to use it as a medium for an obsession, etc. Therefore rehearse a conjuration as aforesaid, and then open the shroud and come forth out of the midst thereof, and then disintegrate that shroud (Form), by the use of a conjuration to the forces of the plane appropriate to the Form, to disintegrate and scatter the particles thereof, but affirming that they shall again be readily attracted at thy command.

But on no account must that shroud of awful Mystery be left without such disintegration, seeing that it would speedily attract an occupant which would become a terrible vampire praying upon him who had called it into being.

And after frequent rehearsals of this operation, the thing may almost be done "per Motem."

The second method of experimentation is that of evocation with the chess set. At Thoth-Hermes, we have experimented with the Knight's move as a sigil and with numerous other methods of evocation with the chess set, but the best method we have found to date is to use the Z2 formula of evocation. This is accomplished by placing the chessboard in the triangle you use for evocation with a single piece on it, the one you wish to evoke. It is placed on the board and square that you require it to manipulate.

To use this method, the adept must be very familiar with the chess squares and their individual functions. The only way this can be accomplished is for him or her to have scryed or astrally projected into each of the squares to record their effects. This takes years when done correctly and is only for the very experienced adept. At Thoth-Hermes, adepts must have personally scryed into all the squares of the Enochian Tablets before they can advance on to stages such as this.

The use of the chessboards and pieces for evocation differs considerably from performing a normal evocation per se (which in itself takes some effort). Here the object is to get the god-form to manipulate the Enochian Servient Square angels to help him perform the desired task. In view of this, you can see that the evocation is in itself multilayered. An example of how this works is to place the Knight Horus, on the Earth Board/Earth Angle, and on the square of the Earth Element, the densest one in all of the tablets. Horus is to be told to exert his power on the angel of the square so that a sticking point or a delaying point in an event can be hurried along. Horus being the Yod Force will instigate the thrust in the direction required.

There are a number of less complex ways to handle this, but the use of the chess piece on the chessboard modifies the current of Horus[1] and that of the chessboard. It then fuses them together into a situation where a type of magical chain reaction occurs. In my opinion, this is a very powerful force to set in motion. The evocation does not specifically relate to any chess game or pivot point but is the use of the magic squares of the chessboard, and the force they represent, guided by a powerful current or god-form.

It must be repeated that these methods are still experimental and a great deal of work needs to be done in this direction. If Enochian chess is played on a regular basis, a link will be established to the individual pieces and each will become a core of power that the adept can tap if needed. Using an effigy such as a chess piece as a power base is as old as antiquity and the roots go back to pre-Egyptian times, with strong links that form the basis of cults that still exist today.

---

1. See *Z-5, Secret Teachings of the Golden Dawn: Book I, The Neophyte Ritual 0=0* by Pat Zalewski for a full description of the current of Horus and other Earth pieces.

Z2 Formula of Evocation Under the Letter Yod[2]

A —The Magic Circle.

B —The Magician, wearing the Great Lamen of the Hierophant; and his scarlet Robe. A Pentacle,[3] whereon is engraved the Sigil[4] of the Spirit to be invoked, has painted on the back of it the circle and cross as shown on the Hierophant's Lamen.

C —The Names and Formulae to be employed.

D —The Symbol of the whole evocation.

E —The Construction of the circle and the placing of all the symbols, etc., employed, in the places properly allotted to them; so as to represent the interior of a G.D. Temple in the Enterer, and the purification and consecration of the actual piece of ground or place, selected for the performance of the Evocation.

F —The Invocation of the Higher Powers. Pentacle formed of three concentric bands, name and Sigil therein, in proper colors, is to be bound thrice with a cord, and shrouded in black, thus bringing into action a Blind Force to be further directed or differentiated in the Process of the Ceremony. Announcement aloud of the Object of the working; naming the Spirit or Spirits, which it is desired to evoke. This is pronounced standing in the center of the Circle and turning towards the quarter from which the Spirit will come.

G—The Name and Sigil of the Spirit, wrapped in a black cloth, or covering, is now placed within the circle, at the point cor-

---

2. This formula as given in the Golden Dawn is flexible and can be manipulated as I have done with the Divination section of the Z2, providing that the original concepts are kept in mind. The formula was never intended to be a hard and fast rule never to be altered; common sense must apply throughout.

3. When applied to a chess game, the Pentacle is usually a seal of the board/Tablet (usually placed above it). These seals can be found in Regardie's *Golden Dawn*.

4. This sigil can literally be a sigil of the name of the Egyptian god-form plus that of the Enochian angel of the square. These sigils can be derived with the Rose Cross method as described in Regardie's *Golden Dawn*.

responding to the West, representing the Candidate. The consecration of Baptism by water and fire of the Sigil then takes place, and the proclamation in a loud and firm voice of the spirit (or spirits) to be evoked.

H—The veiled Sigil is now to be placed at the foot of the Altar. The Magician then calls aloud the Name of the Spirit, summoning him to appear, stating for what purpose the spirit is evoked: what is desired in the operation; why the evocation is performed at this time, and finally solemnly affirming that the Spirit shall be evoked by the Ceremony.

I —Announcement aloud that all is prepared for the commencement of the actual Evocation. If it be a good spirit the Sigil is now to be placed within the White Triangle on the Altar, the Magician places his left hand upon it, raises in his right hand the magical Implement employed (usually the Sword) erect; and commences the Evocation of the Spirit N., to visible appearance. The Magician stands in the Place of the Hierophant during the Obligation, irrespective of the particular quarter of the Spirit. But, if the nature of that Spirit be evil, then the Sigil must be placed without and to the West of the White Triangle and the Magician shall be careful to keep the point of the Magical Sword upon the center of the Sigil.

J —Now let the Magician imagine himself as clothed outwardly with the semblance of the form of the Spirit to be evoked, and in this let him be careful *not to identify himself* with the spirit, which would be dangerous; but only to formulate a species of mask, worn for the time being. And if he knows not the symbolic form of the Spirit, then let him assume the form of an Angel belonging unto the same class of operation, this form being assumed. Then let him pronounce aloud, with a firm and solemn voice, a convenient and potent oration and exorcism of the Spirit unto visible appearance.

At the conclusion of this exorcism, taking the covered Sigil in his left hand, let him smite it thrice with the flat blade of the Magic Sword. Then let him raise on high his arms to their utmost stretch, holding in his left hand the veiled Sigil, and in his right the Sword of Art erect. At the same time stamping thrice upon the ground with his right foot.

K—The veiled and corded Sigil is then to be placed in the Northern part of the Hall at the edge of the Circle, and the Magician employs the oration of the Hierophant, from the throne of the East, modifying it slightly, as follows: "The voice of the Exorcism said unto me, Let me shroud myself in darkness, peradventure thus may I manifest myself in Light, etc." The Magician then proclaims aloud that the Mystic Circumambulation will take place.

L —The Magician takes up the Sigil in his left hand and circumambulates the Magic Circle once, then passes to the South and halts. He stands (having placed the Sigil on the ground) between it and the West, and repeats the oration of the Kerux. And again consecrates it with Water and Fire. Then takes it in his hand, facing westward saying, "Creature of _____, twice consecrate, thou mayest approach the gate of the West."

M—The Magician now moves to the West of the Magical Circle, holds the Sigil in his left hand and the sword in his right, faces Southwest, and again astrally masks himself with the form of the Spirit, and for the first time partially opens the covering of the Sigil, without however entirely removing it. He then smites it once with the flat blade of the sword, saying, in a loud, clear, and firm voice: "Thou canst not pass from concealment unto Manifestation, save by the virtue of the Name Elohim. Before all things are the Chaos and Darkness, and the Gates of the Land of Night. I am He Whose Name is Darkness. I am the Great One of the Path of the Shades. I am the Exorcist in the midst of the Exorcism. Appear thou therefore without fear before me, so pass thou on." He then reveils the Sigil.

N—Take the Sigil to the North, circumambulate first, halt, place Sigil on the ground, stand between it and the East, repeat the oration of the Kerux, again consecrate with Fire and Water. Then take it up, face North, and say "Creature of _____, thrice consecrate, thou mayest approach the Gate of the East."

O —Repeat Section M in Northeast. Magician then passes to East, takes up Sigil in left and Sword in right hand. Assumes the Mask of the Spirit form, smites the Sigil with the Lotus Wand or Sword, and says, "Thou canst not pass from concealment unto manifestation save by virtue of the name YHVH. After the Formless and the Void and the Darkness, then cometh the knowledge of the Light. I am the Light which riseth in the Darkness. I am the Exorcist in the midst of the Exorcism. Appear thou therefore in visible form before me, for I am the Wielder of the Forces of the Balance. Thou hast known me now, so pass thou on to the Cubical Altar of the Universe!"

P —He then recovers Sigil and passes to Altar, laying it thereon as before shown. He then passes to the East of the Altar, holding the Sigil and Sword as already explained. Then doth he rehearse a most potent Conjuration and invocation of the Spirit unto visible appearance, using and reiterating all the Divine, Angelic, and Magical Names appropriate to this end, neither omitting the signs, seals, sigils, lineal figures, signatures and the like from that conjuration.

Q —The Magician now elevates the covered Sigil towards heaven, removes the veil entirely, leaving it yet corded, crying with a loud voice, "Creature of _____, long hast thou dwelt in darkness. Quit the Night and seek the Day." He then replaces it upon the Altar, holds the Magical Sword erect above it, the pommel immediately above the center thereof, and says, "By all the Names, Powers, and Rites already rehearsed, I conjure thee thus into visible appearance." Then the Mystic Words.

R —Saith the Magician, "As Light hidden in the Darkness can manifest therefrom, *so shalt thou* become manifest from concealment unto manifestation."

He then takes up the Sigil, stands to East of Altar, and faces West. He shall then rehearse a long conjuration to the

powers and spirits immediately superior unto that one
which he seeks to invoke, *that they shall force him to man-*
ifest himself unto visible appearance.

He then places the Sigil between the Pillars, himself at
the East facing West, then in the Sign of the Enterer doth
he direct the whole current of his will upon the Sigil. Thus
he continueth until such time as he shall perceive his Will
power to be weakening, when he protects himself from the
reflex of the current by the sign of silence, and drops his
hands. He now looks towards the Quarter that the Spirit is
to appear in, and he should now see the first signs of his
visible manifestation. If he be not thus faintly visible, let
the Magician repeat the conjuration of the Superiors of the
Spirit, from the place of the Throne in the East. And this
conjuration may be repeated thrice, each time ending with
a new projection of Will in the sign of the Enterer, etc. But
if at the third time of repetition he appeareth not, then be
it known that there is an error in the working.

So let the Master of Evocations replace the Sigil upon
the Altar, holding the Sword as usual: and thus doing, let
him address a humble prayer unto the Great Gods of
Heaven to grant unto him the force necessary to correctly
complete that evocation. He is then to take back the Sigil to
between the Pillars, and repeat the former processes, when
assuredly that Spirit will begin to manifest, but in a misty
and ill-defined form.

(But if, as is probable, the Operator be naturally
inclined unto evocation, then might that Spirit perchance
manifest earlier in the Ceremony than this. Still, the Ceremony is to be performed up to this point, whether he be
there or no.)

Now as soon as the Magician shall see the visible manifestation of that Spirit's presence, he shall quit the station
of the Hierophant, and consecrate afresh with Water and
with Fire, the Sigil of the evoked Spirit.

S —Now doth the Master of Evocations remove from the Sigil
the restricting cord, and holding the freed Sigil in his left

hand, he smites it with the flat blade of his sword, exclaiming, "By and in the Names of _____ I do invoke upon thee the power of perfect manifestation unto visible appearance." He then circumambulates the circle thrice holding the Sigil in his Right hand.

T —The Magician, standing in the place of the Hierophant, but turning towards the place of the Spirit, and fixing his attention thereon, now reads a potent Invocation of the Spirit unto visible appearance, having previously placed the Sigil on the ground, within the circle, at the quarter where the Spirit appears.

This Invocation should be some length; and should rehearse and reiterate the Divine and other Names consonant with the working.

That Spirit should now become fully and clearly visible, and should be able to speak with a direct voice, if consonant with his nature. The Magician then proclaims aloud that the Spirit N. hath been duly and properly evoked in accordance with the sacred Rites.

U —The Magician now addresses an Invocation unto the Lords of the plane of the Spirit to compel him to perform that which the Magician shall demand of him.

V —The Magician carefully formulates his demands, questions, etc., and writes down any of the answers that may be advisable. The Master of Evocations now addresses a Conjuration unto the Spirit evoked, binding him to hurt or injure naught connected with him, or his assistants, or the place. And that he deceive in nothing, and that he fail not to perform that which he hath been commanded.

W—He then dismisses that Spirit by any suitable form, such as those used in the higher grades of the Outer. And if he will not go, then shall the Magician compel him by forces contrary to his nature. But he must allow a few minutes for the Spirit to dematerialize the body in which he hath manifested, for he will become less and less material by degrees. And note well that the Magician (or his companions if he have any) shall never quit the circle during the process of evocation, or afterwards, till the Spirit hath quite vanished.

Seeing that in some cases, and with some constitutions, there
may be danger arising from the Astral conditions, and currents established, and without the actual intention of the
Spirit to harm, although if of a low nature, he would probably endeavor to do so. Therefore, before the commencement
of the Evocation, let the operator assure himself that everything which may be necessary, be properly arranged within
the circle.

But if it be actually necessary to interrupt the Process, then let
him stop at that point, veil and re-cord the Sigil if it have
been unbound or uncovered, recite a License to Depart or a
Banishing Formula, and perform the Lesser Banishing Rituals both of the Pentagram and Hexagram. Thus only may
he in comparative safety quit the circle.

Note: If the Spirit is placed into a White Triangle outside the
midheaven, he then will speak the truth of necessity.

Interesting Visitors

One of the methods of invocation is the concept of using a Spirit
to help win the game. This method has been used occasionally
within the Golden Dawn, and I remember one instance during
a game with Pat, my husband, as my opponent. He got very
tired of losing against me, so one day he invoked the Goetic[5]
Angel, Furcas,[6] to aid him in his game play. Astoundingly, Pat
won in two rounds of the game (seven moves)! I was most put
out, and stipulated that future games must be played with one's
own merits.

Another method is the evocation of a Spirit to act as a partner or opponent in game play. This form of evocation differs considerably from the Z2 formula and was popularized by Mathers.

---

5. The *Goetia* is one of the five books of the *Lesser Key of Solomon* that was
used by MacGregor Mathers, and which Aleister Crowley published as his
own work, with a few minor additions.

6. The *Goetia* tells us that this Spirit teaches the arts of philosophy, astrology,
rhetoric, logic, cheiromancy and pyromancy, in all their parts.

The concept here is simply that you make the moves for your invisible opponent. To do this correctly requires, I feel, a very real ability to channel (to use a modern-day term for mediumship), and the player must be very discerning to make sure that imagination is not used in obtaining chess instructions. This is a lot easier if your Spirit has translucently formed to the visible eye. It is rare to have a Spirit so manifested that it can move the material objects (chess pieces) itself.

I tried this latter method myself and found my hand literally moving by itself when I had to move the pieces for the Spirit. This was a process very similar to automatic writing. A most enjoyable game!

Ptah-Kether

*H*ail Ptah, there was given to Thee a power
upon the Earth in its things which were in a
state of inactivity and Thou didst gather
them together after Thou did exist in Thy
form of Ta-Tenen, in Thy becoming the "Uniter of
the Two Worlds" which Thy mouth begot and Thy
hands fashioned.

Homage to Thee, O Ptah, Thou great God
whose form is hidden in the brilliance of Kether.
Thou openest Thy soul, O Father of Fathers of all
the Gods though the Seraphim, Haioth Hakadoth
under the call of Eheie. Thou illuminest Kether
with Thy sight and lightest up the Earth with Thy
brilliant rays in peace.

O Ptah—creater of Gods, He who passeth
through eternity everlastingness of multitudinous
forms—the Hearer of Prayers. The winds come
forth from Thy breath and the celestial Water from
Thy mouth and the staff of life proceeds from Thy
back. Thou makest the Earth to bring forth fruits,
and gods and men have abundance.

Appendix

Enochian Chess Pieces

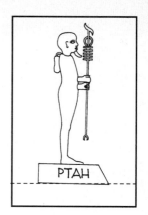

You can make your own Enochian chess pieces using the cut-out figures on the following pages and the Ptah piece above.

1. Color the pieces according to the instructions in the chapter on "Constructing the Chess Pieces," pp. 33–79.

2 For added stability, glue the pages down to shirt cardboard and let dry.

3. Cut out the pieces into rectangular shapes using the heavy lines.

4. Fold on the dotted lines to form bases.

5. Tape or glue coins or other small weights to the bases to make the pieces stand upright.

It might be a good idea to photocopy these pages once or twice and experiment with the copies before you make the final chess sets.

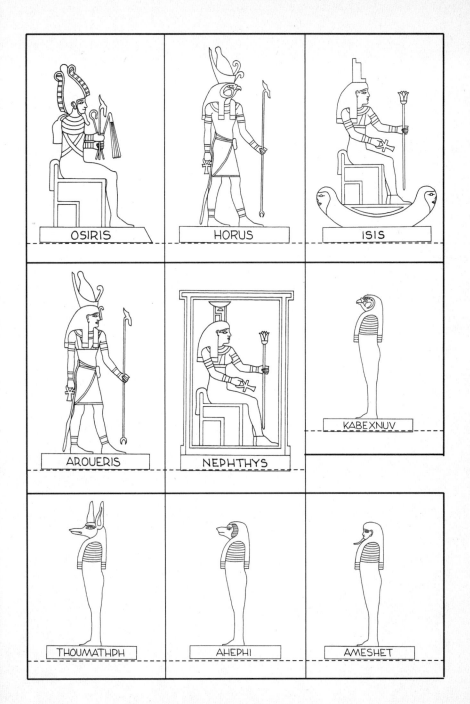

OSIRIS HORUS ISIS

AROUERIS NEPHTHYS KABEXNUV

THOUMATHPH AHEPHI AMESHET

EARTH PANTHEON

325

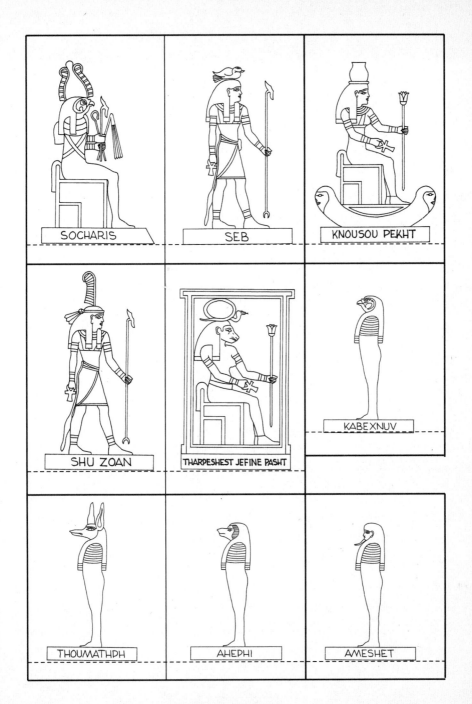

SOCHARIS	SEB	KNOUSOU PEKHT
SHU ZOAN	THARPESHEST JEFINE PASHT	KABEXNUV
THOUMATHPH	AHEPHI	AMESHET

AIR PANTHEON

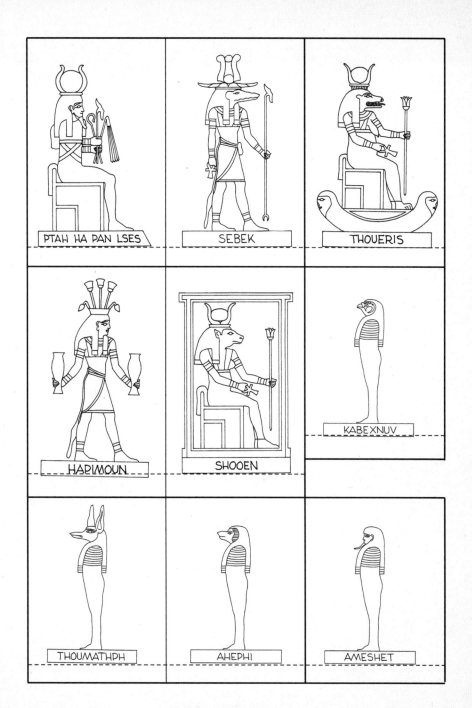

PTAH HA PAN LSES

SEBEK

THOUERIS

HARIMOUN

SHOOEN

KABEXNUV

THOUMATHPH

AHEPHI

AMESHET

WATER PANTHEON

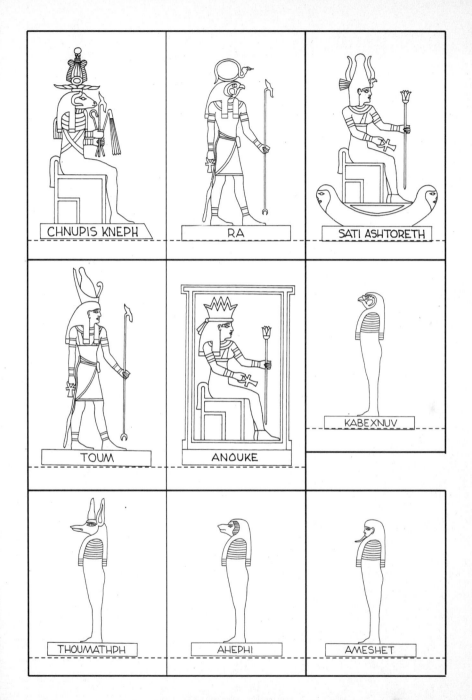

CHNUPIS KNEPH

RA

SATI ASHTORETH

TOUM

ANOUKE

KABEXNUV

THOUMATHPH

AHEPHI

AMESHET

FIRE PANTHEON

331

Bibliography

Bell, R.C. *Board and Table Games from Many Civilizations.* rev. ed. New York: Dover Publications, 1979.

Chernev, Irving. *Combinations: The Heart of Chess.* New York: Dover Publications, 1960.

Cox, Captain Hiram. In *Asiatic Researches* VII, 1799.

Falkener, Edward. *Games Ancient and Oriental, and How to Play Them.* New York: Dover Publications, 1961.

Forbes, Duncan. *The History of Chess.* 1860

Ganguli, Kisari Mohan, trans. *The Mahabharata.* 3rd ed. Munshiram Manoharlal Publishers Ltd, 1975.

Golombek, Harry, ed. *The Penguin Encyclopedia of Chess.* Penguin Books, 1981.

Halevi, Z'ev ben Shimon. *Adam and the Kabbalistic Tree.* London: Rider and Company, 1974.

Harding, T.D. *Better Chess for Average Players.* Oxford University Press, 1978.

Jones, Sir William. In *Asiatic Researches* II, 1788.

Kaplan, Aryeh. *Meditation and Kabbalah*. York Beach, ME: Samuel Weiser, 1982.

Levertoff, Paul P., Maurice Simon and Harry Sperling, trans. *The Zohar*. New York: Bennet Publications, 1959.

Lévi, Éliphas. *The Key of the Mysteries*. trans. Aleister Crowley. London: Rider & Company, 1959.

Mathers, S.L. MacGregor. *The Kabbalah Unveiled*. London: Routledge and Kegan Paul, 1926.

Murray, H.J.R. *History of Chess*. 1913 (Have referred to first sources as quoted by Murray).

Official Rules of Chess. 2nd ed. United States Chess Federation (USCF) Section, and World Chess Federation (FIDE) Section.

Parkhurst, John, M.A. *An Hebrew and English Lexicon*. 2nd ed., London.

Poncé, Charles. *Kabbalah*. San Francisco: Straight Arrow Books, 1973.

Regardie, Israel. *A Practical Guide to Geomantic Divination*. New York: Samuel Weiser, 1972.

Skinner, Stephen. *The Oracle of Geomancy*. Prism Press, 1977.

Skinner, Stephen. *Divination by Geomancy*. London: Routledge & Kegan Paul, 1980.

Waite, A.E. *The Holy Kabbalah*. New Hyde Park, NY: University Books, 1960.

Zukav, Gary. *Dance of the Wu Li Masters*. Flamingo, 1989.

Printed Golden Dawn Sources

McLean, Adam. *Enochian Chess*. Privately printed.

Regardie, Israel. *The Golden Dawn*. St. Paul: Llewellyn Publications, 1971.

Regardie, Israel. *The Complete Golden Dawn System of Magic.* Phoenix: Falcon Press, 1984.

Zalewski, Pat. *Z5, Secret Teachings of the Golden Dawn: Book I, The Neophyte Ritual 0=0.* St. Paul, Llewellyn Publications, 1991.

Zalewski, Pat and Chris. *Z5, Secret Teachings of the Golden Dawn: Book II, The Zelator Ritual 1=10.* St. Paul, Llewellyn Publications, 1992.

Golden Dawn Manuscripts

Brodie-Innes, J.I. Unnamed Enochian manuscript on board association.

Document "S."

Document "T."

Mathers, S.L. MacGregor. "Notes on Rosicrucian Chess."

Pullen-Burry, Rose. "Gods of Egypt and the Enochian Tablets."

Y1 and Y2 copied by Hugh Campbell from Wynn Westcott's chess notebook, issued to the ZAM, 1893.

Zalewski, Pat and Chris. "Enochian Chess," 1st vol., unpublished, 1980.

Thoth-Hermes Temple Manuscripts

Chess Rules, 1980.

Description of Chess Pieces, 1980.

Divination papers, 1–3, 1981.

Evocation of Chess Pieces, 1980

Invocation of Chess God-forms, 1980

Psychology and the Enochian Pyramid Squares.

Various other miscellaneous papers and documents.

STAY IN TOUCH

On the following pages you will find listed, with their current prices, some of the books now available on related subjects. Your book dealer stocks most of these and will stock new titles in the Llewellyn series as they become available. We urge your patronage.

To obtain our full catalog, to keep informed about new titles as they are released and to benefit from informative articles and helpful news, you are invited to write for our bimonthly news magazine/catalog, *Llewellyn's New Worlds of Mind and Spirit*. A sample copy is free, and it will continue coming to you at no cost as long as you are an active mail customer. Or you may subscribe for just $10.00 in U.S.A. and Canada ($20.00 overseas, first class mail). Many bookstores also have *New Worlds* available to their customers. Ask for it.

Stay in touch! In *New Worlds'* pages you will find news and features about new books, tapes and services, announcements of meetings and seminars, articles helpful to our readers, news of authors, products and services, special money-making opportunities, and much more.

Llewellyn's New Worlds of Mind and Spirit
P.O. Box 64383-895, St. Paul, MN 55164-0383, U.S.A.

* * *

TO ORDER BOOKS AND TAPES

If your book dealer does not have the books described on the following pages readily available, you may order them directly from the publisher by sending full price in U.S. funds, plus $3.00 for postage and handling for orders *under* $10.00; $4.00 for orders *over* $10.00. There are no postage and handling charges for orders over $50.00. Postage and handling rates are subject to change. UPS Delivery: We ship UPS whenever possible. Delivery guaranteed. Provide your street address as UPS does not deliver to P.O. Boxes. Allow 4-6 weeks for delivery. UPS to Canada requires a $50.00 minimum order. Orders outside the U.S.A. and Canada: Airmail—add retail price of book; add $5.00 for each non-book item (tapes, etc.); add $1.00 per item for surface mail.

FOR GROUP STUDY AND PURCHASE

Because there is a great deal of interest in group discussion and study of the subject matter of this book, we feel that we should encourage the adoption and use of this particular book by such groups by offering a special quantity price to group leaders or agents.

Our special quantity price for a minimum order of five copies of *Enochian Chess of the Golden Dawn* is $38.85 cash-with-order. This price includes postage and handling within the United States. Minnesota residents must add 6.5% sales tax. For additional quantities, please order in multiples of five. For Canadian and foreign orders, add postage and handling charges as above. Credit card (VISA, MasterCard, American Express) orders are accepted. Charge card orders only ($15.00 minimum order) may be phoned in free within the U.S.A. or Canada by dialing 1-800-THE-MOON. For customer service, call 1-612-291-1970. Mail orders to:

LLEWELLYN PUBLICATIONS
P.O. Box 64383-895, St. Paul, MN 55164-0383, U.S.A.

Prices subject to change without notice.

Z-5: SECRET TEACHINGS OF THE GOLDEN DAWN
Book I: The Neophyte Ritual
by Pat Zalewski

This book is the first in a series on the grade rituals of the Hermetic Order of the Golden Dawn. It is designed to show the type of procedure one encounters when he or she joins a Golden Dawn temple. It focuses on the secret, Inner Order techniques for performing the Neophyte initiation ritual, which is the essence of the Golden Dawn's Z-2 magical instructions.

Z-5 is a tool and a helpful guide based on the observations of a number of Adepts from the Golden Dawn, the Stella Matutina, and the Smaragdum Thalasses. Originally intended as a document restricted to members of the Inner Order of the Thoth-Hermes Temple, the Z-5 material includes many of the "word of mouth" teachings passed on from Inner Order Adepti. These teachings go beyond the step-by-step mechanics of ritual on the mundane level and unveil the deeper meanings, allowing access into the Golden Dawn's "magical current" which is the source of the true power of ritual.

0-87542-897-5, 240 pgs., 6 x 9, illus., softcover   **$12.95**

Z-5: SECRET TEACHINGS OF THE GOLDEN DAWN
Book II: The Zelator Ritual 1=10
by Pat & Chris Zalewski

Two of the Golden Dawn's highest initiates reveal the hidden mysteries of the best-known occult system in the world. Pat and Chris Zalewski show what actually happens when one is initiated into the Golden Dawn's second grade ceremony—the Zelator Ritual.

In the first book in this series, *Z-5 … The Neophyte Ritual 0=0,* Pat Zalewski showed the whole process of initial initiation. Now, in *Z-5 … The Zelator Ritual 1=10,* Pat and his wife Chris take things a step further as the candidate embraces the forces of the Earth Element and the effects it has on him. In this ceremony, the postulant has his aura magnetically earthed and his physical body revitalized.

Unlike any other book written on the Golden Dawn, *Z-5 … 1=10* presents in enormous detail all the higher explanations given on the Zelator Ceremony in one package. For those who want to study ritual magic in a group, this book provides firm guidelines of the dos and don'ts of Hermetic Ritual. For those who wish to utilize magic in the privacy of their own homes, this book explains the shortcuts that can be applied on a solo basis.

0-87542-896-7, 224 pgs., 6 x 9, illus., softcover   **$12.95**

Prices subject to change without notice.

KABBALAH OF THE GOLDEN DAWN
by Pat Zalewski

Of all the material published about the Golden Dawn, one area that has not received the attention it deserves is the Kabbalah—the basis of all Golden Dawn rites. And while the subject of the Kabbalah itself has been well documented from the traditional Hebrew viewpoint, there is less available from the occultist's point of view. Now, *Kabbalah of the Golden Dawn* presents the majority of the Kabbalistic teachings from the Golden Dawn in one unified and fascinating volume. It contains a synthesis of all major Kabbalistic teachings used by the Order, a number of previously unpublished Golden Dawn texts and diagrams, and additional insight into the concepts they contain.

Original Golden Dawn adepts were spoon fed this material over a number of years as they went through the various grade ceremonies. This compact book places all the relevant teachings together for everyone. It does not duplicate already published material on the subject, but adds to and strengthens many areas of previous teachings.

0-87542-873-8, 250 pgs., 6 x 9, softcover **$12.95**

THE EQUINOX & SOLSTICE CEREMONIES
OF THE GOLDEN DAWN
by Chris & Pat Zalewski

Throughout time, the Spring and Fall Equinoxes and Summer and Winter Solstices have been the basic reference points for the seasons and the major times for celebration in both the Christian and Pagan calendars. Yet until now, there has been little in the way of detailed information on the magical effects of the Equinox and Solstice.

The Equinox & Solstice Ceremonies of the Golden Dawn is a valuable contribution to magical literature. It defines and explains the Equinox and Solstice, along with the Golden Dawn concept of them. It presents a scientific evaluation of the magnetic fields they produce, along with the astrological data connecting them and how they relate to spiritual development. It investigates myths and festivals from the time of the Egyptians and how the theology of that time related specifically to the Sun and the change of the seasons. Jewish, Christian, Celtic and Norse festivals are also explored along with the different timing of these ceremonies in different climatic conditions. The authors then present the full Golden Dawn rituals and give their expert commentary, which reveals many unpublished teachings associated with the ceremonies.

0-87542-899-1, 192 pgs., 6 x 9, illus., softcover **$12.95**

Prices subject to change without notice.

GOLDEN DAWN ENOCHIAN MAGIC
by Pat Zalewski

Enochian magic is considered by most magicians to be the most powerful system ever created. Aleister Crowley learned this system of magic from the Hermetic Order of the Golden Dawn, which had developed and expanded the concepts and discoveries of Elizabethan magus John Dee. This book picks up where the published versions of the Enochian material of the Golden Dawn leave off.

Based on the research and unpublished papers of MacGregor Mathers, one of the founders of the Golden Dawn, *Golden Dawn Enochian Magic* opens new avenues of use for this system. New insights are given on such topics as the Sigillum Dei Aemeth, the Angels of the Enochian Aires applied to the 12 tribes of Israel and the Kabbalah, the 91 Governors, the Elemental Tablets as applied to the celestial sphere, and more. This book provides a long-sought break from amateurish and inaccurate books on the subject; it is designed to complement such scholarly classics as *Enochian Invocation* and *Heptarchia Mystica*.

0-87542-898-3, 224 pgs., 5¼ x 8, illus., softcover **$12.95**

GODWIN'S CABALISTIC ENCYCLOPEDIA
A Complete Guide to Cabalistic Magick
by David Godwin

This is the most complete correlation of Hebrew and English ideas ever offered. It is a dictionary of Cabalism arranged, with definitions, alphabetically in Hebrew and numerically. With this book, the practicing Cabalist or student no longer needs access to a large number of books on mysticism, magic and the occult in order to trace down the basic meanings, Hebrew spellings, and enumerations of the hundreds of terms, words, and names that are included in this book.

This book includes: all of the two-letter root words found in Biblical Hebrew, the many names of God, the Planets, the Astrological Signs, Numerous Angels, the Shem ha-Mephorash, the Spirits of the *Goetia,* the correspondences of the 32 Paths, a comparison of the Tarot and the Cabala, a guide to Hebrew Pronunciation, and a complete edition of Aleister Crowley's valuable book *Sepher Sephiroth.*

Here is a book that is a must for the shelf of all Magicians, Cabalists, Astrologers, Tarot students, Thelemites, and those with any interest at all in the spiritual aspects of our universe.

0-87542-292-6, 528 pgs., 6 x 9, softcover **$15.00**

Prices subject to change without notice.

THE GOLDEN DAWN
The Original Account of the Teachings, Rites & Ceremonies of the Hermetic Order
As revealed by Israel Regardie
Complete in one volume with further revision, expansion, and additional notes by Regardie, Cris Monnastre, and others. Expanded with an index of more than 100 pages!

Originally published in four bulky volumes of some 1,200 pages, this 6th Revised and Enlarged Edition has been entirely reset in modern, less space-consuming type, in half the pages (while retaining the original pagination in marginal notation for reference) for greater ease and use.

Corrections of typographical errors perpetuated in the original and subsequent editions have been made, with further revision and additional text and notes by noted scholars and by actual practitioners of the Golden Dawn system of Magick, with an Introduction by the only student ever accepted for personal training by Regardie.

Also included are Initiation Ceremonies, important rituals for consecration and invocation, methods of meditation and magical working based on the Enochian Tablets, studies in the Tarot, and the system of Qabalistic Correspondences that unite the World's religions and magical traditions into a comprehensive and practical whole.

This volume is designed as a study and practice curriculum suited to both group and private practice. Meditation upon, and following with the Active Imagination, the Initiation Ceremonies are fully experiential without need of participation in group or lodge. A very complete reference encyclopedia of Western Magick.
0-87542-663-8, 840 pgs., 6 x 9, illus., softcover   **$19.95**

A GARDEN OF POMEGRANATES
by Israel Regardie

What is the Tree of Life? It's the ground plan of the Qabalistic system—a set of symbols used since ancient times to study the Universe. The Tree of Life is a geometrical arrangement of ten sephiroth, or spheres, each of which is associated with a different archetypal idea, and 22 paths which connect the spheres.This system of primal correspondences has been found the most efficient plan ever devised to classify and organize the characteristics of the self. Israel Regardie has written one of the best and most lucid introductions to the Qabalah. *A Garden of Pomegranates* combines Regardie's own studies with his notes on the works of Aleister Crowley, A. E. Waite, Eliphas Levi and D. H. Lawrence. No longer is the wisdom of the Qabalah to be held secret! The needs of today place the burden of growth upon each and every person . . . each has to undertake the Path as his or her own responsibility, but every help is given in the most ancient and yet most modern teaching here known to humankind.

0-87542-690-5, 160 pgs., 5 1/4 x 8, softcover $8.95

THE MIDDLE PILLAR
by Israel Regardie

Between the two outer pillars of the Qabalistic Tree of Life, the extremes of Mercy and Severity, stands *The Middle Pillar*, signifying one who has achieved equilibrium in his or her own self.

Integration of the human personality is vital to the continuance of creative life. Without it, man lives as an outsider to his own true self. By combining Magic and Psychology in the Middle Pillar Ritual/Exercise (a magical meditation technique), we bring into balance the opposing elements of the psyche while yet holding within their essence and allowing full expression of man's entire being.

In this book, and with this practice, you will learn to: understand the psyche through its correspondences of the Tree of Life; expand self-awareness, thereby intensifying the inner growth process; activate creative and intuitive potentials; understand the individual thought patterns which control every facet of personal behavior; and regain the sense of balance and peace of mind—the equilibrium that everyone needs for physical and psychic health.

0-87542-658-1, 176 pgs., 5-1/4x8, softcover $8.95

SECRETS OF A GOLDEN DAWN TEMPLE
The Alchemy and Crafting of Magickal Implements
by Chic Cicero and Sandra Tabatha Cicero

A Must-Have for Every Student of the Western Magickal Tradition! From its inception 100 years ago, the Hermetic Order of the Golden Dawn continues to be *the* authority on high magick. Yet the books written on the Golden Dawn system have fallen far short in explaining how to construct the tools and implements necessary for ritual. Until now.

Secrets of a Golden Dawn Temple picks up where all the other books leave off. This is the first book to describe *all* Golden Dawn implements and tools in complete detail. Here is a unique compilation of the various tools used, all described in full: wands, ritual clothing, elemental tools, Enochian tablets, altars, temple furniture, banners, lamens, admission badges and much more. This book provides complete step-by-step instructions for the construction of nearly 80 different implements, all displayed in photographs or drawings, along with the exact symbolism behind each and every item. Plus, it gives a ritual or meditation for every magickal instrument presented. It truly is an indispensable guide for any student of Western Magickal Tradition.

0-87542-150-4, 592 pgs., 6 x 9, 16 color plates, softcover $19.95

THE NEW GOLDEN DAWN RITUAL TAROT
Keys to the Rituals, Symbolism, Magic & Divination
by Chic Cicero & Sandra Tabatha Cicero

This is the indispensable companion to Llewellyn's New Golden Dawn Ritual Tarot Deck. It provides a card-by-card analysis of the deck's intricate symbolism, an introduction to the Qabalah, and a section on the use of the deck for practical rituals, meditations and divination procedures. The Tarot newcomer as well as the advanced magician will benefit from this groundbreaking work.

The highlight of the book is the section on rituals. Instructions are included for: ritual baths, Lesser Banishing Ritual of the Pentagram, Tarot deck consecration ritual, using the Tarot for talismans, scrying with the Tarot, dream work with the Tarot, the Golden Dawn method of Tarot divination, and much, much more.

The Golden Dawn is experiencing a widespread revival among New Agers, Wiccans, mystics and ceremonial magicians. This book and companion deck are just what people are looking for: traditional Golden Dawn knowledge with new rituals written by authors with "magickal credentials."

0-87542-139-3, 256 pgs., 6 x 9, illus. $12.95

Prices subject to change without notice.

THE ENOCHIAN WORKBOOK
The Enochian Magickal System Presented in 43 Easy Lessons
by Gerald J. and Betty Schueler

Enochian Magic is an extremely powerful and complex path to spiritual enlightenment. Here, at last, is the first book on the subject written specifically for the beginning student. Ideally suited for those who have tried other books on Enochia and found them to be too difficult, *The Enochian Workbook* presents the basic teachings of Enochian Magic in a clear, easy-to-use workbook.

The authors have employed the latest techniques in educational psychology to help students master the information in this book. The book is comprised of 11 sections, containing a total of 43 lessons, with test questions following each section so students can gauge their progress. You will learn how to conduct selected rituals, skry using a crystal, and use the Enochian Tarot as a focus for productive meditation. Also explore Enochian Chess, Enochian Physics (the laws and models behind how the magic works), and examine the dangers associated with Enochian Magic. Readers who complete the book will be ready to tackle the more complex concepts contained in the other books in the series.

One of the reasons why Enochian Magic is so hard to understand is that it has a special, complex vocabulary. To help beginning students, Enochian terms are explained in simple, everyday words, wherever possible.

0-87542-719-7, 360 pgs., 7 x 10, illus.,
16 color plates, softcover $14.95

ENOCHIAN MAGIC
A Practical Manual
by Gerald J. Schueler

The powerful system of magic introduced in the 16th century by Dr. John Dee, Astrologer Royal to Queen Elizabeth I, and as practiced by Aleister Crowley and the Hermetic Order of the Golden Dawn, is here presented for the first time in a complete, step-by-step form. There has never before been a book that has made Enochian Magic this easy!

In this book you are led carefully along the path from "A brief history of the Enochian Magical System," through "How to Speak Enochian," "How to Invoke," "The Calls," "Egyptian Deities" and "Chief Hazards" to "How to visit the Aethyrs in Spirit Vision (Astral Projection)." Not a step is missed; not a necessary instruction forgotten.

0-87542-710-3, 288 pgs., 5 1/4 x 8, illus., softcover $9.95

Prices subject to change without notice.

AN ADVANCED GUIDE TO ENOCHIAN MAGICK
A Complete Manual of Angelic Magick
by Gerald J. Schueler

This is a sequel to *Enochian Magic: A Practical Manual*. In this book, Schueler provides everything for the serious practitioner of the Enochian system—a system that is complete in itself, and yet easily related to other systems of Qabalistic or Shamanistic magick. All students of the Golden Dawn, Aurum Solis and other mainstream systems of Western practice will find this work a practical "working manual" combining theory with exercises, complete rituals and outlines for multilevel magical operations. New students will find the Enochian system particularly modern, reflective of the new physics; others will be attracted to the feeling of working at the frontiers of the New Age.

The book includes information not only on Enochian Magick, but also on Enochian Meditation and Enochian Healing. It is an ideal book for beginning, intermediate or advanced students of magick and a vital resource and guidebook for occult Orders and Lodges.

0-87542-711-1, 448 pgs., 5 1/4 x 8, illus., softcover   **$12.95**

ENOCHIAN PHYSICS
The Structure of the Magical Universe
by Gerald J. Schueler

Gerald Schueler has taken the latest discoveries of modern physics and compared them to the laws of Enochian Physics. He shows how the magical universe is a natural extension of Einstein's space/time continuum. The only ingredient that Einstein left out was consciousness. When this factor is included, the magical universe is revealed. According to modern physics, matter is a form of energy. In *Enochian Physics* you will see that this same energy, the energy of modern physics, is the very substance, or "matter," of the magical universe.

The book incorporates magick and the latest concepts in the ever-changing field of theoretical physics. Quantum mechanics, black and white holes, alchemy and levitation, quarks and the Big Bang, the four elements and the four elementary forces are all brought together within a Grand Unified System of the magical universe. Included are such tantalizing scientific puzzles as the fluidity of time, the possibility of parallel universes, matter and antimatter, and the fate of the stars and galaxies. Those seeking a clear explanation of magical phenomena such as invisibility, astral travel and psychic healing will find it in the pages of *Enochian Physics*. Anyone practicing magick or interested in how magick works should read this book.

0-87542-712-X, 400 pgs., 5 1/4 x 8, illus., softcover   **$12.95**

Prices subject to change without notice.

ENOCHIAN YOGA
Uniting Humanity and Divinity
by Gerald & Betty Schueler

Here is the only book currently available that combines magick and yoga, and Western and Eastern thought, into a single, easy-to-use system that is suitable for everyone, from beginners to advanced magicians and yogis. Eight graduated paths of development are described, and the book includes a complete description of the subtle Centers and Channels of Enochian Yoga, which are equivalent to the chakras and nadis of kundalini Yoga. The application of the Enochian worlds to the meditation techniques and philosophy of yoga makes this magical development more accessible to those having a cultural or educational background in the Eastern religions. A thorough method for spiritual attainment.

0-87542-718-9, 408 pgs., 5 1/4 x 8, illus., softcover   **$12.95**

THE ENOCHIAN TAROT DECK
Created by Gerald and Betty Schueler
Painted by Sallie Ann Glassman

The Enochian Tarot is a deck of cards which is primarily used to foretell the future. Forecasting the future, however, is only a superficial use of the massive powers of the Enochian Tarot. Here is a powerful tool which allows you to look deep inside your subconscious and "see" the direction your life is taking. The Enochian Tarot is an easy-to-use system of self-discovery which allows you to see your relationship to God and the universe.

The Tarot is your map of life. With it you can choose the road you want to wander. Instead of being an uninformed victim of your subconscious will, you can gather your inner strength and consciously change the path your life is to take. The Tarot is your key to self-determination, and with that key you can open any door.

The Enochian Tarot Deck consists of 86 cards which are divided into two main sections: a Major Arcana and a Minor Arcana. The Major Arcana is a set of 30 picture cards which are also called The Greater Arcana, Trumps, Atouts, or Triumphs. These cards are symbolic representations of various cosmic forces such as Doubt, Intuition, Glory, etc. The Minor Arcana contains 56 cards which represent the Four Enochian Watchtowers. The Minor Arcana is divided into 4 "suits" called Earth, Water, Air, and Fire.

0-87542-708-1, boxed set: 86 cards with booklet   **$12.95**

Prices subject to change without notice.

THE ENOCHIAN TAROT
by Gerald and Betty Schueler

The popular deck of cards known as the Tarot has been used for many centuries for divination, fortunetelling and self-initiation through meditation. The Enochian Tarot, an 86-card deck, is the first to utilize the mystery and magical power inherent in Enochian Magic.

The Enochian Tarot explains in detail the meaningful correspondences behind the structure of this deck. It discusses, for example, the difference between the 22 Paths on the Qabalistic Tree of Life, on which traditional Tarot decks are based, and the 30 Aethyrs of Enochian Magick (the Enochian deck has 8 extra cards because there are 8 more Aethyrs than Paths). The book also includes tables and figures for easy comprehension of an otherwise difficult subject, as well as tips for reading the cards for fun or profit.

The unique system of Enochian Magick was revealed to John Dee, court astrologer to Queen Elizabeth I of England, and his partner Edward Kelly by the Enochian Angels who inhabit the Watchtowers and Aethyrs of the subtle regions of the universe. The authors are foremost authorities on this subject and have published a number of books that have made a fascinating magical system accessible to a wide audience.

0-87542-709-X, 352 pgs., 5-1/4 x 8, illus., softcover $12.95

20TH CENTURY MAGIC AND THE OLD RELIGION
Dion Fortune, Christine Hartley, Charles Seymour
by Alan Richardson

This magical record details the work of two senior magicians—Charles Seymour and Christine Hartley—within Dion Fortune's Society of the Inner Light during the years 1937 to 1939.

Using juxtaposed excerpts from Seymour and Hartley's magical diaries together with biographical prefaces containing unique insights into the background and nature of the Society, Alan Richardson paints a fascinating picture of Dion Fortune and her fellow adepts at the peak of their magical careers.

Originally published as *Dancers to the Gods,* and now with a new introduction and the addition of Seymour's long essay, "The Old Religion," a manual of self-initiation, this new edition retains Dion Fortune's "lost" novels, the past-life identities of her Secret Chiefs, and much more.

The simple act of reading these juxtaposed diaries of a true priest and priestess can cause a resonance with the soul which will ultimately transform those who so desire it.

0-87542-673-5, 256 pgs., 6 x 9, photos, softcover $12.95

Prices subject to change without notice.

MAGICAL GATEWAYS
by Alan Richardson

Originally published as *An Introduction to the Mystical Qabalah* (1974, 1981), *Magical Gateways* is the revised and substantially expanded re-release of of this excellent introduction to the essentials of magic.

It shows magic to be a spiritual system which everyone can use to enhance their lives. Whatever your spiritual path, these tried-and-tested methods will expand your consciousness and broaden your grasp of the Western Esoteric Tradition as it exists today.

Explore the *theories and principles* behind ritual practice (i.e., the Middle Pillar and the Lesser Banishing Ritual) that other books only touch upon. Explore the Qabalah—the Tree of Life—as it applies to daily living, perform astral magic, use the Tarot for self-exploration, relate mythology to your own life to gain greater self-knowledge, revisit past lives, build patterns in your aura, banish unpleasant atmospheres and create gates into other dimensions.

This is the world of *real* magic, in which an understanding of the Qabalah forms the first step in a radical transformation of personal consciousness.

0-87542-681-6, 208 pgs., mass market, illus.　　　　　　　**$4.95**

EARTH GOD RISING
The Return of the Male Mysteries
by Alan Richardson

Today, in an age that is witnessing the return of the Goddess in all ways and on all levels, the idea of one more male deity may appear to be a step backward. But along with looking toward the feminine powers as a cure for our personal and social ills, we must remember to invoke those forgotten and positive aspects of our most ancient God. The Horned God is just, never cruel; firm, but not vindictive. The Horned Gods loves women as equals. He provides the balance needed in this New Age, and he must be invoked as clearly and as ardently as the Goddess to whom he is twin.

The how-to section of this book shows how to make direct contact with your most ancient potentials, as exemplified by the Goddess and the Horned God. Using the simplest of techniques, available to everyone in any circumstance, *Earth God Rising* shows how we can create our own mystery and bring about real magical transformations without the need for groups, gurus, or elaborate ceremonies.

0-87542-672-7, 224 pgs., 5 1/4 x 8, illus., softcover　　　　**$9.95**

Prices subject to change without notice.

ANCIENT MAGICKS FOR A NEW AGE
Rituals from the Merlin Temple, the Magick of the Dragon Kings
by Alan Richardson and Geoff Hughes

With two sets of personal magickal diaries, this book details the work of magicians from two different eras. In it, you can learn what a particular magician is experiencing in this day and age, how to follow a similar path of your own, and discover correlations to the workings of traditional adepti from almost half a century ago.

The first set of diaries are from Christine Hartley and show the magick performed within the Merlin Temple of the Stella Matutina, an offshoot of the Hermetic Order of the Golden Dawn, in the years 1940–42. The second set are from Geoff Hughes and detail his magickal work during 1984-86. Although he was not at that time a member of any formal group, the magick he practiced was under the same aegis as Hartley's. The third section of this book, written by Hughes, shows how you can become your own Priest or Priestess and make contact with Merlin.

The magick of Christine Hartley and Geoff Hughes are like the poles of some hidden battery that lies beneath the Earth and beneath the years. There is a current flowing between them, and the energy is there for you to tap.

0-87542-671-9, 320 pgs., 6 x 9, illus., softcover   **$12.95**

TEMPLE MAGIC
Building the Personal Temple: Gateway to Inner Worlds
by William Gray

This important book on occultism deals specifically with problems and details you are likely to encounter in temple practice. Learn how a temple should look, how a temple should function, what a ceremonialist should wear, what physical postures best promote the ideal spiritual-mental attitude, and how magic is worked in a temple.

Temple Magic has been written specifically for the instruction and guidance of esoteric ceremonialists by someone who spent a lifetime in spiritual service to his natural Inner Way. There are few comparable works in existence, and this book in particular deals with up-to-date techniques of constructing and using a workable temple dedicated to the furtherance of the Western Inner Tradition. In simple yet adequate language, it helps any individual understand and promote the spiritual structure of our esoteric inheritance. It is a book by a specialist for those who are intending to be specialists.

0-87542-274-8, 288 pgs,, 5 1/4 x 8, illus., softcover   **$7.95**

GROWING THE TREE WITHIN:
Patterns of the Unconscious Revealed by the Qabalah
by William Gray

The Qabalah, or Tree of Life, has been the basic genetic pattern of Western esotericism, and it shows us mortals how to make our climb steadily back to Heaven. When we study the Qabalah, open ourselves to it and work with it as an Inner Activity, we gain wisdom that will illuminate our individual paths to perfection. Qabalah means "getting wise" in the broadest possible sense.

Formerly titled *The Talking Tree,* this book presents an exhaustive and systematic analysis of the 22 Paths of the Tree of Life. It includes a detailed and comprehensive study of the symbolism of the Tarot cards in which author William Gray presents a viable yet unorthodox method of allocating the Major Arcana to the Paths. Of particular interest is his attempt at reaching a better understanding of the nature of the English alphabet and its correspondence to the Tree of Life.

Gray contends that the "traditional" Tree is a living spirit that needs to be in a continual state of evolution and improvement. It is the duty of all those who love and work with it to cultivate and develop it with every care. This includes both pruning off dead wood and training new growth in the right directions for future fruiting. *Growing the Tree Within* does precisely that.

0-87542-268-3, 468 pgs., 6 x 9, illus., softcover   **$14.95**

BETWEEN GOOD AND EVIL
Polarities of Power
by William G. Gray

Between Good and Evil provides new insight that can help you take the forces of Darkness that naturally exist within us and transform them into spiritual light. It will help you discover how you can deal constructively, rather than destructively, with the unavoidable problem of Evil. Our lives depend on which way we direct our energy— whether we made the Devil in ourselves serve the God, or the other way around. We must use our Good intentions to understand and exploit the Evil energies that would otherwise prove fatal to us.

In order to confront and control our "demons," Gray has revived a centuries-old magical ritual technique called the "Abramelin Experience": a practical step-by-step process in which you call upon your Holy Guardian Angel to assist in converting Evil into Good. By following the richly detailed explanation of this "spiritual alchemy," you will learn how to positively channel your negative energies into a path leading directly to a re-union with Divinity.

0-87542-273-X, 272 pgs., 5 1/4x 8, softcover   **$9.95**

Prices subject to change without notice.

MAGICIAN'S COMPANION
A Practical and Encyclopedic Guide to
Magical and Religious Symbolism
by Bill Whitcomb

The Magician's Companion is a "desk reference" overflowing with a wide range of occult and esoteric materials absolutely indispensable to anyone engaged in the magickal arts!

The magical knowledge of our ancestors comprises an intricate and elegant technology of the mind and imagination. This book attempts to make the ancient systems accessible, understandable and useful to modern magicians by categorizing and cross-referencing the major magical symbol-systems (i.e., world views on inner and outer levels). Students of religion, mysticism, mythology, symbolic art, literature, and even cryptography will find this work of value.

This comprehensive book discusses and compares over 35 magical models (e.g., the Trinities, the Taoist Psychic Centers, Enochian magic, the qabala, the Worlds of the Hopi Indians). Also included are discussions of the theory and practice of magic and ritual; sections on alchemy, magical alphabets, talismans, sigils, magical herbs and plants; suggested programs of study; an extensive glossary and bibliography; and much more.

0-87542-868-1, 522 pgs., 7 x 10, illus., softcover $19.95

ATTAINMENT THROUGH MAGIC
by William G. Gray

In this newly titled re-release of the classic *A Self Made by Magic*, the author presents a "Self-Seeking System" of powerful magical practice designed to help seekers become better and more fulfilled souls. The source material is taken from standard procedures familiar to most students of the Western Inner Tradition, procedures that encourage the best of our potential while diminishing or eliminating our worst characteristics. To that end, Gray deals extensively with the dangers and detriments of maleficent or "black" magic.

The lessons follow the pattern of the Life-Tree, and guide the student through the four elements and their connection of Truth, the Ten Principles of "Spheres" of the Life-Tree, and the associations which bind these together. Gray includes an in-depth study of the Archangelic concepts with exercises to "make the Archangels come true" for us through the systematic use of appropriate words of power.

0-87542-298-5, 308 pgs., 5 1/4 x 8, illus., softcover $9.95

Prices subject to change without notice.

THE KEY OF IT ALL
BOOK ONE: THE EASTERN MYSTERIES
An Encyclopedic Guide to the Sacred Languages & Magical Systems of the World
by David Allen Hulse

The Key of It All series clarifies and extends the knowledge established by all previous books on occult magick. Book One catalogs and distills, in hundreds of tables of secret symbolism, the true alphabet magick of every ancient Eastern magickal tradition. Unlike the current rash of publications which do no more than recapitulate Regardie or Crowley, *The Key of It All* series establishes a new level of competence in all fields of magick both East and West.

Key 1: Cuneiform—the oldest tradition ascribing number to word; the symbolism of base 60 used in Babylonian and Sumerian Cuneiform; the first God and Goddess names associated to number.

Key 2: Hebrew—a complete exposition of the rules governing the Hebrew Qabalah; the evolution of the Tree of Life; an analysis of the *Book of Formation,* the oldest key to the symbolic meaning of the Hebrew alphabet.

Key 3: Arabic—the similarity between the Hebrew and Arabic Qabalahs; the secret Quranic symbolism for the Arabic alphabet; the Persian alphabet code; the philosophical numbering system of G.I. Gurdjieff.

Key 4: Sanskrit—the secret Vedic number codes for Sanskrit; the digital word-numbers; the symbolism of the seven chakras and their numerical key.

Key 5: Tibetan—the secret number lore for Tibetan as inspired by the Sanskrit codes; the secret symbols for the Tibetan alphabet; the six major schools of Tattva philosophy.

Key 6: Chinese—the Taoist calligraphic stroke count technique for number Chinese characters; Chinese Taoist number philosophy; the I Ching, the Japanese language and its parallels to the Chinese number system.

0-87542-318-3, 592 pgs., 7 x 10, tables, charts, softcover $19.95